DI058782

CRISIS MANAGEMENT IN A COMPLEX WORLD

CRISIS MANAGEMENT IN A COMPLEX WORLD

Dawn R. Gilpin and Priscilla J. Murphy

OXFORD

UNIVERSITY PRESS

2008

HD
49
,G55
2008

OXFORD
UNIVERSITY PRESS

Oxford University Press, Inc., publishes works that further
Oxford University's objective of excellence
in research, scholarship, and education.

Oxford   New York
Auckland   Cape Town   Dar es Salaam   Hong Kong   Karachi
Kuala Lumpur   Madrid   Melbourne   Mexico City   Nairobi
New Delhi   Shanghai   Taipei   Toronto

With offices in
Argentina   Austria   Brazil   Chile   Czech Republic   France   Greece
Guatemala   Hungary   Italy   Japan   Poland   Portugal   Singapore
South Korea   Switzerland   Thailand   Turkey   Ukraine   Vietnam

Published by Oxford University Press, Inc.
198 Madison Avenue, New York, New York 10016

www.oup.com

Oxford is a registered trademark of Oxford University Press

Library of Congress Cataloging-in-Publication Data
Gilpin, Dawn R.
Crisis management in a complex world / Dawn R. Gilpin
and Priscilla J. Murphy.
    p. cm.
Includes bibliographical references and index.
ISBN 978-0-19-532872-1
1. Crisis management. I. Murphy, Priscilla J. II. Title.
HD49.G55 2008
658.4'056—dc22   2007040014

9 8 7 6 5 4 3 2 1

Printed in the United States of America
on acid-free paper

ACKNOWLEDGMENTS

We want to thank our external reviewers, whose comments and suggestions vastly improved the quality of this book, and our editor John Rauschenberg and production editor Gwen Colvin, whose knowledge, understanding, and judiciousness made the publication process such a pleasure. Catherine Rae also deserves a special mention for her patient and helpful guidance through the various stages of production.

We also want to thank Kelly Mendoza, Suman Mishra, and Kelly Ryan, three doctoral students in Temple University's Mass Media and Communication program. They contributed valuable background material on crises in the Catholic Church, Enron, and NASA, as well as the Chinese pet food scandal.

Dawn is especially grateful to the Department of Journalism of the University of Memphis for their support at the beginning of this project. Rick Fischer and Jim Redmond merit special appreciation for gamely wading through the tortuous pages of those early drafts—proof that there can indeed be such a thing as too much complexity. Should they dare to hazard another look, she hopes they will agree that it has improved considerably in the interim.

Dawn also extends her sincere thanks to Dario Parisini, who certainly knows a thing or two about both complexity and crisis himself; Kathleen Doherty, an anchor of stability in a turbulent world for more years than either of us would like to admit; and Sue Robinson, who somehow could always intuit when crisis reduction was the better strategy. Your support and friendship have been invaluable.

Priscilla particularly appreciates the encouragement of her husband, Fred Murphy, whose interest in the mathematics of decision making prompted her journey along convoluted paths through game theory, chaos theory, and complexity theory.

We both want to thank other family members, friends, and colleagues, whose lives were made considerably more complex during the time we were researching, writing, and constantly talking to them about this book. We promise to give them a break—at least until the next project.

CONTENTS

CRISIS MANAGEMENT IN A COMPLEX WORLD

Introduction

A Paradigm Shift in Crisis Management

Consider the following crises:

On August 14, 2003, a snapped tree limb triggered the largest electrical blackout that North America has ever experienced. About 60 million people in the northeastern United States and southern Canada lost power, equivalent to the entire population of France or Britain. Looting broke out in several major cities darkened by the blackout, which included New York, Detroit, Cleveland, and Toronto. Economic losses totaled about $12 billion. An official with PJM Interconnection, a consortium that coordinates East Coast power transmission, commented, "Nobody saw this coming....None of us drew the proper conclusions about what was going to happen." (Behr & Barbaro, 2003)

In June 1999, five European countries banned Coca-Cola from store shelves after nearly 200 people, many of them children, became sick from drinking Coke. Two separate batches of ill-smelling but non-toxic Coke in France and Belgium became linked in media coverage. The story acquired further negative associations because it followed on the heels of earlier media coverage of a Belgian food scare involving sheep feed tainted with cancer-causing dioxin. That association, in turn, encouraged connections with mad cow disease, all worsened by the European public's anxieties about genetically altered foods—illogical, unscientific, and not amenable to public relations mitigation. Media coverage of the debacle reversed prior positive depictions of Coke, which had until then enjoyed a good reputation in Europe. (Murphy, 2000; Taylor, 2000)

In December 2006, former Enron CEO Jeffrey Skilling began serving a 24-year jail term for leading his firm into an $11 billion scandal. With more than 21,000 employees in 40 countries, Enron once was one of the fastest growing energy companies in the world, the seventh largest corporation in the United States. However, exposure of financial malfeasance under Skilling initiated a "corporate meltdown" in 2001 that destroyed Enron and damaged major corporations with which it had done business, including the accounting firm Arthur Andersen and the securities firm Merrill Lynch. Legislative and reputational fallout from the Enron scandals spread throughout the American business community, involving such corporations as WorldCom, Xerox, Halliburton, ImClone, Kmart, Lucent, and Tyco International. Enron, once listed among *Fortune* magazine's "most admired" companies, has become a symbol for corporate corruption. (Conrad, 2003; Seeger & Ulmer, 2003)

As different as these three crises are, they share important fundamentals. Within a matter of days or weeks, each crisis radically redefined the reputation of a person, a company, or an industry in ways that would take years to reverse—if indeed they could be improved at all. Each one involved the spread of a crisis situation along routes that either could not have been anticipated or could not be controlled once set in motion. In each case, highly competent public relations professionals proved unable to modify the triggering events or channel the crises along less damaging lines. These factors raise one of the central questions of crisis management: To what extent can communicators actually perform their expected role to anticipate and head off crises or to guide their organizations through crises with the least possible damage to reputation?

In this book, we address that question by emphasizing the role of contingency, uncertainty, and happenstance; the unexpected confluence of unrelated events; and the destabilizing influence of rapidly changing circumstances. These are all central factors in crises, and most of the crisis literature seeks to mitigate them by simplifying the decision environment and standardizing decision making. In contrast, our approach maintains a vision of the changeable and complex nature of crises, and it looks for ways to operate within that very real-world environment of confusion, unforeseen events, and missing information. This approach fundamentally differs from the dominant paradigms of crisis communication.

Because of their potential for cataclysmic damage, crises have become one of the most extensively studied phenomena in public relations. The trend in such studies has been toward scientific management, endowing public relations with increasingly specific techniques for crisis anticipation and response. The implication is that if public relations professionals diligently follow these prescriptive steps, they can avoid or mitigate nearly every crisis.

A dominant paradigm has emerged within the crisis communication literature. Organizations are urged to prepare as much as possible during noncrisis times so that they will be able to act swiftly and effectively to prevent and manage any untoward situations that arise. This preparation process generally puts the emphasis on gathering and analyzing information about the organization's environment before any crisis occurs. Indeed, many authors rank environmental monitoring and establishing clear internal and external communication channels among the most important aspects of crisis preparedness (Coombs, 2007; Mitroff & Anagnos, 2001; Regester & Larkin, 2005). These and other experts argue that early awareness of potential crisis situations is one of the best forms of defense for organizations, and therefore they urge managers to invest considerable material and human resources in these areas. During the crisis, most experts emphasize dissemination of information, as well as monitoring audience reactions and concerns (Barton, 1993, 2001; Fearn-Banks, 2007; Fink, 1986; Ulmer, Sellnow, & Seeger, 2007). After a crisis has passed, organizations are encouraged to study their experience and draw lessons to be used in the future (Fishman, 1999; O'Rourke, 1996; Smallman & Weir, 1999).

In this book, however, we argue that successful crisis management is not guaranteed by scientific planning and prescriptive decision making. Rather, the nature of the organization, the crisis, and the environment exert important influences on outcomes, influences that even the most skilled professional cannot fully control but can learn to work with adeptly. In fact, overly rigid crisis planning procedures can raise false expectations among managers that make communication less effective when a crisis hits or make public relations staff appear incompetent if they do not achieve success by following these procedures. For example, Hearit and Courtright (2004) described an "information engineering approach" to crisis planning that sees "crises as objective events whose meaning is both predetermined and self-evident" (p. 204). They argued that this type of approach presents a limited view of crises as simple calculations involving factors such as crisis type and locus of responsibility. Furthermore, in this view crises are the result of forces external to the organization that require a direct and identifiable response. Thus crises visit from outside and, in most current approaches, can be handled primarily by external communications, such as media relations.

This emphasis on external factors means that most crisis communication literature does not pay enough attention to how information travels within and between organizations or how knowledge develops beyond the level of information. In addition, there needs to be more attention to how organizations find out about, make sense of, make decisions for, and learn from rapidly changing situations such as those encountered in a crisis. The ability to prepare for, manage, and comprehend the aftermath of crises relies heavily on the creation and retention of knowledge through organizational learning (Appelbaum & Goransson, 1997; Nonaka & Konno, 1998). Therefore, we need a stronger connection between crisis management and knowledge management that addresses how individuals and groups acquire and transfer knowledge and information within an organization.

Finally, the scientific management of crises encourages a focus on prediction and control that can easily overstate predictability. This detailed planning approach often deliberately oversimplifies the complex: By reducing the uncertainty of the situation to a set of rules and steps, the perceived risk is reduced, and the world is made to appear more controllable (Dörner, 1996). However, this approach deemphasizes the multiplicity of other factors that can aggravate organizational crises. To use our opening examples, in the case of the Coke scare in Europe, public relations staff could neither predict nor control the subconscious association between tainted Coke and mad cow disease. Nor could Enron's public relations staff have predicted that the very practices that earned the company half a dozen "most innovative" and "most admired" awards from *Fortune* magazine would suddenly drag down both Enron and its affiliates ("Enron Named Most Innovative," 2001). As Weick (2001) observed, apparently minor problems can spiral from "small, volitional beginnings" into major crisis situations as "small events are carried forward, cumulate with other events, and over time systematically construct an environment that is a rare combination of unexpected simultaneous failures" (p. 228).

This book's approach to crises follows more from Weick's observation than from most experts' advice about crisis communication. Our approach emphasizes coping with the unexpected and uncertain; it depends on evolving learning as much as advance planning; it builds on concepts from psychology and physics, in addition to communication and business; and it views crises as largely endogenous to organizations in both cause and cure.

Our basic model is complexity theory, or the study of interaction processes within complex systems, including social systems such as organizations. We begin with a fundamental definition of a complex system as one in which "the interaction among constituents of the system, and the interaction between the system and its environment, are of such a nature that the system as a whole cannot be fully understood simply by analyzing its components. Moreover, these relationships are not fixed, but shift and change, often as a result of self-organisation" (Cilliers, 1998, pp. viii–ix). This definition captures the sense of contingency, of rapid change, of limited predictability and control, that characterize organizational crises. It is the foundation for multiple additional characteristics of complex systems that will be described in chapter 3.

Given its focus on organizational relationships, complexity theory has attracted widespread attention among organizational theorists, especially the management community (Ashmos, Duchon, & McDaniel, 2000; Dent, 1999; Haeckel, 1999; Lissack, 1997; Lissack & Roos, 1999; McElroy, 2000; McKelvey, 1999; Stacey, 2001; van Uden, Richardson, & Cilliers, 2001). However, it can pose serious challenges to embedded organizational practices. Complexity theory accepts and embraces uncertainty, ambiguity, conflict, and error to an uncomfortable extent for those accustomed to seeking linear predictability and control (Mirvis, 1996).

At the same time, by acknowledging the disorder of everyday occurrences rather than attempting to simplify them for clarity, complexity theory offers a potentially powerful tool for managers who must face a multifaceted and rapidly changing world. Complexity theory has particular relevance to organizational crises because of its focus on uncertainty and unpredictability and the central role it affords relationships and the communicative process. It thereby creates a link between crisis management and organizational learning, and it suggests new ways for organizations to approach both these areas from a practical standpoint. A complexity-based approach emphasizes flexibility and alertness over standardized or preplanned response to threats; it takes into account the unpredictable nature of crises as they unfold; and it suggests how organizations can best learn from their own experiences and those of others.

Like many others, we differentiate between the terms *crisis management* and *crisis communication*. Despite our roots in communication, in this book we prefer to speak in terms of "management" rather than "communication." We do so for several reasons.

First, we want to distinguish our approach from the tactical emphasis of much crisis literature, which is action-oriented, favoring what to do rather than why crises happen and how to mitigate them in the long run (see Kersten, 2005). In that pragmatic view, communication can appear to be simply tactical. Instead, we wanted to emphasize the comprehensive mind-set involved in crises—a mind-set that penetrates all activities of an organization, that both sets crises in motion to begin with and governs how organizations respond to them. We initially hesitated to use the term *management* because it implies a level of control that, we argue, does not exist in most crisis situations. However, *management* also implies a comprehensive, strategic worldview that we believe is fundamental to understanding crises.

Second, the implications of the complexity and expert learning approaches we advocate in this book go far beyond crisis situations. If fully implemented, our complexity-based model would be enacted in everyday business practices and even organizational structure. Ultimately, an organization capable of this type of crisis management may be best poised to confront challenges of every kind in the business environment—demonstrating competent management in a general sense.

One way to develop a new perspective on organizational problems is to "take an existing knowledge management issue and associated organic practice, reviewing it in the context of complexity theory, and applying the revisions in a visible way that on articulation enables a shift in thinking and understanding" (Snowden, 2000, p. 55). With these recommendations in mind, this book pursues four aims. First, we look at the evolution of crisis communication during the past 20 years, showing how a dominant paradigm of planning and control came to be established. Second, we offer an overview of complexity theory, showing how it may be applied to organizations in general and to crisis management and learning in particular. Third, we examine the role of knowledge and learning in organizations from a new perspective, that of complex responsive processes. Fourth, we critique the most commonly accepted approaches to crisis management—particularly the role of information, knowledge, and learning—from the perspective of complexity-based thinking. Finally, we use the tools provided by complexity theory to suggest a new approach to crisis management and to propose ways in which this complexity-based framework may inform practical applications to organizational behavior before, during, and after crises.

Part I

COMPLEXITY, CRISIS, AND CONTROL

Case History

The Spinach Contamination Crisis

In September 2006, an outbreak of *E. coli* infections swept through the United States, resulting in 199 cases of illness in 26 states, plus three deaths (Burros, 2007). The Food and Drug Administration (FDA) issued a warning to consumers to avoid bagged and other fresh spinach, including salad mixes containing spinach leaves, and six producers issued a nationwide recall of their products. The outbreak was eventually traced to four farms in California's Salinas Valley, whose produce was packed and distributed under more than 30 different brand names throughout the country and also exported to Canada. The bacteria allegedly originated at a nearby cattle ranch, although the exact means of contamination has not yet been determined as of this writing (see Burros, 2007).

The story of the outbreak first broke on September 15 and was covered by newspapers around the country. Somewhat ironically, just days before, the *Los Angeles Times* had run an article about the broader problem of recurring *E. coli* contamination from California produce, noting that the FDA had ordered heightened inspections to attempt to explain the phenomenon. The article also mentioned the difficulty of performing such investigations after an outbreak, explaining that "it can be weeks before an infected person is properly diagnosed and even longer before public health officials determine that there is an outbreak" (Lin, 2006, p. B1) and further noted that contaminated crops may well have been tilled under by the time an investigation is under way.

These statements proved prophetic but also understated the ramifications of produce contamination. Initial accounts of the problem indicated that victims had been identified in Michigan, Wisconsin, Connecticut, Idaho, Indiana, New Mexico, Oregon, and Utah. The first victims had become infected near the end of August, 2 to 3 weeks before the story was publicized ("Feds: Don't Eat Your Spinach," 2006). Both the elapsed time and the vast territory affected by the contamination complicated investigators' efforts to pinpoint its source.

Although the FDA ban ultimately remained in effect for less than 3 weeks, the spinach crisis had widespread and lasting effects. The outbreak affected conventional and organic growers of various types of produce, processed food manufacturers, distributors from Whole Foods to regular supermarket chains to small independent grocers, farmers' markets, restaurants, and others. Reported packaged spinach sales in December 2006 were down 37% from the same period in 2005, despite the FDA having lifted its ban more than 2 months earlier. Costco did not begin selling spinach again until January 2007 and instituted its own quality control measures aimed at preventing future incidences of contamination (Schmit, 2007).

The spinach contamination illustrates the dense interconnectedness of players in the food system, a complex system consisting of producers, handlers, distributors, restaurateurs, consumers, and regulators. Crisis issues in this system frequently originate at the point of consumption, when outbreaks of food-borne illness or deaths trigger an investigation into the sources of contaminated or tainted foods (see, e.g., Fearn-Banks, 2007; Gonzalez-Herrero & Pratt, 1995; Paraskevas, 2006). In part as a result of the effects of this increasingly complex production and supply system, food safety concerns are growing among consumers (Hosansky, 2002; Pollan, 2006). Situations such as mad cow disease and the avian flu both represent serious health and economic threats, as do the recent issues with pet food containing melamine-contaminated rice, wheat, and corn gluten imported as additives from countries as far-flung as China and South Africa (see, e.g., Hosansky, 2002; Reeves, 2002; Weise & Schmit, 2007; see part III of this book for more discussion of the pet food crisis).

These examples illustrate another side effect of complex organizational systems, namely that crises often cannot be contained within a single organization, geographical area, or economic sector. The spinach contamination issue is thus a form of organizational crisis that is not contained within a single organization but affects an interlocking set of actors in various domains.

The next two chapters in this section provide an overview of current crisis management literature and theories of complexity. The outbreak of E. coli-contaminated spinach offers an example of some of the limitations of mainstream crisis management approaches and a first glimpse at how theories of complexity can help researchers and practitioners gain a better understanding of the ways crises emerge and evolve.

2

Crisis Communication

The Evolution of a Field

Organizations have been responding to crises since the very first tribe faced a drought, death of a chief, or enemy attack. However, organizational crisis management is a relatively new specialization for both academic study and professional practice. During its rapid evolution over the past 20 years, the field of crisis communication has been fed by multiple disciplines, each with its own theoretical focus, definitional issues, teleological assumptions, and practical recommendations. In this chapter we look briefly at the evolution of the field and examine its dominant perspectives.

Definitional Issues

One of the first matters to address, and one that may never be entirely resolved, is the definition of what constitutes a crisis. Many authors have noted the paradox inherent in a crisis: the simultaneous potential for both destruction and opportunity. At its inception in the early days of medicine, the term *crisis* referred to the critical turning point of an illness when the patient's fate hung in the balance. Since then it has come to mean "a relatively short period of confusion or turbulence which leads to a transition from one [state] to another" (Burke, 2000, p. 203).

The Chinese term for crisis is often mentioned because it combines the ideographs for "danger" and "opportunity" (Fink, 1986). The Western view of crisis shares this ambivalence, with most crisis definitions invoking this duality. Hence Fearn-Banks (2007) defined a crisis as "a major occurrence with a potentially negative outcome affecting an organization, company, or industry, as well as its publics, products, services, or good name" (p. 2). However, she also noted that effective management of, and communication about, crises can actually improve an organization's reputation. Similarly, Bronn and Olson (1999) saw crises as the product

13

of "either a threat or opportunity that arises from internal or external issues that may have a major impact on an organization" (p. 355).

The particular factors emphasized in a given definition of crisis differ widely, as they reflect divergent views of both causes and solutions. Some authors have emphasized the role of human agency in defining a crisis. For example, Linke (1989) identified four types of crises according to how much time they allowed for managerial response. The first type is an *exploding* crisis, such as an accident or natural disaster, a specific event with instantaneous consequences. The second is an *immediate* crisis, such as a government hearing or a TV news report, that catches the organization by surprise but still leaves some time to prepare a response. The third is a *building* crisis, such as layoffs or an upcoming Congressional vote, which an organization can anticipate and take steps to influence. Finally there is a *continuing* crisis, such as asbestos liability or public debates on issues such as gun control or stem-cell research, in which the crisis builds slowly and will not easily dissipate.

Others have extended the construct of crisis to include not simply a description of the event per se and how it is managed but also its effect on the members of the organization and other stakeholders. Indeed, many authors agree that a situation becomes a crisis when one or more stakeholder groups perceive it as such. A rumor, or simply the perception of a "crisis event," is sufficient to trigger a response, regardless of whether the rumor or perception is grounded in fact (Coombs, 2007; Fearn-Banks, 2007). As Weick (1995) noted, meaning is not intrinsic to an experience but lies "in the kind of attention that is directed to this experience" (p. 26). Thus how an event is perceived and how it affects the people linked to an organization, both individually and as a group, will determine whether or not it is classified as a crisis and how it is subsequently handled. Lerbinger (1997) pointed out that when a crisis follows a slow, cumulative buildup, the crisis threshold is more likely to be defined by outsiders—media, regulators, whistle-blowers, activists—and also more likely to involve managers who have ignored early warning signals.

The spinach contamination described in the introduction to this chapter illustrates the limitations of some of these definitions of crises and how each tends to focus attention on certain aspects while neglecting others. For example, one facet viewed differently by various scholars is timing: The first victims were affected in late August, health officials began investigating in early September, and the outbreak first became known to the general public in mid-September. Furthermore, the problem of recurring *E. coli* contamination of California produce had already been tagged by federal officials as a matter for investigation. Where, then, does one place the beginning of the crisis? Would it be considered a crisis defined by outsiders or by one or more of the organizations directly involved? For public health specialists and California growers, the spinach outbreak might be seen as part of a larger pattern or ongoing issue, whereas for much of the public it emerged suddenly and without warning. Those who knew or knew of the early victims would have yet another perspective on the timing of the crisis.

Responding further to these issues of timing and warning, researchers have defined crises by their psychological attributes, particularly what it feels like to be involved in a crisis from a manager's point of view. Hence Lerbinger (1997) and Lagadec (1993) described three psychological issues that beset managers facing a crisis: extreme time pressures to act, lack of clarity about what is the best action to take, and an element of surprise. A crisis definition by Pearson and Clair (1998) similarly highlights the subjective perception of organizational crisis: "An organizational crisis is a low-probability, high-impact situation that is perceived by critical stakeholders to threaten the viability of the organization and that is subjectively experienced by these individuals as personally and socially threatening" (p. 66). That description comes close to Morin's view of a crisis as "always a progression of disorders, instabilities and hazards" in which the immediate future is uncertain (1992, p. 14). It leads to Weick's (1993) term for the psychological impact of crisis as a *cosmology episode* that jolts an individual's entire belief system. Although not everyone involved in the spinach contamination was surprised, it is safe to assume that it was considered a serious threat by stakeholders ranging from growers to distributors to consumers and shook the nation's confidence in the safety of the food system.

Crises can also be defined according to cause. This approach was taken by Lerbinger (1997), who organized his examination of crises around seven different types: (1) *natural,* (2) *technological,* (3) *crises of confrontation,* (4) *crises of malevolence,* (5) *skewed management values,* (6) *deception,* and (7) *management misconduct.* A similar, though simplified, approach was taken by Small (1991), who reduced Lerbinger's seven types of crises to four categories. Small's first type of crisis is *technological* and involves flaws in equipment design, major accidents at industrial facilities, product recalls, mishaps involving hazardous wastes, and transportation disasters. His second category of crisis is *societal,* ranging from kidnapping to war to sabotage (crises of "confrontation" and "malevolence," in Lerbinger's phrase [pp. 112, 144]). The third type of crisis is *natural disaster,* and the fourth is *managerial* or *systemic* types of crises, such as charges of wrongdoing by a corporation or its officers, plant shutdowns, worker layoffs, charges of excessive profits, business rumors, and allegations of illegal dealings by an organization in a foreign country. All but the last of these cause-related definitions encourage a view of crisis in terms of events impinging from the outside, to which the organization then reacts.

Other authors have favored crisis definitions that emphasize business impacts. Hence Barton (1993, 2001) listed 14 kinds of crisis events that commonly affect businesses, ranging from embezzlement and environmental accidents to employee shootings and bankruptcy. Meyers and Holusha (1986), authors of one of the earliest books on crises, identified nine types of business crises: (1) *public perception*, (2) *sudden market shift*, (3) *product failure*, (4) *top management succession*, (5) *cash*, (6) *industrial relations*, (7) *hostile takeover*, (8) *adverse international events*, and (9) *regulation and deregulation*. More recently, Mitroff (2004) and many of his coauthors (e.g., Mitroff & Anagnos, 2001; Mitroff & Pearson, 1993; Pauchant & Mitroff, 1992) designed a complex taxonomy of crises according to the type of business event initiated. They proposed six clusters or crisis categories: (1) *economic attacks* on proprietary information that come from outside the firm; (2) *information attacks* that come from outside and directly threaten the firm's economic well-being; (3) "*breaks*," or internal malfunctions; (4) *megadamage*, referring to major catastrophes such as Bhopal or Chernobyl; (5) "*psycho*" crises such as terrorism, sabotage, or product tampering; and (6) *occupational health diseases*: slow-onset, simmering crises such as asbestos liability or Gulf War syndrome. Approaching crises from the victims' angle, Gottschalk (1993) categorized three types of crisis according to who gets hurt: *business calamities*, such as bankruptcies or oil spills; *consumer troubles*, such as defective products; and *human tragedies,* such as employee violence or airplane crashes.

No matter what attributes they choose to highlight, all crisis taxonomists emphasize that their categories are not mutually exclusive. For example, the 1986 gas leak that killed nearly 4,000 people in Bhopal, India, was a technological disaster but was quickly compounded by bad crisis management on the part of Union Carbide and became a managerial crisis (Weick, 1988). Similarly, 2005's Hurricane Katrina was a natural disaster compounded by managerial incompetence at all levels of government. The *E. coli* contamination combined multiple, uncertain causes with structural factors that exacerbated the crisis, such as the produce packing and distribution system that allowed the contaminated spinach to be distributed throughout the country. Despite this linkage, some authors seek to separate these aspects, making a critical distinction between a natural disaster, emergency, or technological crisis on the one hand and a "crisis of legitimacy" on the other (Massey, 2001). Hence Mitroff and Anagnos (2001) described crises as "man-made or human-caused" events, rather than natural disasters, in order to distinguish the crisis management field from risk and emergency management.

In contrast, we contend that managerial attitudes and behaviors before, during, and after crises have a direct link to the crisis of legitimacy that ensues. For example, Fearn-Banks (2007) defined crisis management as "a process of strategic planning for a crisis or negative turning point" that is linked to crisis communication as "the dialog between the organization and its publics prior to, during, and after the negative occurrence" (p. 2). She thereby defined both management and communication as parts of the same process. Similarly, although Coombs's authoritative book on crises (2007) focused almost exclusively on communication issues, he referred to his approach as "crisis management." Like those authors, we do not separate communication from other management actions. That is one reason why this book adopts the practices of most other crisis literature by considering communication as one component—albeit the central one—in a larger complex of crisis management.

This inclusiveness is important because the particular features emphasized in a given definition of crisis can have a profound impact on the resulting scholarly theories and on the behaviors manifested by the organization. Pearson and Clair (1998) noted that discussions of organizational crises vary considerably according to the different disciplines or perspectives referenced by authors. They identified three broad perspectives—psychological, social-political, and technological-structural—and examined the effect of each approach on the "4Cs" for crisis studies: the *causes* attributed for crises within each discipline; the *consequences* of crises; the *cautionary* measures advocated to prevent crises or minimize impact; and the *coping* techniques suggested in response to crisis occurrences. (A brief summary of their classification is presented in table 2.1.) They concluded that crisis management has suffered from a fragmented paradigm, and they recommended that scholars and practitioners attempt to synthesize the three approaches into a single, multidimensional perspective. This chapter, and this book as a whole, attempts such an approach by examining mainstream assumptions about crisis communication in the light of a metatheory of complex systems.

Evolution of the Crisis Communication Discipline

Most authors trace the origin of the crisis communication field to the first Tylenol tampering case in 1982 (Alexander, 2000; Mitroff & Anagnos, 2001; Mitroff, Harrington, & Gai, 1996). Impressed by Johnson & Johnson's ability to retrieve both market share and reputation in the wake of this potentially disastrous crisis, scholars and practitioners began a type of reverse engineering process to examine how it had been done and attempted to replicate these results in other crisis situations (Murray & Shohen, 1992).

As the field has matured, its assumptions have become increasingly complex, and it is possible to discern phases of development in which the emphasis shifted. In the broadest sense, during the 1980s the field was concerned mainly with tactical advice that prescribed specific plans and checklists. During the 1990s, crisis specialists began to give more attention to strategic issues, noting the impacts of contingency and uncertainty along with the possibility of multiple outcomes. Most recently, those who study crisis have focused increasingly on organizational culture and transformation. Elements from each phase have carried over into the next so that it is possible to speak of a "dominant" view of crisis communication representing an accretion of 20 years of study. Overall, crisis specialists have given increasing attention to the open-endedness

Table 2.1. Three Approaches to Crisis Management
(Pearson & Clair, 1998)

	Psychological Approach	Social-Political Approach	Technological-Structural Approach
Causes	Cognitive or behavioral limitations or errors, in individuals or groups	Breakdown of shared understandings and social structures	Tightly coupled, densely interactive technological and managerial structures that foster complex and unpredictable interactions
Consequences	Shattered assumptions about organization and/or its members, feeling threatened or otherwise insecure, victimization of affected individuals	Dissolution of shared values, beliefs, structures, roles	More or less widespread disaster and destruction, including self-destruction
Cautionary Measures	Understanding vulnerability and potential harm	Flexibility in norms and behaviors that guide interaction, mutual respect, wisdom	Avoidance of risky and/or poorly understood technology or "fail-safe" structures designed to limit risks
Coping Techniques	Readjusting beliefs, assumptions, behaviors, and emotions	Reconstruction of adjusted meanings, collective adaptation	Emergency intervention to assist victims and repair structural damage

of crisis, the role played by multiple stakeholders, and the interaction between internal and external drivers of crisis. This evolution points toward a model of crisis as a complex adaptive system.

The Tactical Approach

Tactical, "how-to" approaches to crisis communication planning began to appear in the literature in the late 1970s (Smith, 1979) and increased in popularity throughout the 1980s. This development came mainly in response to a series of high-profile crises: the 1979 Three Mile Island incident, the 1982 Tylenol poisonings, the 1984 Bhopal disaster, the Challenger and Chernobyl accidents in 1986, and the Exxon Valdez oil spill in 1989. The Tylenol case is often cited as an example of excellent crisis management even though Johnson & Johnson had no specific crisis plan in place prior to the incident (Fearn-Banks, 2007; Mitroff & Anagnos, 2001; Murray & Shohen, 1992).

Despite J&J's success, beginning in the 1980s authors generally emphasized the need for detailed planning. Many early writings focused primarily on the crisis communication plan, or crisis management plan (CMP; Brewton, 1987; Ramée, 1987; Smith, 1979). Perhaps as a result of increased public attention to crises, the communication aspects of the plan emphasized information diffusion, mainly media relations and the need to develop carefully worded press releases, to compile media contact lists, and to carry out spokesperson training as a cornerstone of crisis preparation efforts (Fugel, 1996; Hearit, 1994; Murray & Shohen, 1992; Shell, 1993; Spencer, 1989). Although necessary, this emphasis on careful planning promoted a somewhat mechanical approach to crisis management, with instructions on preparing telephone trees, checklists, and step-by-step contingency plans (Fearn-Banks, 2007; Murray & Shohen, 1992).

This approach to crisis management generally focuses on the metaphor of a crisis "life cycle" (Fink, 1986; Gonzalez-Herrero & Pratt, 1995), and it breaks the crisis down into discrete stages that follow a linear sequence. The number of specific stages identified in these models varies from author to author, but most can be combined into three general stages: precrisis, crisis, and postcrisis (Coombs, 2007).

The Strategic Approach

Early descriptions of the crisis life cycle tended to see the final, postcrisis stage as the end of the crisis management function (Fink, 1986). However, after a few years the trend moved toward a continuous, cyclical perspective on crisis. Especially during the 1990s, authors began to view the crisis plan alone as insufficient to safeguard a company's reputational and tangible assets, and they shifted their focus toward preventive action (Coombs, 2007; Gonzalez-Herrero & Pratt, 1995; Mitroff et al., 1996).

Thus as the field matured, practitioners and scholars began paying more attention to the different needs of the individual stages of the crisis life cycle, focusing on areas such as issues management and environmental scanning (Gonzalez-Herrero & Pratt, 1995; Kash & Darling, 1998; Regester & Larkin, 2005); response strategies and messages for different types of crises (Benoit, 1997; D'Aveni & Macmillan, 1990; Hearit, 1994; Sellnow & Ulmer, 1995); and practice simulations and recovery (Burnett, 1998; Ramée, 1987).

This current period of crisis communication takes more of a strategic approach than the prior tactics-driven phase of the 1970s and 1980s. For example, Millar and Heath (2004) saw crises as consisting of two dimensions: technical/managerial and rhetorical. Both dimensions have to do with planned actions and statements that position the organization in relation to its stakeholders' perceptions and its own needs, that "responsibly and ethically address stakeholder concerns, issues, and need for control" (Millar & Heath, 2004, p. 8), and that "demonstrate persuasively that the organization understands the crisis and has the resources—intellectual, managerial, financial, rhetorical, and ethical" to restore the crisis situation to an "acceptable" state of affairs (p. 11). The acknowledgement of mutual pressures from, as well as toward, stakeholder perceptions, coupled with an emphasis on understanding the symbolic dimensions of crises, place current approaches to crisis management in the realm of strategy rather than tactics.

The ongoing nature of current crisis management practices also emphasizes the strategic approach. Crisis management has become a circular process that starts and ends with the "default" stage of intelligence gathering and monitoring, what Mitroff et al. (1996) and Coombs (2007) referred to as "signal detection," aimed at early discovery of potential crises through careful internal and external monitoring. This approach also focuses on the postcrisis stage, advocating careful post hoc evaluation to clarify the lessons learned and incorporate them into the plan for future use (Fishman, 1999; O'Rourke, 1996; Smallman & Weir, 1999). According to this perspective, crisis prevention, detection, and management become an integral part of the company's way of doing business, rather than a separate and distinct project to be handled only when a crisis actually strikes (Mitroff & Anagnos, 2001). Crisis planning as a subset or form of strategic planning (Burnett, 1998; Ren, 2000) has become the prevailing approach. In fact, this paradigm has become so widely adopted that it has even been used to evaluate the relative professionalism of public relations practitioners overall (Bronn & Olson, 1999).

The Adaptive Approach

Although it is still the dominant approach to crises, the strategic perspective has expanded focus as the cultural and organizational foundations of crisis have claimed increasing attention. Most recently, crisis studies have begun to emphasize the interaction between internal and external stakeholders, cultural drivers of crisis, and the social construction of crisis. Compared with the earlier days of crisis communication, there is less emphasis on viewing crises in asymmetrical terms as situations in which an audience is fed information tailored to protect the company's interests. The trend to view crises in strategic terms, in which audience viewpoints are sounded through issues management, is developing into a relational view of crisis, with ongoing interaction between internal and external stakeholders.

One recent trend in crisis management scholarship focuses on developing strong, positive relationships with various stakeholder groups as a preventive measure or attenuating factor in the event of a crisis (Caponigro, 2000; Coombs, 2000; Gonzalez-Herrero & Pratt, 1995). Indeed, Irvine and Millar (1996) found that the vast majority of organizational crises were not the result of technical failures or environmental damage but were instead the direct result of the organization's inability to develop and maintain positive relationships with key internal and external stakeholders. Coombs (2000) proposed an analytical approach in which response strategies are adjusted based on factors that include relational history with key stakeholder groups, the locus of responsibility for the crisis trigger event, and relative "stability," or frequency, of crises. Similarly, the contingency theory developed by Cameron and his colleagues argued that organizations' stances toward their publics during crises are influenced by dozens of relational considerations ranging from legal concerns to decision makers' personality traits to internal-external trust levels (Cancel, Cameron, Sallot, & Mitrook, 1997; Cancel, Mitrook, & Cameron, 1999). They pointed out that interactions between organizations and their publics "result from combinations of variables at work...that may change according to the dynamics of the situation"; and therefore, crisis decisions result from the interaction between a "matrix" of variables rather than flowing linearly from one or several variables (Yarbrough, Cameron, Sallot, & McWilliams, 1998, pp. 40, 41).

All of these crisis theorists rely on the concept of relationships as repeated local interactions that allow organizations and publics to adapt to one another. Although they do not use the term, the process they describe fundamentally characterizes the behavior of complex adaptive systems, with their "interaction among constituents" in "relationships [that] are not fixed, but shift and change" (Cilliers, 1998, pp. viii–ix). The next chapter discusses the traits of complex systems in greater detail, and subsequent chapters explore the similarities between such systems and organizational crises.

A related stream of inquiry has examined the role of sensemaking in crisis perception and response. Defined as "the reciprocal interaction of information seeking, meaning ascription, and action" (Thomas, Clark, & Gioia, 1993, p. 240), sensemaking clearly shares assumptions with crisis preparation activities such as issues management. It can also shed light on audiences' constructions of the motivations and effects of organizations' actions. Operating from this viewpoint, sensemaking scholarship often examines case studies of organizational crises from a context-sensitive standpoint (e.g., Murphy, 2001; Sellnow & Seeger, 2001; Smith, 2000; Weick, 1993). For example, Ulmer et al. (2007) reviewed the National Weather Service's response to the 1997 flooding of the Red River Valley and concluded that the organization had failed to properly make sense of events as they unfolded. They found that National Weather Service reports during the crisis did not reflect the rapid changes and complexity of the situation over the vast geographic area involved. The reports downplayed the uncertainty of weather predictions, which hindered the effectiveness of response efforts, as emergency volunteers found themselves having to repeatedly change the location and extent of their sandbagging and dike-building actions. This sensemaking failure ultimately meant that the reports contained too many inaccuracies to prove reliable or useful to many of the citizens and communities affected by the floods, which exacerbated the final damage. Better contextual awareness and sensitivity to changing conditions on the part of both the National Weather Service and citizens in flood-prone areas could have produced a more effective overall response to the disaster.

Overall, crisis management studies have evolved through accretion. Most current work maintains the focus on careful planning, usually written, with which the field originated. However, an increasing number of authors have supplemented the more mechanistic aspects of planning, or manipulative aspects of strategic issues management, with an adaptive approach that examines flaws in organizational culture, unintended consequences, and blind spots or seemingly irrational behavior. What is also needed, we contend, is a theoretical framework that takes into account crises with multiple or uncertain points of origin, rather than the more typical "organization-centric" view that is inadequate when applied to complex situations such as the spinach contamination or Hurricane Katrina.

In the next chapter we examine theories of complex systems. We argue that complex adaptive systems are a natural evolution of the current trend toward acknowledging the uncertainties inherent in crises as social constructions with multiple possible outcomes. In later chapters we show how complexity theory can be used to harness this uncertainty, multifariousness, and lack of control in the service of ongoing adaptive learning that helps organizations to respond to crises more adeptly and effectively than before.

3

Theories of Complexity

Like other social sciences, the communication field has a long tradition of theories and models adopted from the natural sciences. Some scholars (e.g., Introna, 2003) caution against too readily making that translation, on the grounds that social and natural sciences are incommensurable in many respects. However, other scholars (e.g., McKie, 2001) argue that adopting the rigidity and quantitative bias of the hard sciences has actually worked to "retard" the social sciences (p. 81). These scholars consider that a complexity-based perspective provides a more accurate view of both natural and social sciences than does traditional reductionism.

Urry (2003), for example, noted that a number of scientists from both domains—including such scholars as Ilya Prigogine and Immanuel Wallerstein—have advocated "breaking down the division between 'natural' and 'social' science through seeing both domains as characterized by 'complexity'" (p. 12). Bridging natural and social sciences thus involves seeing both domains as expressions of the same underlying worldview, not "conceiving of humanity as mechanical, but rather instead conceiving of nature as active and creative" (Wallerstein, 1996; as cited in Urry, 2003, pp. 12–13). This point of view creates a middle ground between the use of complexity theory strictly as metaphor and the insistence that it be quantitatively operationalized, and it is this view we adopt here.

Efforts to utilize theories imported from the complexity sciences have also challenged scholars' understanding in a more immediate fashion. This is still an emerging body of knowledge in which the same terms are defined by researchers in multiple ways, often using unfamiliar scientific terminology or loosely adapting the terminology to suit particular needs. Hence Letiche (2000) noted: "Complexity theorists can discuss emergence and self-organization—as well as 'complex adaptive systems,' 'attractors/bifurcations,' and the 'edge of chaos'—and actually be referring to very different universes of discourse" (p. 545; also see Price, 1997). This lack of cohesion also explains why we generally refer to multiple theories of complexity, or more simply "complexity," as an umbrella term to refer to this group of perspectives.

To avoid contributing to further lexical confusion, in this chapter we define major concepts in complexity theory, giving an overview of its foundations and describing the most important theoretical perspectives currently being explored. Throughout, we link complexity with crisis management, laying out the approach that will guide our discussion in the remainder of this book.

Complexity Theories and Complex Systems

There is no single definition of complexity theory. Instead, scholars have advanced various definitions according to which aspects of the theoretical perspective they wish to emphasize. For example, focusing on complexity's societal implications, Murphy (2000) defined complexity theory as "the study of many individual actors who interact locally in an effort to adapt to their immediate situation. These local adaptations, however, accumulate to form large-scale patterns that affect the greater society, often in ways that could not have been anticipated" (p. 450). Taking a different tack, the unpredictability of complex systems was emphasized by Richardson and Cilliers (2001), who defined complex systems as "comprised of a large number of entities that display a high level of nonlinear interactivity" (p. 8). Connectivity and interdependence were accentuated in a parsimonious definition by van Uden et al. (2001): "Complexity science basically tells us that everything is connected to everything else" (p. 57). Other authors have compiled lists of features that characterize complex systems, and we join them by elaborating our own set of defining principles that distinguish a complexity approach from other perspectives.

Seven Principles of Complex Systems

Despite the differing emphases of these definitions, all complex systems show consistent distinguishing features that are important for crisis management. These are summarized here to provide principles for interpreting complex behavior that we use in the remainder of this book. Seven of the basic features of complex systems are also summarized in table 3.1.

Principle #1: Interacting Agents

First, *complex systems are composed of individual elements, or agents.* In crisis management terms, these may be persons (members of a crisis planning team, a reporter on a given beat), organizations (a corporation

Table 3.1. Distinguishing Features of Complex Systems

1. Complex systems are composed of individual elements/agents.
2. Agents' interactions alter the system over time.
   • Interactions are local.
   • Interactions are rule-based.
   • Interactions are recurrent.
   • Interactions produce adaptability.
   • Interactions are nonlinear.
3. Complex systems are self-organizing.
4. Complex systems are unstable.
5. Complex systems are dynamic, with their history an essential feature.
6. Complex systems have permeable and ill-defined boundaries.
7. Complex systems are irreducible.

or not-for-profit undergoing a crisis), or an entire industry group (the Securities Industry Association or the nuclear power industry). However, having multiple individual elements is not in itself sufficient to constitute complexity: A closed system that consists of many elements may be merely complicated, not complex. For example, a space shuttle is a merely complicated system containing a large number of interacting parts, whereas a soufflé is complex, despite having fewer distinct ingredients, because its ingredients are irreversibly (sometimes unpredictably) transformed during its preparation. Similarly, a crisis planning team is not like an assembly line. In pooling their vantage points, crisis team members may generate novel ways to cope with the organization's problems so that the final approach to a crisis may be quite different from what the members expected at the beginning of the process. In contrast, individuals on an assembly line interact to create a predesigned product, and unanticipated outcomes constitute defective goods.

Principle #2: Adaptability

This principle of interaction generates a second feature of complex systems: *The agents in a complex system interact in ways that alter the system itself over time.* These interactions need not be physical; they may also relate to sharing information (Cilliers, 1998). This feature has a number of corollaries:

• *Interactions are local.* They have a relatively short range, primarily affecting neighboring agents. No individual agent has complete knowledge about the behavior of the system as a whole, only the information received locally. In fact, as crisis management teams know well, it is not feasible to explore all possible courses of action; it is feasible, however, to explore the most immediate context. In a typical example of selective planning, Fink (1986) designed a method to prioritize specific potential crises that require immediate planning by combining probability of occurrence with expected impact on reputation and bottom line. Only the most immediate and damaging crises were selected for planning.

Complexity theorist Stuart Kauffman (2000) examined the dynamics of local interaction from the standpoint of biological evolution. He termed this local exploration "the adjacent possible" (p. 142), emphasizing that change transpires and diffuses step by step. Through gradual expansion of the adjacent possible, large-scale changes emerge over time. As Cilliers (1998) noted, local interaction "does not preclude wide-ranging influence— since the interaction is rich, the route from one element to any other can usually be covered in a few steps. As a result, the influence gets modulated along the way. It can be enhanced, suppressed or altered in a number of ways" (p. 4). Therefore, the behavior of the system is not a direct result of the number of interactions among individual elements but of the patterns that emerge from these interactions. Crisis managers apply this principle when they do environmental surveillance: They rarely focus on a single individual in the environment but look for patterns built up from individual reactions—customer response, legislative initiatives, or media coverage.

- *Interactions are rule-based.* They do not follow fixed regulation by a higher echelon (such as senior management) but are dynamically developed by the agents themselves in the course of their interaction. At the same time, the context of the interaction— organizational, economic, cultural—provides some constraints for the local interactions.

  In terms of crisis management, Marra (2004) argued that the existence of a crisis communication plan is not synonymous with successful crisis management. Rather, he used two crises—one at AT&T and one at the University of Maryland—to show that successful crisis communication depends first on the decision-making autonomy of individual agents (such as public relations staff) and second on an organizational culture of open communication. He concluded that tactical details are secondary compared with "a supportive organizational philosophy" (p. 324). Marra's study showed in pragmatic terms that rules for interaction are developed on the micro level with interaction between agents as a situation unfolds but are patterned by macro-level organizational expectations and context.

- *Interactions are recurrent.* Effects of interaction are "looped," meaning they can feed back at any point in the system, either positively (to encourage change) or negatively (to encourage stability). Recurrent interactions and the type of feedback can be beneficial or harmful. For example, Mitleton-Kelly (2003) pointed out that excessive planning can function as a repressively stabilizing form of negative feedback: "Although the intention of change management interventions is to create new ways of working, they may block or constrain emergent patterns of behaviour if they attempt to excessively design and control outcomes" (p. 35). On the other hand, when an organization has gone deeply into crisis, negative feedback could help to stabilize it. For example, Williams and Olaniran (1994) argued that Exxon's mismanagement of the Valdez crisis showed "hypervigilance" whereby the company tried one approach after another in quick succession, never settling down to a stable state in which communication could be effective.

- *Interactions produce adaptability.* In a complex system, adaptation is mutual and multifaceted. That means that the system does not simply accommodate an outside environment, as general systems theory contends. Instead, the parts of the whole—including staff, technologies, cultural norms, institutional and legal structures—adapt to one another in an ongoing process. At its best, adaptability can generate new patterns of behavior that enable an organization to operate more effectively than it would have by maintaining invariable behaviors. Hence Ashby (1954) proposed the law of requisite variety, whereby "the range and variety of stimuli that impinge upon a system from its environment [must] be in some way reflected in the range and variety of the system's repertoire of responses" (Boisot, 2003, p. 187). Thus, in a rapidly changing environment, the most effective organizations are those that generate a rich variety of possible responses, because "another way of stating Ross Ashby's law is to say that the complexity of a system must be adequate to the complexity of its environment that it finds itself in" (Boisot, 2003, p. 187).

  Crisis planning teams attempt to enact the law of requisite variety when they specify the broadest range of possible crisis types, audience reactions, and organizational responses. In the case of the spinach *E. coli* outbreak described earlier in this section, an extensive array of individual and coordinated responses were necessary on the part of growers, handlers, restaurants, supermarkets and other distributors, policy makers, public health agencies, and consumers, all distributed over a vast geographical area. This instance shows how the instability and interconnectedness of complex systems makes it impossible to fully specify their potential directions.

- *Interactions are nonlinear.* The results of individual interactions are unpredictable: Small causes can have a profound impact on the system, and large events may have minimal effect. As is discussed later on, the nonlinearity of the system is especially destabilizing when an organization is operating in "far from equilibrium" (far from stable norms) conditions typical of a crisis mode. This characteristic suggests why, in such crisis environments, small events often appear to tip media coverage into the negative, or why all the organization's communication efforts sometimes seem powerless to stem the momentum of public opinion.

Principle #3: Self-Organization

Returning to the general characteristics of complex systems, a third feature is that *they are self-organizing*. Agents learn from their interactions, adapting to each other based on the feedback received, in an ongoing process known as "coevolution." What they learn cannot be specifically predicted, as it emerges from individual and shared history, as well as ongoing interaction. Eventually these small local moves amount to patterns. Theorists often refer to the outcome of coevolution as "emergence"—that is, unpredictable patterns of order that appear through a process of self-organization. Varela (1995), for example, asserted that emergence refers to the point at which a system's local interactions become global patterns encompassing all individual agents.

This feature of emergence—of unpredictable self-organization—accounts for the often-made observation that if a system is truly complex, it is more than the sum of its parts because of the interaction among those parts (van Uden et al., 2001). That is the reason that, no matter how complete our familiarity with its components, a complex system does not allow us to predict with certainty how or in what direction the system as a whole will develop (Boje, 2000). For example, Fink (1986) described crises as "overdetermined": "for any one effect there may be five causes, and for any one cause there may be five effects" (as cited in Lagadec, 1993, p. 64). Indeed, given their local vision, the agents themselves may not be aware of the themes patterning their behavior. Hence Thomsen (1995) spoke of environmental scanning in terms not of rational analysis but rather of a "sixth sense," a "heightened sensitivity," and being "magically aware" of patterns and correspondences that emerge from the business environment (p. 109).

Some authors speak of recurrent patterns in complex systems in terms of "fractals." Fractal mathematics is a specific type of nonlinear calculation that uses a series of recursive equations to create patterns that remain invariable regardless of scale. Fractal equations produce graphical representations that show how very slight alterations in interactions among the elements of a complex system will, over time, develop into patterns that evolve in a nonlinear yet regular fashion. These replicas are immune to the problem of scale because they consist of infinite sets of nested interactions that produce identical patterns. Because they portray an iterative process that results from incremental evolution, fractal representations also incorporate the essential element of time and show how the history of a given system plays a role in reaching its present state.

One example commonly used to illustrate fractal-like phenomena is that of the cloud: Water droplets self-organize into regular and identifiable patterns, yet it is impossible to predict exactly what form a cloud will take. This principle holds true whether we are examining the steam from a teapot, eyeing a storm cloud in the sky above, or viewing

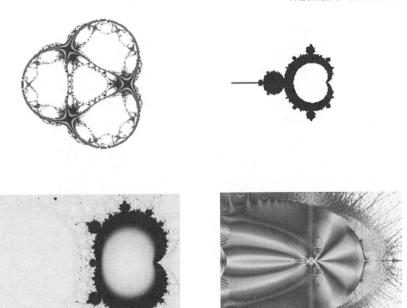

Figure 3.1. Various Types of Fractal Renderings

satellite photographs of global weather patterns: The scale may change, but the underlying phenomenon remains the same. Figure 3.1 shows a few examples of different kinds of fractal patterns, rendered in two and three dimensions.

The mapping of fractal patterns also provides a means of conceptualizing the qualitative features of systems. Because they are multilayered, fractal patterns lend themselves to examining behaviors and relationships through various tiers of an organization, at the individual, group, division, organization-wide, and extraorganizational levels (Ferdig, 2000). Several authors have advocated the use of fractals to model social and organizational processes (Murphy, 2000; Urry, 2003). For example, Stacey (2001) described complex responsive processes as fractal interactions in order to emphasize that individuals and groups inhabit the same plane— rather than existing on separate ontological levels, as traditional social science holds—and are merely variations in scale that depend on the level of examination used to observe the system. Viewed as longitudinal maps, fractals can be seen as visual representations of developing patterns in the "adjacent possible" over time. Nonetheless, the use of fractal images to represent complex processes is purely descriptive, not predictive. Patterns may become visible after the fact, but the very nature of complex adaptive systems and complex responsive processes precludes accurate prediction.

Principle #4: Instability

The principle of coevolution, expressed through fractal patterns, brings up a fourth general characteristic of complex systems: *They are unstable*. A complex system is constantly evolving, requiring an ongoing flow of energy. In complexity-based thinking, stability is not a desired state; indeed, it is possible only when the system ceases to be complex. Thus any attempt at representation that does not include the dimension of time can be considered only an incomplete vision of the system or, at best, a snapshot of a specific point in time. This sense of moment-to-moment instability also expresses the most challenging characteristics of a crisis mode: the need to act in an atmosphere of uncertainty and "feeling of powerlessness and extreme danger" that result from "intervening in any way... [in] a sensitive system in which everything is interrelated, [and] can have drastic and unexpected results" (Lagadec, 1993, p. 178).

Principle #5: Influence of History

A fifth general characteristic of complex systems is a corollary to this instability and coevolution: *Complex systems are dynamic*—that is, their history is an essential feature of their emergent patterns. Because the evolution of the system is the result of iterative interaction between its agents, past history helps to produce present behavior. The memory of a complex system is present at the level of individual elements, such as the experiences and personal opinions of organizational members, as well as at the macroscopic level in the rituals and other features of a shared culture (Richardson, Mathieson, & Cilliers, 2000). Hence, Marra (2004) argued that organizational culture, rather than a specific crisis plan, is one of several factors that determine successful crisis communication. In a fractal-like replication, organizational history puts its stamp on all aspects of a crisis, at all levels of an organization.

However, the influence of history does not mean that a system is predictable. Contrary to the well-known adage, in a complex system those who do not remember the past are not condemned to repeat it, at least not in identical ways. Interactions between agents are repeated in a recursive and reflexive manner that allows variations to build up over time. Hence even organizational situations that are governed by highly structured and repetitive procedures may not always be carried out in exactly the same manner. Over time, the procedural rules themselves may be changed to reflect actual practice—or the subtle variation may produce unforeseen consequences, positive or negative. This type of realization made it possible for Finch and Welker (2004) to argue that improvisational responses to possible crisis simulations are superior to overly specified crisis plans because they allow for variations to build up around the basic core of crisis management processes, resulting in a range of adaptive responses that meet the requirement to match a turbulent environment with requisite variety.

Principle #6: Permeable Boundaries

As a sixth general principle, *complex systems have permeable and ill-defined boundaries*. Here complexity-based thinking departs from other social science approaches, notably general systems theory, that assume the existence of distinct borders between a system and its environment, even though systems are constantly adapting to their changing environments. Complex systems theory revises this perspective. It defines complex systems as open, in the sense that the environment provides feedback used in local interactions. However, a complex system never simply adapts passively to its environment; it evolves its own rules, as its component agents make local decisions using information from the environment as part of the decision-making mix. These decisions in turn bring about changes in the environment. In this sense, the environment is not external to the system but integral to the system itself. Corporate executives have discovered this principle as legal, regulatory, and media environments have become increasingly intolerant of any malfeasance; if crises of legitimacy are to be avoided, these contexts need to be treated as "participants" in corporate strategies. From this standpoint, what is commonly called "executive hubris" is substantially the inability to see how context impinges on agents' actions.

When organizations are seen as complex systems, delineating their boundaries becomes problematical. In fact, boundaries are not an inherent feature of complex systems but are imposed by the observer in order to fix some limits on the scope of a system that would make it feasible to study. Yet if everything is interconnected, as van Uden et al. (2001) claim, where does the organization begin and end? One corollary of complexity theory is that separating the part from the whole necessarily means sacrificing some portion of meaning. However, the inability to allow a part to stand for the whole or to describe the whole as the sum of its parts means that sampling becomes a difficult challenge. One solution is to view complexity science as the study of *parts* of complex systems, acknowledging up front that some sacrifices must be made in order to get at the parts that interest us (van Uden et al., 2001). Another solution is the approach advocated in this book, which is to focus on relationships, seeing the organization as an ongoing process and series of interactions rather than organization-as-autonomous-thing. This approach seems most appropriate for a field such as public relations—the study of relations between publics—and a topic such as crisis management, which is itself highly dependent on relationships.

Principle #7: Irreducibility

This interweaving of relationships, environment, history, and individual self-interest makes it particularly hard to define discrete borders for a complex system and leads to a seventh characteristic: *Complex systems are irreducible*. If a system is truly complex, it is more than the sum of its parts. If a system may be accurately and completely described by reducing it to its component parts, then it is merely complicated. Therefore, in order to understand a complex system, it is necessary to trace out the entire history of the system; it is not possible to reduce the system to its component parts or to allow a sample to stand in for the whole. This concept of incompressibility has been described as "the single most important aspect of complex systems" (van Uden et al., 2001, p. 57). However, the irreducibility of a complex system raises serious problems for crisis planners. As we discuss later, traditional crisis planning that schematizes and simplifies potential crisis situations into their generic components runs counter to the need to situate complex systems in terms of history, context, and relationship networks.

In order to define complex systems clearly, we have laid out seven separate principles: interacting agents, adaptability, self-organization, instability, influence of history, permeable boundaries, and irreducibility. However, none of these seven principles operates in isolation; all have a compounding effect on one another. The spinach crisis provides an example of this interaction: It shows how events unfolded in a system of many interacting agents, with a history of *E. coli* contamination in California produce known to certain agents but not others. Boundaries between supermarkets, small grocers, and restaurants became insignificant, because the contamination affected both organic and conventional spinach (in many cases sold under different labels by the same handler), as well as both wholesale and retail distribution channels. Geographical boundaries also became less significant, as the spinach was distributed over at least eight different states, few of which shared borders with each other or with the point of origin. The economic effects have been severe, as the food system adapted to a temporary acute shortage of spinach and has not returned to previous consumption levels; this reduced demand will affect growers for at least another crop cycle. Cultural, economic, and regulatory factors mutually interacted to compound the effects of the contamination and the evolution of the crisis.

How one goes about the systematic study of such situations from a complexity perspective depends on the type of approach adopted. The next section discusses some of the main points of view with regard to how complexity theories may be applied in organizational research and the social sciences in general.

Three Approaches to Complexity Theories

As the preceding sections made clear, complexity theory has elements common to a wide variety of disciplines in both hard sciences and social sciences. There is no one theory of complexity, and numerous schools of thought have emerged within the complexity sciences. Some of these schools propose very different ideas about what complexity means, how it can be applied, and what methods are appropriate for studying it. These schools have tended to separate into three broad approaches: reductionist complexity science, soft complexity science, and complexity-based thinking (Richardson & Cilliers, 2001).

Reductionist Complexity Science

As its name implies, the primary aim of "reductionist" complexity science is to describe naturally occurring phenomena in terms of a limited number of universal laws, in the tradition of classic positivist science (Richardson & Cilliers, 2001). The realist approach taken by reductionists attempts to circumvent human subjectivity by isolating testable, generalizable laws that are believed to reflect natural reality in an objective state. However, in creating certainty, this approach risks self-contradiction. For instance, Richardson and Cilliers (2001) remarked that, although most of the complexity science literature explicitly acknowledges the break from a Newtonian or mechanistic approach, it still relies on a positivist method that emphasizes universal commonalities more than idiosyncratic differences between systems. Similarly, Daneke (1997) noted that many attempts to apply nonlinear science methodologies to the social realm have fallen back on neoclassical economic theory and the concept of "rational choice" as a motivation for human action.

Soft Complexity Science

In direct contrast to the reductionist approach, "soft" complexity science asserts a sharp distinction between social reality and the natural world. Therefore, any theory originating in nature, such as complexity, can be used only metaphorically to enrich our understanding of social interaction. Supporters of this view reject the notion that the complexity sciences can be applied with scientific rigor to human social situations but do see the rich lexicon of the field as a source of new concepts that can be explored in terms of language and meaning. Introna (2003), for example, maintained that social and natural sciences are incommensurable but that complexity theory might be used as a metaphor to understand aspects of social reality—as long as we avoid "stretching" the science metaphor to reach conclusions about social life that cannot be supported by structural similarity.

Complexity-Based Thinking

A third approach to complexity science accepts the limitations to transferability implied by complexity theory in favor of a radical epistemological shift that recognizes the contingent nature of all knowledge (Richardson & Cilliers, 2001). Proponents refer to this approach as "complexity-based thinking" that includes both hard science and philosophy under the same rubric. In essence, complexity-based thinking requires that we abandon the quest for exact knowledge or universal absolutes and seek instead the limitations and boundaries of our knowledge, by whatever means are most appropriate for the situation at hand.

Although it may seem less rigid than the other two approaches to complexity, complexity-based thinking has firm methodological corollaries. Primarily the approach dictates that "complex matters demand a methodological pluralism" (Richardson & Cilliers, 2001, p. 12), without privileging one method or approach over another as "more scientific." This methodological pluralism is not the same as triangulation, in which various methods are used to confirm the validity of empirical findings. Instead, each approach to a given problem is treated singularly, and the results are combined to provide a richer portrayal of the object of inquiry, including any inherent paradoxes or conflicts they may contain (Miller, 2001; Taylor & Trujillo, 2001). Richardson and Cilliers (2001) explained the need for multiple approaches as a matter of relative goodness of fit: Because knowledge can only ever be partial, pluralism offers a way of seeking the best possible explanation for phenomena in any given set of circumstances. Within the complexity paradigm, knowledge is always localized and multifaceted. Instead of offering single solutions, complexity theory offers "diverse avenues for discovering what may end up being a multiplicity of answers that are differentially sensitive to and grounded in specific circumstances, conditions, people, times, and places" (Cooksey, 2001, p. 84). This insistence on pluralism that characterizes complexity-based thinking carries back to Ashby's (1954) law of requisite variety. Faced with partial knowledge and a rapidly changing environment in crisis situations, managers cannot hope to specify all possible solutions to a crisis. However, they can apply complexity-based thinking to a turbulent environment, ensuring that they can rapidly brainstorm multiple possible actions depending on how the crisis evolves.

Armed with these basic principles of complexity and possibilities for their application to social systems, in the next chapter we move on to address some of the special challenges these theories pose to researchers and practitioners. In particular, we begin to compare approaches to crisis management and principles of complexity. The similarities and differences that emerge from this comparison pave the way for our later analysis and propositions for change, discussed in part III.

4

Predictability and Control in Complex Systems

The traditional crisis planning process described in chapter 2 depends on the ability of managers to predict and control multiple features of crisis situations: how organizations will behave during a crisis, how publics will respond to efforts to contain or repair the crisis, and how the company's actions will affect subsequent outcomes. In contrast, the complexity view described in chapter 3 substantially limits actors' ability to either predict or control all the interacting elements that make up a complex system. This chapter focuses on that key difference between the two paradigms, looking more closely at the features of complex systems that elude control.

Interaction Among Components of Complex Systems

Traditionally, prediction and control are made possible by establishing linear cause-and-effect relationships in a system. However, complex systems consist of such densely interconnected relationships that this type of linearity is difficult or impossible to establish. Cause and effect in complex systems are produced by myriad interactions among aggregate networks rather than by the linear causal chains of other types of systems (van Uden et al., 2001). As a corollary of this unstable and non-linear behavior, the effects of change may be highly unpredictable, so that small changes over time can produce disproportionately large consequences, major shocks can result in relatively small consequences, and there may be multiple possible outcomes, not an inevitable path from a cause to its effect (see Byrne, 1998).

The unpredictability of future developments is further heightened by the influence of past history. A system can never escape its past, as even small-scale changes accumulate in ways that are impossible to disembed from the whole fabric of the system at a later point in time. Hence any determination of the current state of a complex system must necessarily take its previous states into account as well (van Uden et al., 2001). Still another factor amplifying unpredictability is the discontinuous pace of change, which may take place gradually or with calamitous abruptness. Even systems that have a superficial appearance of stability, such as most organizations, may suffer sudden discontinuities. For example, Tyler (2005) argued that a crisis "disrupts the official story" and "may open that official narrative up to public contest," allowing alternate narratives to "erupt" and spoil or transform the previously dominant image of the organization (p. 567).

Yet another way in which complex systems elude prediction is by challenging traditional statistical methods. Statistics normally allow researchers to make inferences based on the occurrence of given phenomena within a sample representing the universe being studied. As Byrne (1998) pointed out, this is in essence an effort to predict and control the future: "Once we can predict, we can engineer the world and make it work in the ways we want it to. We can turn from reflection to engagement" (p. 19). This probability-based view requires acceptance of causal relationships among selected variables that can be explored within a sample.

However, there are several reasons that complex systems cannot, by nature, be subjected to traditional linear analysis in any meaningful fashion. Because complex systems are holistic, they are not amenable to letting a part stand for the whole, and therefore one cannot have confidence in traditional statistical sampling. Furthermore, linear approaches assume a momentary state of the system that can be traced back or reversed to produce an account of the system's effects over time. But in nonlinear systems, attempts to reverse fail because it is impossible to precisely account for the effects of complex interactions at various points in time. In addition, the incompressibility of complex systems means that any model that represents such a system must be equally complex. That requirement violates one of the basic assumptions of the analytical method: "If something is too complex to be grasped as a whole, it is divided into manageable units which can be analysed separately and then put together again"; but because complex systems involve not only variables but also relationships, "in 'cutting up' a system, the analytical method destroys what it seeks to understand" (Cilliers, 1998, pp. 1–2). Complexity theory thus forces us to evaluate to what extent deliberate reductionism—in sampling, in choice of variables, in schematic models— impoverishes our analysis so that it does not help us understand the present or predict the future.

Thus managerial efforts to control and predict are constrained in multiple ways by the instability of complex systems, a factor that underlies the uncertainty and rapidly shifting circumstances of crisis situations. However, complex systems, like crises, are not completely random: They have a logic of their own that is not always amenable to the schematic process of traditional crisis planning, largely because of the ability of complex systems to self-organize.

Attractors: The Logic of Self-Organization

As Price (1997) observed, "one of the basic insights of complexity theory is that dynamic systems tend to evolve in the direction of increased complexity over time" (p. 9). Yet this increase in complexity does not necessarily lead to chaos, decline, or exhaustion. Nobel Prize–winning chemist Ilya Prigogine developed a concept of *dissipative structures* that explained why certain open systems do not dissolve into entropy but, rather, renew and self-organize into complex systems with their own logic (Abel, 1998). These dissipative systems go beyond mere adaptation to external or internal conditions: They are capable of complete, independent self-organization. Typically, a dissipative system will disperse energy until it reaches a transition state at which it may either self-destruct or self-organize into a new, emergent form.

One key difference between these systems and classic Newtonian models of systems is that, in dissipative structures, time is no longer considered reversible (Abel, 1998). Each successive development emerges from a specific set of previous developments in a given temporally and spatially situated context, but not in a linear sequence that can simply be folded or unfolded. This contextual path dependency is one reason that, from the perspective of dissipative structures, the study of complex systems cannot be carried out in isolation from the system's own unique past. As complex systems enact their history by transitioning among phases or areas of change, they are governed by "attractors," recurrent patterns of behavior that exert a pull on the system. The system may be drawn into a certain attractor domain as it travels through "phase space," a history of the system showing the range of options available at any given moment.

Three types of attractors are particularly relevant to organizations. First, there are "stable" attractors: simple behavioral trajectories, including stable equilibria (point attractors) and periodic behavior (cyclic attractors). Stable attractors are composed of forces that interact independently or in a linear manner (Poole, Van de Ven, Dooley, & Holmes, 2000). In communication terms, these might consist of activities that are done daily (e.g., news summaries) or periodically (e.g., quarterly dividend releases). Second, there are "unstable" attractors: erratic, unpredictable, and irregular behaviors that eventually cycle out of control, flinging the system out of its current trajectory. In communication terms, such attractors might represent crisis triggers, or issues that are allowed to simmer until a serious conflict erupts and threatens the reputation, even the existence, of the organization.

The third type of attractor is the "strange" attractor, describing behaviors that look random in the short term but that, through multiple interactions, gradually acquire an organized pattern over time (Ferdig, 2000; Kauffman, 1995; Richardson, Mathieson, & Cilliers, 2000; Stacey, Griffin, & Shaw, 2000; Urry, 2003). In communication terms, such attractors might model the type of crisis that seems intractable to communication, appropriating seemingly unrelated causes over time, so that its mature form little resembles, and could not have been predicted from, its inception. Gerlach's (1987) description of an accelerating environmental crisis suggests this type of attractor. The movement started with a handful of Minnesota farmers who wanted to stop a power line from crossing their land and, to do so, forged relationships with a diverse set of community members, from church leaders to activists. The result was a group that "developed not only an ideology of stopping the line, but also of protecting the family farm and rural life, of promoting alternative energy technologies, of challenging big business, and—as women began to lead in the protest—of advancing women's liberation" (Gerlach, 1987, cited in Murphy, 1996, p. 104).

Ultimately, these disparate groups were linked by concern over institutional, not electrical, power, an ideological core that functioned as an attractor to govern and coordinate the behavior of individual interest groups. However, "the attractor is often clear only after the fact" (Murphy, 1996, p. 104); traces of it are not evident in either the initial trigger or a casual sample of group member opinions as circumstances unfolded. In a similar fashion, the problems experienced by Coca-Cola in Europe appear to have been shaped by an attractor of which most people were aware only dimly, if at all: that is, ill-smelling Coke became associated with dioxin in animal food, then with mad cow disease. The underlying attractor may have been the European public's uneasiness about genetically altered foods, much in the news at that time, placing all these issues in an attractor basin of unwholesome, "unnatural," or even toxic results produced by human interference in the food chain.

The concept of strange attractors is often applied to both chaos theory and complexity theory, and this practice encourages a general penchant to conflate the two fields. Particularly in communication, chaos theory has been used to talk about crisis situations. The two theories do share many characteristics: Both involve attractors, bifurcation, unpredictability, and nonlinearity. However, complexity is not the same as chaos. Goldberg and Markóczy (2000) noted that "the study of chaos generally involves the study of extremely simple nonlinear systems that lead to extremely complicated behavior"—the creation of disorder out of regimented repetition—whereas complexity moves in the opposite direction, being "generally about the (simple) interactions of many things (often repeated) leading to higher level patterns" of coherence (p. 75). Therefore, "complexity science aims to explain the emergence of order—it is really *order-creation science*" (McKelvey, 2003, p. 108; italics in original). This evolution of recognizable patterns makes complexity science especially appealing to the social scientist interested in studying emergent phenomena, the manifestation of overall order from the confusion of myriad local interactions.

In contrast, Poole et al. (2000) pointed out that true chaos involves iteration of the same simple algorithm or behavior over and over, and thus true chaos is characterized by very few degrees of freedom. In fact, "the presence of chaos in observed organizational states is characteristic of an organizational system where, either through control and/or cooperation, independence and autonomy between individuals has been lost" (p. 334). Even though complex systems may at times appear chaotic and disorderly, such behavior is one possible manifestation, rather than a typical characteristic, of complex systems—it is merely one of many possible trajectories that autonomous agent interactions might create (van Uden et al., 2001). Thus, whereas chaotic systems have few degrees of freedom, complex systems have many (McKelvey, 2003). For all these reasons, we prefer to speak of organizations in terms of complex, rather than chaotic, systems.

Returning to the idea of attractors, to describe the numerous possible paths that a complex system might take and the suddenness of change, some find it useful to think in terms of a "phase space," often depicted as a map containing all the possible states a system could be in. The phase space is composed of "attractor basins," discrete areas of behavior, attitudes, or values that capture a system for a while. These basins are proximate to, or even overlap with, one another. As a result, the closer a system edges toward their boundaries, the greater the likelihood that the system will spring into the neighboring basin, causing it to adopt the behaviors that typify its attractor (van Uden et al., 2001). This process may not be gradual; it can take the form of a sudden hop, which complexity theorists often term a "bifurcation point."

Thus, as a complex system moves through time, it occasionally encounters these critical points of instability known as bifurcation points. These are junctures at which the system is forced to veer into one of several directions, thereby changing its evolutionary course (Byrne, 1998; Frederick, 1998; Stacey et al., 2000). These junctures correspond to the boundary zones between attractor basins. Bifurcation points are the triggers for self-organization in complex entities, moments at which "a new coherent pattern suddenly emerges without any blueprint, one that cannot be explained by, or reduced to, or predicted from, the nature of the system's component entities" (Stacey et al., 2000, p. 94). Because of the nonlinearity of a complex system, even a minimal disturbance within the system may be sufficient to nudge it into a different attractor basin (van Uden et al., 2001).

Reputational crises often take the form of these sudden leaps from one "attractor basin," or organizational image held by the public, to another. This process can be seen in media coverage of the National Aeronautics and Space Administration (NASA) after the first shuttle disaster in 1986, in which the space agency went from being considered a bastion of "the right stuff" (Wolfe, 1979) to a failed organization that could not produce a working space telescope or land instruments on Mars (Murphy, 1996). Thus multiple, radically different outcomes can arise from a fork in what was previously perceived to be a cohesive, predictable narrative. Both identities—the "right stuff" image presented to the public and the internal culture of uncontrolled risk taking—were part of NASA from the start, with the "noise" of a dysfunctional organizational culture building to a radical bifurcation point in the 1986 Challenger disaster. The bifurcation point is the moment at which everything changes, and the differences lie in the attractor basin into which the organization slips.

Within the context of organizations, factors such as institutional forms, societal and organizational norms, stakeholder needs, or industry conventions may all form attractor basins that exert a pull on the organization, drawing it into a given pattern. Variations in these patterns depend on the myriad human, historical, and environmental factors that are unique to the organization—that specific portion of a complex system—being examined. In this spirit, van Uden et al. (2001) suggested that organizing can itself serve as "an attempt to stay away from the boundaries of the attractor basin" (p. 64). Using that same metaphor, traditional crisis planning may be seen as an effort to "stay away from the boundaries" where unwanted endogenous (e.g., executive misjudgment) or exogenous (e.g., media coverage) events might destabilize the organization's hold on one attractor basin and push it into another. Later in this book, we argue that complexity-based crisis management includes the ability to react adaptively when the organization slips or is pushed into such a basin at a bifurcation point. For now, we argue that this adaptivity is impaired by traditional management assumptions that attempt to impose control in ways and on situations that are not amenable to it.

Scientific Management and Systems Theory

Systems-based thinking underlies many of these efforts to exert control. Some researchers view complexity theory itself as an extension of systems thinking (Mathews, White, & Long, 1999; McElroy, 2000). In fact, the two fields do share certain qualities, mainly a sense of context and totality expressed through attention to the environment and the contribution of parts to the whole. However, complexity theory differs from systems theory in ways that involve managerial control and are therefore important for crisis management.

Primarily, systems theory has preserved a concern with regulation that comes from its early roots. General systems theory, developed in the 1940s by Austrian biologist Ludwig von Bertalanffy, was concerned with the regulatory mechanisms of organisms and between organisms and the environment. It became closely associated with cybernetics and systems dynamics, giving the approach an engineering perspective (Stacey et al., 2000). These schools of thought intersected with concepts from scientific management from the early part of the twentieth century. That approach took a mechanistic view, dividing the organization into distinct activities, objectively defined and governed by clear rules and principles in order to produce measurable output. Management scientists saw themselves as located outside the system, designing rational processes to achieve predetermined goals.

Although these earlier concepts have now become far more sophisticated, the systems approach still retains its emphasis on control. In particular, systems thinking relies on the goal of homeostasis, or the tendency to move toward a state of stable equilibrium. The environment has substantial influence, but it remains separate from the organization. The system boundaries are seen as permeable to interaction with the environment to the extent necessary to maintain stability. Within this schema, managers assume the roles of task definition and boundary control, taking timely action to correct for change, preserve equilibrium, and regulate the system to achieve its maximum potential. Applying efficient, linear causality, managers intervene at "leverage points" to control the dynamics within the system. System feedback does cause changes in patterns of behavior within an organization, but the feedback does not change the dynamics themselves; the system continues to operate in essentially the same manner as before, simply with more information (Stacey et al., 2000).

Although a systems approach may be an effective tool for structuring problems within a known set of options, we think it is an unrealistic approach to crisis management. The assumptions of distinct boundaries between organizational entities and their environments is a risky one in the relationship-driven context of crises. In addition, the notion of control dampens human agency in ways that reduce system adaptability. This is a severe limitation when it comes to dealing with the unknown, the rapidly changing, the uncertain, when people need the autonomy to make effective decisions that traverse functional restrictions when the system does not work as expected.

Despite these limitations, the rationalism of systems theory has made it an attractive framework for much crisis planning. For example, systems assume a set of rational rules and procedures that are designed by managers and followed by other organization members, such as a series of steps that become the official plan. This is often the case with traditional crisis plans: first, identification of a core group of crises to plan for; second, consideration of alternative plans to contain the crises; third, codification of the plans in a manual.

Were this rationalism and control truly the case, crises would not be a problem. Yet rules and procedures account for only a portion of what takes place within an organization, and an organization's interaction with other entities can seldom be stabilized for long. More realistic is the view expressed by Urry (2003) that equilibrium is not just difficult to impose and maintain; it is also not a natural state: "Ecological systems are always on the edge of chaos without a 'natural' tendency towards equilibrium" (p. 32). In a complex system—whether a living being or a society—complete stability is hardly desirable because it represents an inert state, equivalent to stagnation or even death. Instead of equilibrium, managers and researchers necessarily struggle with the unique challenges presented by a system that, by definition, involves novel and unforeseeable change in a far-from-equilibrium state.

Redefining Prediction

From the standpoint of the functionalist scientific tradition, an inability to accurately predict future behavior often appears to signal inadequacy (Abel, 1998). Hence Urry (2003) argued that "much social science is premised upon the successful achievement of an agent's or system's goals and objectives" (p. 13). Yet from a complexity viewpoint, "social life is full of what we may term 'relative failure'" as a "'necessary consequence of incompleteness' and of the inability to establish and sustain complete control" over the complex realm of the social (Malpas & Wickham, 1995, pp. 39–40, as cited in Urry, 2003, p. 14). Complexity-based thinking, therefore, does not expect rigorously accurate prediction nor view its lack as a shortcoming.

Surprise, uncertainty, and a lack of determinacy are fundamental properties of complex systems, including societies and organizations. When it comes to crisis management, we may need to develop a tolerance for looser causality, lighter controls, and limited predictability. In this spirit, Poole and Van de Ven (1989) asserted "that theorists need not be completely consistent; that seemingly opposed viewpoints can inform one another; that models are, after all, just models, incapable of fully capturing the 'buzzing, booming confusion,' no matter how strongly logical arrogance tries to convince theorists otherwise" (p. 566).

Despite such words as *confusion,* the unpredictable nature of events does not require completely abandoning the principle of causality. Managers need not give up all efforts to understand, predict, or manage, but, rather, to redefine their expectations. Complexity is not randomness but a kind of plural causality. Complexity theories, particularly as applied to social organizations, maintain rigorous logical and mathematical underpinnings. These are simply pluralistic rather than the univocal approach favored by mainstream science, as the study of complex systems requires the use of multiple perspectives (van Uden et al., 2001). Endogenous and exogenous factors interact in complex ways to bring about subsequent events; hence the need to maintain a broad view of the history and scope of a system that includes its multifarious possibilities.

With respect to prediction, complexity-based thinking urges us not to abandon any hope of predicting but rather to rethink what we expect from that effort. Prediction is indeed possible within complex systems as long as we make a subtle but significant shift in our attitude, considering forecasting as "not the ability to foretell specific, well-defined events (in space and time), but, at best, the ability to foretell the range of possible behaviours the system might adopt" (van Uden et al., 2001, p. 63). Therefore, we are not looking to chart a clear path to an outcome but rather to develop a menu of contingencies. In addition, although complexity science does not allow us to predict specific outcomes, it may be useful in forecasting the complete breakdown of system structures, which tend to occur after multiple bifurcations (Price, 1997). We should also limit our predictions to the short term, as myriad interactions among agents will quickly multiply longer-term possibilities far beyond our capacity to model them (Richardson, Cilliers, & Lissack, 2000). As Fink (1986) pointed out with respect to organizational crises, "for any one effect there may be five causes, and for any one cause there may be five effects" (as cited in Lagadec, 1993, p. 64).

These are not necessarily severe limitations if we shift our aims from the positivist demand for accuracy within narrowly defined constraints to a goal more in line with the character of complexity theory: deeper understanding of localized situations. Instead of a master plan for crises, we would be more attentive to the local, the short term, and the contingent. This approach redefines strategy in terms of quick response and organizational learning. The ability to learn and act quickly is so central to crisis management in a complex environment that we consider it at length in part II.

Part II

THE COMPLEXITY OF KNOWLEDGE AND LEARNING

Case History

Knowledge, Uncertainty, and Expertise

NASA

Perhaps no other organization has commanded more respect, from both the public and the world's scientific community, than has the National Aeronautics and Space Administration (NASA). Established in 1958, NASA quickly made a reputation for cutting-edge technologies and successful space missions. In 1979, journalist Tom Wolfe labeled NASA's can-do, risk-taking culture as "the right stuff." However, NASA today faces serious funding and leadership challenges, not to mention a tarnished reputation. Far from exhibiting the right stuff, NASA is now associated with multiple mission failures, in particular the vivid shuttle disasters of Challenger (1986) and Columbia (2003).

NASA's current state stands in stark contrast to its glory days in the 1960s and 1970s. A favorite agency of President John F. Kennedy—himself a near-mythical hero to many Americans—NASA soon became an organization that could do no wrong. With the Apollo space program, NASA undertook to land humans on the surface of the moon and bring them back safely to earth, and it accomplished that mission on July 20, 1969. The agency's success in carrying out this extraordinarily difficult task helped establish U.S. technological superiority on a global scale and also garnered NASA wide admiration for its accomplishments.

There were, of course, problems in the background. A grisly cockpit fire killed three Apollo astronauts in 1967; disaster was barely averted in 1970, when the Apollo 13 spacecraft not only failed to reach the moon but also nearly failed to come home after an onboard explosion crippled the controls. However, faced with manifold technological uncertainties, as well as known risks, NASA largely managed to conclude its Apollo missions with spectacular success.

The Apollo program was not only successful, but it was also expensive, costing the U.S. government billions of dollars. Under pressure to cut costs, in the 1970s and 1980s NASA focused on building frequently launchable and mostly reusable vehicles: the space shuttles. The first shuttle launched was Columbia, in April 1981.

The space shuttle program appeared to be doing well. However, reusability and lower costs proved an expensive combination, as NASA engineers constantly pushed the envelope on risks and constantly succeeded, setting in motion a risk escalation culture that Vaughan (1996) described as "the social organization of a mistake" (p. 394). Finally, on January 28, 1986, the shuttle Challenger exploded during the program's 25th mission. The accident resulted from a leak in one of two solid rocket boosters that ignited the main liquid fuel tank, a failure that had been anticipated and discussed prior to the decision to launch. It killed all seven crew members and completely destroyed the shuttle in a tragedy televised before the eyes of millions of people around the world.

This failure provoked intense debate about the cost of the space missions, both human and financial. A hiatus in the shuttle program followed, during which a special presidential commission investigated the accident. In June 1986, the Rogers Commission found that NASA's organizational culture and decision-making processes had been key contributing factors to the accident. The Commission concluded that "there was a serious flaw in the decision making process leading up to the launch of [the Challenger]. A well structured and managed system emphasizing safety would have flagged the rising doubts about the Solid Rocket Booster joint seal" whose failure had caused the accident (Report of the Presidential Commission on the Space Shuttle Challenger Accident, 1986).

After the Challenger disaster, NASA turned its attention to revamping its shuttle program. It also pursued a variety of unmanned missions that included the Hubble Space Telescope and the International Space Station. However, public excitement about NASA projects had started to fade. During much of the 1990s, NASA faced shrinking annual budgets, a situation that reflected public debate about whether a program perceived as problematic should be given priority (O'Toole, 1999). As a result, NASA pioneered a "faster, better, cheaper" approach that allowed it to engage in a wide variety of aerospace programs while keeping down costs (Canizares, 1999). This approach, too, was criticized when the Mars Climate Orbiter and Mars Polar Lander were lost in 1999 (O'Toole, 1999; Canizares, 1999).

In February 2003, public debate resurged when disaster befell the space shuttle Columbia during the program's 113th mission. After much anticipation and delay, Columbia finally completed its mission, only to break up in a spectacularly horrific manner, again televised around the world, during the ship's reentry into the earth's atmosphere. Like the Challenger disaster, the Columbia accident killed the seven astronauts on board and proved extremely damaging to the entire NASA program. NASA once again faced severe criticism, and once again the investment in space programs and its future were debated.

After 7 months of analysis, the Columbia Accident Investigation Board (CAIB) released its report in August 2003, finding that the causes of the accident were both physical and organizational. The physical cause was failure of the shuttle's protective heat shield, which had been struck during takeoff by a large piece of foam insulation that fell from the external fuel tank. The CAIB report concluded that "while NASA's present Space Shuttle is not inherently unsafe, a number of mechanical fixes are required to make the Shuttle safer in the short term" (Brown, 2003). Worse, the report also concluded that there were organizational failures: "NASA's management system is unsafe to manage the shuttle system beyond the short term and...the agency does not have a strong safety culture" (Brown, 2003). The report highlighted some of the fundamental flaws in communication and decision making: "organizational barriers that prevented effective communication of critical safety information and stifled professional differences of opinion; lack of integrated management across program elements; and the evolution of an informal chain of command and decision-making processes that operated outside the organizations" (Columbia Accident Investigation Board, 2003, p. 9).

Despite years of organizational analysis and redesign between the two shuttle disasters of 1986 and 2003, NASA's culture still undermined its ability to control risk. In fact, well before the Columbia launch, the agency had put in place painstakingly detailed procedures that it considered adequate to prevent future disasters. The failure of these plans and procedures illustrates most of the shortcomings of crisis planning. Chief among these dangers are overreliance on the formal plan and procedures, inability to see the total picture, and, above all, a homogenous organizational culture that saw no necessity to question the way decisions were made (for thorough analyses of the NASA decision-making process, see Tompkins, 2005; Vaughan, 1996).

Although the NASA crises were more dramatic than many others, the cognitive shortcomings that led to the crises are common to many other organizations and may in fact be the norm, not the exception. In the section that follows, we consider these problems with knowledge and learning, ignorance and uncertainty, expertise and sensemaking. We combine the theories of complexity and organizational learning to show how these two theoretical strands offer insights into crisis management.

5

The Complexity of Information and Assimilation

Knowledge and Ignorance

Most people think of a crisis as an event, a situation that has gone wrong. However, equally important is how that situation is interpreted by stakeholders across the spectrum and how they make decisions based on their interpretations. That is the topic of this chapter and the starting point for our recasting of crisis management from a complexity perspective.

In one way or another, all crisis situations involve problems with information, knowledge, and understanding; and all audiences affected by a crisis have problems processing information. In particular, the media's gatekeeping function commonly fails in the early stages of crisis, so that all information gets into the story regardless of accuracy (Scanlon, Tuukka, & Morton, 1978). That gatekeeping failure can have widespread impact. According to Poulsen (1996), for example, Britain's 1996 mad cow disease story turned into a "media avalanche" because it developed quickly and got coverage in multiple media across national boundaries, "despite the fact that the factual basis may have been misunderstood and [was] out of proportion to the coverage received" (p. 5). That information processing problem facilitated further calamities down the road: beef boycotts, bankruptcies, and political name calling.

For an organization's nonmedia stakeholders, the most salient quality of a crisis is also its uncertainty—as to what is happening, what the organization is doing to resolve the problem, and what the crisis means to them (Millar & Heath, 2004; Ulmer et al., 2007). Similarly, managers within the organization experience crises in terms of confusion, information flows far higher than can be processed, and loss of control over judgments and decisions, often producing what Weick (1993) referred to as a *cosmology episode*, a fundamental questioning of prior beliefs and opinions.

Most people agree that knowledge, learning, and sensemaking are essential components of crisis management. Typically, pragmatic crisis literature focuses on knowledge in the sense of structuring and processing data. This type of approach teaches managers how to identify potential crises, classify them, and prioritize them; how to list publics and key contacts, with messages tailored to each; how to classify events according to culpability and respond accordingly (e.g., Barton, 1993, 2001; Coombs, 2007; Fearn-Banks, 2007; Fink, 1986; Mitroff & Pearson, 1993). Each one of these activities inherently recognizes that acquiring and organizing information is a central part of good decision making under duress. However, the pragmatic approach deemphasizes the dynamic learning and sensemaking aspects of managing a crisis. It puts the emphasis on preplanning the strategy and distilling it into a set of tactics, so that managers, overwhelmed by mountains of information during a crisis, can act without having to build strategy and tactics from the ground up. This approach places learning and sensemaking before and after a crisis, in the form of issues management and postcrisis debriefing, but not during a crisis when tactics have primacy.

Some authors think that this focus on tactics during a crisis does not lead to optimal outcomes in the long haul. For example, Bechler (2004) remarked that because most of the crisis research "has focused on effective crisis response mechanisms and the need for crisis containment, crisis situations have been treated as isolated events rather than necessary correctives that are interrelated with the culture and history of the organization or industry" (p. 63). Rather than viewing a crisis as a single, anomalous incident, he recommended a "historical cultural context" that seeks to deconstruct "problematic organizational behaviors that over time have become 'acceptable' and embedded within the culture," so that "decision-making becomes 'contextually' understood rather than 'incidentally' understood" (pp. 73, 74). This context-sensitive decision making is important because crises often emerge from patterns of organizational behavior over time: "They are intertwined and interrelated; to understand one you have to be able to study the other" (p. 71). The Challenger and Columbia disasters recounted in the opening of this section offer an example of the potentially severe consequences of failing to adequately address an organization's entrenched culture and historical patterns of decision making.

Lagadec (1993) made a similar observation when he described crises caused by marketplace rumors as emerging from ill-understood cultural perceptions. From this standpoint, for example, recurrent urban legends that claim that fast food is made from rodents actually express consumers' deep-seated concerns that such food is unwholesome and literally "junk" food. Such legends will not subside until fast-food companies deal with consumers' concerns about nutrition, not with immediate rumors about vermin. Poulsen (1996) noted a similar "cocktail of discourses" fuelling the public panic about mad cow disease: "A link emerges between a fatal, mysterious and perhaps contagious disease and the strong, deep-seated emotions which 'animal-eats-animal' arouses [*sic*]" (p. 5). In such situations, in which personal experience, media coverage, knowledge, and emotions coalesce around a specific news item, it would be easy to miss the underlying cause of crisis—in complexity terminology, its attractor—without the ability to see historically and contextually (Murphy, 1996).

This understanding of crisis as embedded in context comes very close to the complexity model of crisis that we described in part I. There we pointed out that because crises often behave like complex systems, detailed planning has only limited efficacy in controlling them; crises have the potential to self-organize into such a large number of possible avenues that it is impracticable to try to plan each one tactically. Rather, we recommended a type of historical-contextual decision making that aims beyond tactics and information toward understanding and sensemaking.

In this chapter, we lay the foundations for this contextual decision making by looking more closely at managerial information processing: what constitutes knowledge; how knowledge is communicated around an organization; and how cultivated expertise can fill in for uncertain or incomplete knowledge. Learning, sensemaking, and decision making are the focus of the chapters that follow.

Characteristics of Knowledge

We begin with a bundle of related terms: *data, information, knowledge, expertise,* and *learning.* Each is fundamental to good decision making. But what are the differences between these forms of cognition, and what does each contribute to decision making in an organizational exigency?

Some authors use the terms *information* and *knowledge* interchangeably (Marquardt, 1996) or without articulating the difference between them even when using the terms separately. For others, knowledge is a catchphrase that encompasses all other elements of decision making. Along these lines, a general definition of knowledge was proposed by Davenport and Prusak (1998):

> Knowledge is a fluid mix of framed experience, values, contextual information, and expert insight that provides a framework for evaluating and incorporating new experiences and information. It originates and is applied in the minds of knowers. In organizations, it often becomes embedded not only in documents or repositories, but also in organizational routines, processes, practices and norms. (p. 5)

As this comprehensive definition implies, knowledge goes well beyond informational characteristics to include values, experiences, and organizational culture. Here we discuss six core characteristics of knowledge: It is actionable; it is situated; it combines theory with practice; it can be tacit or explicit (or both); it can have both individual and collective elements; and it can be particular or holistic.

1. Knowledge Is Actionable

The first characteristic of knowledge is that it is structured to be usable. Hence McCampbell, Clare, and Gitters (1999) stated that knowledge is "information that must be processed, understood and acted upon" (p. 174). Tsoukas (2000) also saw the difference between information and knowledge as a matter of structuring: "As individuals increase and refine their capacity for making distinctions...they increase their capacity for knowing. Knowledge is what is retained as a result of this process" (p. 106). Knowledge, then, turns unstructured information or data into interpreted, actionable intelligence.

Tsoukas and Vladimirou (2001) elaborated on these qualities when they placed knowledge along a continuum ranging from data (which situate items or events as a sequence) to information (which arranges data to show relationships and context) to knowledge (which requires an appraisal of the relative significance of the information based on a given perspective). The continuum shows a progressive increase in the extent of human involvement, with data consisting of discrete bits subjected to no human intervention at one end and to socially generated knowledge at the other. Data and information require knowledge in order to be interpreted and applied to any given situation, because without the appropriate knowledge they remain meaningless (Stenmark, 2001).

According to this scheme, knowledge involves the application of judgment, which in turn requires the individual to draw distinctions, a skill that invokes both theory and experience (Tsoukas & Vladimirou, 2001). One may be taught a series of general rules but be unsure or unable to apply them in situations that do not clearly match the categories learned (Brown & Duguid, 2000). For example, a book may explain the techniques for diagnosing and repairing an engine, but an inexperienced mechanic will not always be able to distinguish between similar diagnoses or know when a given screw has been tightened properly. Similarly, a staff member new to an organization may find a detailed, prescriptive crisis plan simply bewildering, because he or she has not yet absorbed the collective knowledge that is often labeled "institutional memory." This collective knowledge resides in individual cognitive processes, as well as action networks, or relations among agents based on individual behaviors and collective routines (Heiss, 2006). Without an awareness of the shared understandings of the community, even the most detailed procedures may baffle rather than enlighten. Novices must learn to understand collectively defined categories and standards before they can transform the information into applicable knowledge. Therefore the application of judgment also requires location within a "collectively generated and sustained domain of action" (Tsoukas & Vladimirou, 2001, p. 977). This is the situated quality, the second characteristic of knowledge.

2. Knowledge Is Locally Situated

Knowledge is local; it is peculiar to its site of origin. From this perspective, Nonaka and Konno (1998) described the difference between information and knowledge as primarily one of context: According to their existentialist approach, knowledge is embedded in "shared spaces" that may be physical or virtual. These spaces foster the acquisition of knowledge, filtered through one's own experience or reflections. Knowledge that is separated from this space becomes information, which can then be supplied to others outside the environment. Thus knowledge is local, whereas information is transportable and unsituated.

A complexity perspective also supports this insistence that knowledge is situated. Complexity-based thinking argues against the decontextualization of knowledge, the claim that notions taken from one "shared space" may be applied interchangeably to other contexts. Hence in Chapter 3 we pointed out that one important characteristic of a complex adaptive system is the local nature of interactions among its agents. No agent has complete knowledge about the behavior of the system as a whole; although agents are presumed intelligent, "that intelligence is local to their position on the landscape" (Levinthal & Warglien, 1999, p. 345). The local, but diffusive, qualities of knowledge resemble the effect of local interactions between the large number of individual agents in a complex system. Kauffman (2000) termed this local exploration "the adjacent possible" (p. 142), from which knowledge spreads to "a new adjacent possible, accessible from the enlarged actual that includes the novel discoveries from the former adjacent possible" (Mitleton-Kelly, 2003, pp. 36–37). In other words, knowledge spreads incrementally through local interactions between agents in shared spaces, accreting small changes as it goes. Without this commonality, knowledge does not diffuse.

3. Knowledge Combines Theory With Application

A comparable local/general dichotomy can be seen in the third characteristic of knowledge, which revives two terms first used in early modern Europe: *ars* and *scientia*—not quite *art* and *science,* but analogous to *practice* and *theory* (Burke, 2000). In organizational knowledge terms, we might consider *ars*, or practice, comparable to our own experiential knowledge, whereas *scientia* is comparable to knowledge that is transmitted to us from information sources—print, electronic, or personal. Along similar lines, Gherardi (1999) referred to a difference between *propositional knowledge* and *practical knowledge*. Propositional knowledge refers to what some might call "book learning," or knowledge spelled out and made explicit (*scientia*). In contrast, practical knowledge comes closer to experience (*ars*).

4. Knowledge Can Be Tacit or Explicit

Related to these distinctions, a fourth characteristic of knowledge is whether it is *tacit* or *explicit*. Definitions of these terms vary, but for the most part, explicit knowledge "can be expressed in words and numbers and shared in the form of data, scientific formulae, specifications, manuals, and the like" (Nonaka & Konno, 1998, p. 42). Explicit knowledge is therefore easy to codify and communicate through formal systems. In contrast, tacit knowledge resists codification and transmission, since it is highly dependent on the individual's personal and subjective context of experience and values (Nonaka & Konno, 1998).

As these remarks suggest, many consider that explicit knowledge can be shared as information, whereas tacit knowledge is so subjective that it resists precise communication. In fact, Michael Polanyi (1961)—generally seen as the originator of the tacit-explicit distinction—asserted that by definition tacit knowledge cannot be made explicit because of its inherently personal character. Similarly, Cook and Brown (1999) remarked on a drawback of the term *tacit*, which seems to imply "that any such knowledge must be 'hidden' from our understanding or 'inaccessible' for practical purposes" (p. 384). They and others have argued that explicit and tacit knowledge are distinct forms of knowledge that cannot be "converted" into one another (Brown & Duguid, 2000; King & Ranft, 2001; Stenmark, 2001; Tsoukas & Vladimirou, 2001).

The example Cook and Brown (1999) used to illustrate their view of tacit knowledge is riding a bicycle. A bicyclist may not be able to respond to direct questions about, for instance, how to remain upright. She tacitly knows how to do so as a result of experience. An engineer may explain that the wheels of a moving bicycle are effectively gyroscopes that require a force to overcome their tendency to remain in the plane of rotation and how the rider shifts his or her weight to provide this force. However, possession of this knowledge does not indicate whether a person is actually capable of remaining upright on a bicycle; it merely denotes an understanding of the physical and engineering principles involved. Many capable bike riders cannot provide such a description, yet lack of such explicit knowledge does not hinder their ability to ride. The two kinds of knowledge may exist either separately or together, but tacit knowledge is the type required in order to perform the physical activity of bicycling—indeed, it is the result of having practiced bike riding, as it can be acquired only by interacting with the domain in question.

Although explicit and tacit knowledge are distinct according to this outlook, each may aid in acquiring the other. For instance, someone might practice riding a bicycle mindfully in order to describe the experience in words and thus state in explicit terms how a bike rider stays upright. This description may be of some use to a beginner, but it cannot replace the tacit knowledge that every aspiring bicyclist must acquire individually through practice. Cook and Brown (1999) argued that this process cannot be described as "converting" tacit knowledge into explicit knowledge because the end product does not in any way replace the tacit knowledge—which is still necessary in order to practice the activity— nor was the explicit knowledge merely uncovered from a preexisting state "hidden" within the tacit knowledge. When an experienced rider describes how to ride a bike, he uses tacit knowledge to generate explicit knowledge about bicycle riding, which may then be applied in a variety of ways as a separate entity. In essence, this conceptualization integrates *ars* and *scientia*, stating that they must both be present in order to reflect the richest possible knowledge. Similarly, others have asserted that the two forms of knowledge—tacit and explicit—must coexist and cooperate as two sides of the same process (Stacey, 2001; Tsoukas & Vladimirou, 2001). In organizations, purely tacit or purely explicit knowledge is unusual; most often experiential knowledge occupies an intermediate position along a continuum (Dixon, 2000), just as bicycle riding instructions combine both aspects of knowledge.

Although doctrinaire, these debates about tacit and explicit knowledge try to get at problems that hold particular interest for crisis planners: How transferable is knowledge? In what form is it most effectively transferred? Crisis scholars have dealt with similar issues, particularly in differentiating technical and symbolic approaches to crisis. For example, Hearit and Courtright (2004) criticized an "objectivist" or "materialist" view of crisis communication as "information transfer" whereby crisis communication is conceptualized as a "'conduit' through which meanings are 'transferred' from one person to another" (p. 204). The technical approach tends to focus on the transmission of explicit information, generally in the form of a detailed crisis plan that contains scripts for as many contingencies as possible. This approach implies a view of information as a commodity that can be handed from person to person. Other scholars have favored a symbolic approach to crisis communication that emphasizes crises as socially constructed by people both inside and outside the organization (Hearit & Courtright, 2004). This approach favors a holistic view, looking at organizational culture during a crisis for patterns of dysfunctional attitudes that produced conflict and crisis with stakeholders (Bechler, 2004). In both the Challenger and Columbia disasters the failure of known safety issues to generate preventive action highlights both the information-sharing and cultural aspects of knowledge transfer in a crisis situation.

These views of knowledge are expressed in two main streams of knowledge literature, the *commodity view* and the *community view* (Stenmark, 2001). The commodity view sees knowledge as a "thing" that exists separately from the knower, an object that can be manipulated, broken into discrete parts, stored, indexed, and transferred between people and groups. The community view sees knowledge as a process enacted through social intercourse, something that exists solely within the context of a given relationship and cannot be disconnected from the knower or from a given environment. Community knowledge is highly situated knowledge.

Boisot (2003) approached these views of knowledge from a complexity perspective to describe how firms organize and share information. He contrasted the world of Zen Buddhism, "a world in which knowledge is highly personal and hard to articulate," with the world of bond traders, "where all knowledge relevant to trading has been codified and abstracted into prices and quantities. This knowledge, in contrast to that held by Zen masters, can diffuse from screen to screen instantaneously and on a global scale. Face-to-face relationships and interpersonal trust are not necessary" (Boisot, 2003, pp. 188–89). Like bond traders, the knowledge management field in general prefers the commodity view of knowledge. Hence, according to Mårtensson (2000), the greatest contribution by the field of knowledge management has been its effort to "transpose tacit knowledge into explicit information, which will lead to greater possibilities to manage and control knowledge effectively" (pp. 212–13). Information and knowledge in this context are often expressed in economic terminology. For example, Laudon and Starbuck (1996) compared knowledge to an "inventory" of information that goes well beyond a mere "accumulation of information: It is an organized collection that reflects the intentions of the humans who create and interpret it. Thus, knowledge resembles an organized portfolio of assets" (p. 3924).

Writings that focus on "managing intellectual capital" adopt this commodity-based view of knowledge and its role in the organization (Carneiro, 2000; Dawson, 2000; McCampbell et al., 1999; Pérez-Bustamante, 1999). However, this "bond trader" focus can create a problem for the "Zen masters" because it fails to account for the social, community knowledge that, in a complex system, amounts to more than the sum of its parts. This collectivity constitutes another important aspect of knowledge.

5. Knowledge Can Be Both Individual and Collective

So far we have looked at four characteristics of knowledge: It is structured, it is situated, it has elements of both theory and practice, and to varying degrees it can be explicit or tacit, raising issues about its transmissibility between individuals and groups. This is where the fifth characteristic of knowledge comes in: It incorporates both individual and collective elements. Generally, authors agree that knowledge at an organizational level amounts to more than the sum of many knowledgeable individuals; it is a collective phenomenon within communities and therefore "cannot be represented as the aggregation of individual knowledge" (Snowden, 2000, p. 53). Instead, collective knowledge is qualitatively different from individual knowledge, not simply an outgrowth of it.

Group knowledge has characteristics and functions that clearly distinguish it from individual knowledge. Groups, including organizations, have socially constructed, shared assumptions that encompass far more meaning on the group level than on an individual level. One example of this group knowledge is the "body of knowledge" of a given trade or discipline. There is no need to assume that all members of the group possess the same knowledge or the same level of knowledge. Instead, groups themselves have access to knowledge based on the actions undertaken collectively, which is "epistemically distinct from work done by an individual in it, as informed by the knowledge he or she possesses" (Cook & Brown 1999, p. 386).

From this perspective, the organization provides three bases for knowledge: a group of actors, a physical or social context, and "a particular set of concepts (or cognitive categories) and the propositions expressing the relationship between concepts" (Tsoukas & Vladimirou, 2001, p. 980). Similarly, Heiss (2006) described organizations as consisting of three types of interlinked metanetworks: knowledge domains, social networks among organizational members, and routine practices. However, she observed that these networks primarily exist in the form of "idiosyncratic cognitive maps" (p. 3) in the minds of organizational actors and are constantly updated. Knowledge is therefore situated not in the facts themselves as much as in the interaction among individual organizational members and their shared perceptions, practices, and experiences.

This collective definition of organizational knowledge is highly compatible with complexity theory. In essence, a group is an incompressible complex system, one whose characteristics cannot be described simply as the sum of its parts, because the collectively shared organizational knowledge is qualitatively different from the knowledge possessed by each individual within the group. As in other complex systems, local interactions between constituent actors result in patterns that are repeated with subtle changes over time, as the group makes its way through "phase space," or organizational history. The group is not a static entity—a collection of individuals—but rather a dynamic whole whose actions and knowledge may not be meaningfully or usefully reduced to an account of actions taken by the individuals in them.

As with complex systems, history is important to group knowledge. Groups that work together regularly develop a sort of "transactive memory," a means for members to jointly encode, store, and retrieve information (King & Ranft, 2001; Rulke & Rau, 2000). The benefits of such a system are twofold, as it allows members to share not only information as such but also an awareness of what knowledge individual members possess. This kind of distributed cognition occurs in settings in which agents "act independently yet recognize that they have interdependencies" (Boland, Tenkasi, & Te'eni, 1994, p. 456). As a result, groups need "an effective transactive memory system...to retrieve the knowledge needed from an expert in the group in a timely fashion," whereas an ineffective transactive memory "could leave the group with either a fruitless search for the needed knowledge or flawed information from 'nonexperts'" (Rulke & Rau, 2000, pp. 374–75). This is the same concern addressed by crisis management teams with members selected to include all germane areas of expertise across the organization.

In fact, if we view organizations as "distributed knowledge systems" (Gherardi, 1999, p. 113), this conceptualization has clear consequences for how we approach any team-based activity, especially one requiring tight coordination. Gherardi pointed out, for instance, that in such a system "no single agent can fully specify in advance what kind of practical knowledge is going to be relevant in a situated course of action" (1999, p. 113). Therefore, within a group context, an essential part of knowledge involves awareness of where to find information as the need arises and knowing who has the necessary skills for a given task. The crisis management team is set up to maximize this transactive memory system by requiring that managers who are ordinarily widely distributed throughout the organization interact repeatedly to share their expertise (Barton, 2001; Coombs, 2007).

6. Knowledge Is Both Particular and Holistic

The emphasis on collective knowledge leads to the final characteristic of knowledge that we discuss: Knowledge has both particular and holistic modes. Although Polanyi (1961) did not use these labels, we have adopted his dichotomy of knowledge, which alternates between detailed examination of the individual parts of an entity and the study of the relationships between those parts within the whole.

The *particular* mode of knowledge is essentially based on analysis, breaking entities down into smaller parts, such as the buildings and roads of an urban layout or the symptoms of a disease. Such partitioning has clear benefits, as it makes phenomena more tractable to analysis. For that reason, as we saw in chapter 2, crisis experts usually partition crisis life cycles into discrete phases. However, Polanyi (1961) identified two weaknesses in this approach. First, some particulars are always left unspecified; and second, even when particulars can be identified, they are always transformed to some extent by their isolation in an analysis. We have already seen that the structure of complex systems raises similar concerns: The rule of incompressibility means that the part cannot stand for the whole, and therefore the individual variable studied in isolation does not necessarily reflect what is actually happening in the system.

The reverse of the particular mode is the *holistic* mode of knowledge, which focuses on relationships between the parts and their joint role in forming a comprehensive entity. This conceptualization comes very close to the fractal approach previously described in relationship to complex systems. Both focus on the history, or "phase space," of a system and the relationships that form repeated patterns in a system as it moves through time. This fractal view tends to highlight relationships between discrete events and societal trends, looking at them as expressing the same fractal social patterns with variations on scale that depend on the level of observation used to observe the system: individual, organizational, or societal. The holistic or fractal conceptualization is particularly useful with respect to crisis planning, and especially issues management, which demands a high level of context sensitivity. Therefore, "in a process similar to analyzing fractal patterns, issues managers look for relationships between emerging social concerns, and then seek correspondences between industry or organizational actions on a micro scale, and the social context on a macro scale" (Murphy, 1996, p. 103). Issues management requires the ability to switch back and forth between holistic and particular modes of knowledge.

Polanyi (1961) described the particular and holistic modes of knowledge as complementary yet contradictory, operating on a sliding scale whereby having more of one capability always means having less of the other. This distinction returns us to the basic division between the "bond trader" and the "Zen master." According to Boisot (2003), the Zen view of the world allows "absorption" of complex phenomena—a holistic form of understanding—but it limits the transmissibility of knowledge. Conversely, the bond-trader view of the world encourages "reduction" of complex phenomena to data and information bits that are less rich but more easily and rapidly transmitted.

Crisis situations require rapid transmission of information, yet we have seen that without a grasp of historical context, crisis communication can miss the mark, aimed at the wrong publics or tangential concerns. Therefore, we next consider the complementary roles of both kinds of knowledge, first the world of the bond trader—knowledge managed as a commodity—and then the world of the Zen master—knowledge managed as a social process.

Knowledge Management

When the knowledge management movement first started in the 1980s, it mainly focused on improving the efficiency and productivity of "knowledge workers" by enhancing business processes. Most commonly the improvement came through the use of information technology systems to aid in storing, codifying, and retrieving information (McElroy, 2000). Capturing an organization's collective expertise in databases continues to be a key part of knowledge management. This capture could help organizations "to 'know what they actually know' and then marshal and exploit this knowledge in a systematic way" (Mårtensson, 2000, p. 208).

However, this storage-and-retrieval model suffers the limitations of technology, since a focus on data and information leaches away potentially rich context. Especially when it is linked with the information technology (IT) systems used in organizations, this outlook introduces a number of problems. First, it biases the handling of knowledge in organizations to fit the available technology solutions, directing action "towards problems that these information systems can handle rather than those experienced by participants" (Nidumolu, Subramani, & Aldrich, 2001, p. 116). Put another way, when the only tool is a hammer, all problems will look like nails. Second, IT-centered information handling favors top-down, manager-driven initiatives that focus on measurable outcomes (Nidumolu et al., 2001). This bias is also reflected in some crisis literature, in which companies are advised to measure the success of their crisis management efforts by customer survey scores, content analyses of media coverage, and stock prices—important, but not exclusive, indicators. Third, the IT approach can fail if "errors in the analysis, storage, retrieval and reapplication of past experience" lead to "under- and over-generalizations of its relevance and to self-fulfilling prophesies" (Mirvis, 1996, p. 16). Union Carbide's 1986 toxic gas leak in Bhopal is a case in point, as detached cost-benefit calculations half a world away promoted, at the Indian plant, neglect, indifference, safety violations, then disaster.

An additional problem raised by IT approaches to knowledge has to do with the classification and storage of information in readily accessible and retrievable forms. One reason for this process is the desire to create a centralized repository of information scattered throughout the organization, what is often referred to as "dispersed knowledge" (Becker, 2001). However, many IT-oriented scholars acknowledge that it is impossible to centralize an organization's knowledge in its entirety (Becker, 2001), so this effort may not fulfill its anticipated usefulness. As Marra (2003) noted with respect to formal crisis plans, such forms of knowledge tend to remain on the shelf.

Even though access to information is crucial when time is limited, this type of database thinking has conditioned the way organizations approach many problems today. There is a tendency to break situations down into parts that may be labeled and cross-indexed for rapid retrieval. Knowledge management is no exception. However, the problem with using this approach in situations that are complex, rather than merely complicated, is the loss of contextual and qualitative meaning (Snowden, 2000; Weick, 1993). As we have seen, complex systems are more than the sum of their parts; their meaning resides in the relationships between their components, rather than within individual components in isolation, and that is the reason that complex systems are considered to be incompressible.

These differing outlooks on knowledge have resisted synthesis and, overall, knowledge theorists remain divided into the two camps, either bond traders or Zen masters. Thus for many, organizational knowledge primarily consists of information, in which case knowledge management tends to focus on how to store, retrieve, and share this information

(Dawson, 2000; Farr, 2000; Levett & Guenov, 2000; Nidumolu et al., 2001; Pérez-Bustamante, 1999). For others, knowledge management is instead a matter of guiding complex social processes (Brown & Duguid, 2000; Cook & Brown, 1999; Tsoukas & Vladimirou, 2001).

Knowledge Management as Social Process

In social terms, knowledge management is primarily a dynamic process of turning an unreflective practice into a reflective one. This transformation takes place by elucidating the rules guiding the activities of the practice, by helping to shape collective understandings, and by facilitating the emergence of heuristic knowledge that will guide future decisions by organization members. In this manner, knowledge management becomes a subtle mode of "sustaining and strengthening social processes" (Tsoukas & Vladimirou, 2001, p. 991) rather than focusing principally on the flow of information. At the same time, it reflects a pragmatic emphasis on action, whereby "new knowledge is created primarily through ongoing interactions and improvisations that an organization's employees undertake in order to perform their jobs" (Nidumolu et al., 2001, p. 119). Within this framework, knowledge and learning have an emergent quality, and managers avoid the purposive, information-centric approach. Their role is instead to facilitate interaction and learning through both individual and group actions.

For the management of knowledge dispersed throughout organizations, this relational approach gives a very different perspective from an IT approach. Along these lines, Becker (2001) identified three key problems created by the distribution of knowledge (both explicit and tacit) within organizations. The first is the problem of *large numbers*—the fragmentation of knowledge into small, dispersed units that taxes organizational resources and prevents members from having a clear overview. Dispersed knowledge also creates *asymmetries,* or unequal distribution of knowledge that leads to uneven development of learning skills and, in turn, irregular constraints on further development. Finally, dispersal exacerbates the problem of *uncertainty,* signifying that "neither the probabilities of the different alternative choices nor all the different alternatives are known.... They are indeterminate and emerging. Therefore, the basis for taking decisions is not clear" (Becker, 2001, p. 1040). This dispersal and uncertainty were key factors in the 1986 explosion of the Challenger space shuttle. Calling the problem "structural secrecy," Vaughan (1996) argued that knowledge was so fragmented and dispersed around NASA that no single person possessed enough knowledge of the shuttle's complicated mechanics to make a good decision about launching in cold weather; no one person could see the total pattern of small compromises in safety that mitigated against the launch.

As the Challenger example shows, all three problems with dispersed knowledge—large numbers, asymmetries, and uncertainty—come to the fore in crisis situations. From a complex systems perspective, it would be futile to attempt to overcome their effects entirely, but one might work with these constraints, rather than against them, by providing the means to limit their negative effects. Becker's (2001) solutions to the difficulties raised by dispersed knowledge focus not on capturing and storing information but rather on facilitating access to knowledge by enhancing social networks. He described this strategy as "a shift from direct knowledge—'know how' or 'know what'—to indirect knowledge: 'know whom'" (p. 1041). This approach encourages the development of knowledge and expertise at the group level. It also underlies the reasoning behind recommendations to form crisis management teams, to bring together sources of expertise from across the organization whose knowledge can be tapped on short notice during fast-breaking crises.

As regards uncertainty reduction, Becker (2001) recognized that it is necessary to distinguish between two fundamentally different types of uncertainty before devising the appropriate information strategy. *Stochastic uncertainty* describes a situation in which specific probabilities for an array of possible outcomes are known. This kind of uncertainty may be effectively reduced by increasing the amount of information available to the decision maker. The other form of uncertainty, *structural uncertainty,* is often referred to as "ambiguity" because the probabilities of various potential outcomes remain unclear. Unlike stochastic uncertainty, ambiguity is generally intensified by an increase in information (Becker, 2001; Busby, 1999; Weick, 1995). In these situations, managers may benefit from the holistic combination of skill and expertise, or "knowing."

Knowledge Versus Knowing

In the previous sections we looked at multiple characteristics and forms of knowledge: its dependence on local interactions; its combination of tacit and explicit, individual and collective; its transmissibility. These various forms and functions all find a place in two interrelated knowledge frameworks proposed by Cook and Brown (1999): the "epistemology of possession" and the "epistemology of practice." Possession and practice concepts help to synthesize the various forms of knowledge examined in the previous sections and clarify their roles in both individual and group settings.

The epistemology of possession implies that knowledge is an object that can be possessed by individuals or a group. In contrast, the epistemology of practice comprises coordinated, meaningful actions undertaken by individuals and groups informed by a particular collective context; these meaningful actions simultaneously generate and make use of knowledge. Thus the epistemology of practice refers not to abstract knowledge (tacit or explicit) but to the *application* of that knowledge, the *ars* rather than the *scientia*, tangible activity performed in the real world. This application of knowledge is termed "knowing" and refers to the epistemological dimension of action itself, at both the individual and group levels; "knowing is dynamic, concrete, and relational" (Cook & Brown, 1999, p. 387). In other words, "knowledge" involves possession, whereas "knowing" involves interaction between one or more knowers and the world; its significance is found in relationships. Conceptualized in this way, knowledge becomes a tool for knowing. In turn, the practice of knowing is disciplined by the constraints of knowledge, as well as the physical and social environment.

As proposed by Cook and Brown (1999), this construct applied mainly to individual knowing. However, Gherardi (1999) applied the conceptualization to organizations as well. She used the term "learning-in-organizing" to shift the emphasis toward the emergence of knowledge—hence, learning—as a "collective accomplishment," in contrast to the cognitive view of "knowing as internalization of knowledge and learning as acquisition of 'given' knowledge" (p. 112). Likewise, Polanyi (1961) observed that *knowing* and *doing* (what Cook and Brown call *knowledge* and *knowing*) are usually found in concert.

The pragmatic focus on action and interaction as necessary to knowing runs parallel to interactions in complex systems. Knowing and knowledge influence one another through a series of generative micro interactions, a recursive process. Because the interaction between knower and domain allows both the acquisition of knowledge and its use, this "generative dance" goes well beyond mere knowledge-as-structured-information, opening up the potential for the creation of new knowledge (Cook & Brown, 1999, p. 390). Novelty may emerge at any point through unique combinations of individual and group experience, situational demands, and human judgment (Tsoukas & Vladimirou, 2001). As previously pointed out, this process has affinities with Kauffman's "adjacent possible," whereby local knowledge is diffused and transformed during interactions between neighboring agents. It also has affinities with a fractal view of the world, in which very slight alterations in interactions among elements of a complex system over time develop subtly different yet related patterns.

Another aspect of this view of knowing is its inherently situated character. Knowing is inextricably linked to a given place and time and to the people who take part in it. The emphasis on location and interacting with tools and the environment is a key attribute of the epistemology of practice. Hence authors often discuss the physical setting—or situated nature of knowing—when describing mastery or expertise in a given domain. For instance, Tyre and von Hippel (1997) investigated how engineers used location to solve problems with newly implemented technology at an integrated circuit board factory. They found that the engineers were able to identify patterns and signs of anomaly thanks to their technical expertise. However, they noted that "this skill was necessarily situated: to discover a clue means to pick out as noteworthy some aspect of the specific setting that is not obvious to everyone" (1997, p. 76).

This ability to perceive slight anomalies in massive amounts of data is also reminiscent of environmental scanning that relies on pattern recognition rather than highly specified variables—a fractal approach. Whether they are issues managers or engineers, persons who possess knowledge are able to enact knowing that reflects a certain degree of accomplishment or skill, based on their ability to distinguish cues from the physical and social environment. In other words, "knowledgeable action involves recognizing and using embedded clues" (Tyre & von Hippel, 1997, p. 76), what Tsoukas and Vladimirou (2001) called the ability to *draw distinctions*. Some authors refer to this level of skill and knowledge as "expertise" (Canon-Bowers, Salas, & Pruitt, 1996; Khatri & Ng, 2000; Klein, 1998; Schmitt, 1997). We will have more to say about expertise later in this book.

Ignorance   The previous sections dealt with information and knowledge, but lack of knowledge is at least as important in crisis situations. As we have seen, one of the most salient characteristics of crises is their high levels of uncertainty, or lack of information. These qualities make it important to understand not just knowledge but its absence: ignorance.

The fifteenth-century philosopher and Catholic cardinal Nicholas of Cusa developed the concept of "learned ignorance" (*de docta ignorantia*) to describe the recognition of ignorance as a vital component of wisdom, "a reasonable way of combining knowledge and ignorance through awareness of limitations of knowledge" (Harvey, Novicevic, Buckley, & Ferris, 2001, p. 450). Reasoning from a position of ignorance, or understanding both what is not known and what is necessary in order to fill the gap, is vital in order to rapidly reframe volatile contexts for decision making. This skill is also an essential element of what we term *expertise*.

Not all ignorance is productive, however. Harvey et al. (2001) identified four basic types of ignorance: pluralistic, populistic, probabilistic, and pragmatic. Each is dysfunctional in its own way, and each is relevant to a different type of crisis management. In *pluralistic* ignorance, people who disagree with policies or practices shared by the group publicly adopt those same policies or practices to avoid creating dissent, believing that they are unique in their disagreement. In an organizational setting, for instance, members may keep silent about their disagreement with organizational procedures of dubious utility or ethics, in the perhaps mistaken belief that everyone else finds them acceptable. Thus, in pluralistic ignorance, compliance with behavior is taken as a surface representation of deeper acceptance. Those who suffer from pluralistic ignorance continue to perpetuate the illusion of agreement while remaining unaware that it is an illusion. Indeed, they often compensate for their private lack of acceptance by voicing strong public commitment to the very practices with which they disagree, as proof of their "membership in good standing" within the organization.

Harvey et al. (2001) speculated that pluralistic ignorance might characterize the behavior of individuals in teams in organizations with strong corporate cultures—behavior that may be "politically manipulated by managers in terms of shifting accountability and interest-driven performance evaluation" (p. 453). Something of this sort may have been operating at Enron, where, according to Seeger and Ulmer (2003), CEO Jeffrey Skilling imposed on employees "values of greed and excess and a view that standard notions of right and wrong and traditional business principles simply did not apply" (p. 72). The "prevailing Enron culture of no bad news, also functioned to create self-censorship and self-persuasion" (Seeger & Ulmer, 2003, p. 74) so that managers lost their ability to discern warnings of upcoming crisis and proved powerless when the financial implosion hit Enron.

Within the context of crisis, Janis (1972) also wrote about pluralistic ignorance in his analysis of the "groupthink" planning process that doomed the 1961 Bay of Pigs invasion by Cuban exiles armed by the U.S. government. That poorly conceived attempt to overthrow Castro's government not only failed in a military sense but also had widening repercussions in damaging United States-Cuba relations and laying the ground for the Cuban missile crisis the following year. Before the Bay of Pigs invasion, planning was marred by the overriding sense of euphoria surrounding the Kennedy administration. There was an unwritten rule: "no criticism." Dissenters were told it was "too late to oppose" the Bay of Pigs invasion plan. Their memos protesting the plan never reached the top; planning meetings were set up so that participants felt embarrassed to object (Lagadec, 1993). Clearly such pluralistic ignorance represses the variety of viewpoints that current crisis management practices promote.

The second type of ignorance, *populistic* ignorance, is a social phenomenon in which a group shares a common misperception or lack of knowledge about a given issue or topic. The collective nature of populistic ignorance contributes to its rapid diffusion and relative strength. False rumors are a common example of this type of ignorance; they indicate that, especially in crisis situations, stakeholders' shared ignorance may overpower their shared knowledge and also diffuse faster than their shared knowledge (Harvey et al., 2001). The media often play a key role in spreading populistic ignorance by perpetuating collectively shared norms and beliefs. Within organizations, populistic ignorance is most likely to develop in a strong organizational culture that prizes conformity and points to past successes as the source of corporate knowledge. In such a culture, those who find themselves in disagreement may suffer from pluralistic ignorance and publicly espouse the majority view without acknowledging their private disagreement. In this way, the ignorance becomes increasingly embedded within the organization and is used to interpret subsequent events and make decisions; it becomes populistic ignorance.

The organizational culture at NASA prior to the Challenger disaster illustrates the relationship between populistic ignorance and crisis. Five years before the shuttle explosion, it was general knowledge at NASA that the rocket booster O-rings were causing problems. However, the space program was accustomed to "acceptable risks" that had not led to disasters in the past, and pushing the envelope of risk was a standard procedure in NASA's culture. Therefore, "what NASA had created was a closed culture that...'normalized deviance' so that to the outside world decisions that were obviously questionable were seen by NASA's management as prudent and reasonable" (Gladwell, 1996, p. 34). The NASA culture thus perpetuated populistic ignorance, a collectively shared misperception that led directly to the Challenger breakup.

The third type of ignorance, *probabilistic* ignorance, arises when judgment becomes skewed due to incomplete, inaccurate, or outdated information. This kind of ignorance is the product of societal and educational norms that lead people, consciously or subconsciously, to seek out deterministic rules that guide experience rather than reassessing circumstances as they change and considering alternatives to past behaviors. It is especially insidious in the sort of complex and dynamic environment in which crises thrive, as people can become desensitized to changes in context. This inattention leads to errors in learning as people who are "ignorant of their ignorance" (Harvey et al., 2001, p. 456) regularly draw inconsistent conclusions to which they become increasingly attached over time, in a sort of spiral of increasing ignorance.

Probabilistic ignorance was certainly a factor in the 1986 Challenger shuttle disaster. During the subsequent hearings on the shuttle's explosion, engineers discovered that the decision rules NASA had used for years to judge the safety of the O-rings were based on entirely untested data. As one engineer remarked, "I was referencing a non-existent data base" (Vaughan, 1996, p. 392). Unbeknownst to the decision makers, "this launch decision had become dissociated from its creators and the engineering process behind its creation. They had followed it repeatedly, taking for granted the interpretive work that other engineers had done. They did not realize that Thiokol had not tested the boosters" (Vaughan, 1996, p. 391).

Probabilistic ignorance also led to crisis and tragedy in the fishing town of Minimata, Japan, in the 1950s. Economically dependent on a neighboring chemical plant that discharged mercury into a local bay, the population of Minimata still looked to the sea for its main nutrition, initially not voicing the suspicion that the sea was making them sick. In fact, "the local population had always considered eating fish as the remedy for bad health—even when the fish became contaminated. The sicker people got, the more they felt they should eat fish, and the greater the dose of poison they absorbed" (Lagadec, 1993, pp. 48–49). Eventually, the townspeople's health problems came up against the chemical company's refusal to admit culpability; the result was riots, vandalism, and compensatory payments to victims, a full-blown crisis for community and industry alike.

Finally, the fourth type of ignorance, *pragmatic* ignorance, arises in complex and volatile situations in which unambiguous, reliable information is unavailable yet in which one or more decisions must be made. In such situations, inaction can have consequences equally as serious as those of incorrect action (Harvey et al., 2001). This type of ignorance is especially pernicious to companies in crisis that hunker down and say nothing—such as Exxon in the initial days after the 1989 Valdez spill, or the Soviet government for nearly 3 days after the 1986 Chernobyl accident. If they are not to be paralyzed into inaction, managers who recognize their pragmatic ignorance are forced to take action based on the best information at hand. Mitleton-Kelly (2003) described this situation in terms of living in a complex adaptive system that forces managers "to *change their rules of interaction*; to *act on limited local knowledge*, without knowing what the system as a whole is doing" (p. 27; italics in original). In the same spirit, Holder (2004) argued that the controversial decision by Union Carbide's CEO Warren Anderson to visit Bhopal immediately after his company's lethal gas leak was justified because "it was 'doing something' and perhaps more effective in the long run than taking no action" (p. 55), even though Anderson had little information or aid to offer.

Learning occurs when people openly confront their ignorance. Just as artists prepare to draw an object by examining not its structure but the empty space around it, organizations and individuals may gain knowledge by examining their ignorance (Stocking, 1998). In an organizational context, the optimum situation is that of *managing from knowing* (Harvey et al., 2001). In this condition, managers have two options: (1) They can combine their knowledge and knowing with an awareness of what is not known and how it may be obtained, as one might do with a crisis management team. (2) Otherwise, managers might use their pragmatic ignorance as a tool for action even when the required information is unavailable. Managing from knowing, or learned ignorance, is therefore essentially a form of expertise that helps managers deal with missing or equivocal information. It requires both the ability to recognize, and open acknowledgement of, areas of ignorance. It is a capability that can be achieved only through processes of learning, discussed in the next chapter.

6

The Complexity of Understanding

Constructive and Deviant Learning

In the preceding chapter, we looked at knowledge as a collectively generated endeavor, a blend of information and experience with gaps and imperfections that require completion by means of educated guesses or hunches. Here we look at those characteristics with particular reference to organizations and teams. How does group learning come about? How do organizations learn quickly during crises and glean valuable knowledge from failures?

The idea of collective learning—of organizations as "systems that learn"—originated in the early 1960s with studies of how organizations process information and make decisions (Laudon & Starbuck, 1996). In the broadest terms, learning involves both the acquisition and the creation of knowledge. Particularly in crisis situations, management teams need to learn fast in order to master rapidly changing environments.

Three aspects of learning are especially important in these exigencies. First, learning is both an individual and a social process, one that "takes place as much in people's minds as in the social relations among them, in the oral, written and 'visual' texts which convey ideas and knowledge from one context to another" (Gherardi, 1999, p. 111). The second aspect of learning involves change. Learning is said to have taken place when an individual's or group's attitudes, perspectives, or behaviors are altered (Blackler & McDonald, 2000; Cope & Watts, 2000). Finally, learning is tied up with the concept of identity. Brown and Starkey (2000) described learning as "an ongoing search for a time-and context-sensitive identity" (p. 110) and its management as a means of promoting "critical reflection upon individual and organizational identity" (p. 114). Keeping these factors in mind, in the following sections we consider the impact of group orientation, change, and identity on organizational learning.

Learning in Organizations

Some researchers view organizational learning as an extension of individual learning. Therefore, they define group learning as the aggregate of that of its members (Mirvis, 1996; Senge, 1990). However, this viewpoint differs from our own approach to knowledge, sensemaking, and decision making, in which we focus on the group, not the individual, as representing the emergent properties of complexity. Other researchers also put the emphasis on groups, viewing organizational learning as a "multilayered intersubjective phenomenon" (Oswick, Anthony, Keenoy, & Mangham, 2000, p. 888) that is "emergent, distributed, and resident in people, practices, artifacts and symbols" (Nidumolu et al., 2001, p. 118). This approach is occasionally termed the "situated" theory of organizational learning. It shifts attention away from the individuals within the group and toward the group itself—the context of its activities and the physical and social setting in which it operates (Nidumolu et al., 2001). Our discussion of organizational learning proceeds from this concept of group learning as an emergent phenomenon that cannot be summed up as an aggregation of individual learning.

In addition to the dichotomy between individual and group learning, theories of organizational learning also expose a dichotomy between complete agreement and toleration of multiple points of view. Some authors bypass conflict among viewpoints by recommending "team learning" as "free and creative exploration of complex and subtle issues, a deep 'listening' to one another and suspending of one's own views" (Senge, 1990, p. 237). Their objective is to create a cohesive and uncontested outcome, a univocal perspective.

Others have identified collaborative dialogue as a distinguishing feature of organizational learning (Koschmann, 1999; Oswick et al., 2000; Tyre & von Hippel, 1997). This approach to learning is less orderly than reaching consensus. It distinguishes the simple transfer of information from truly dialogic interaction with its own emergent properties of understanding and potential for creating knowledge. If human interaction is mainly an information process, "meaning is already possessed, and the reason I talk is to get it to others, hoping to change their choices" (Deetz, 1995, p. 97). But dialogic interaction "suggests that meaning is always incomplete and partial, and the reason I talk with others is to better understand what I and they mean, hoping to find new and more satisfying ways of being together" (Deetz, 1995, pp. 97–98). Thus organizational learning based on dialogue does not involve stitching together diverse but equivalent accounts and viewpoints. Instead, it becomes an exploration of differences between varying levels of expertise and a range of communication abilities: to frame arguments, to communicate thoughts and opinions, and to conduct debate in an organizational context.

Group learning is further enriched by a mixture of practices that are socially distributed throughout the organization: historical effects, social and physical artifacts, and contextual situations. The tensions generated by this interplay are what create learning over time. Organizational learning then becomes "a complex mix of intersubjective and generic sensemaking, heedful and decentered collaboration, enrolment and performance, apprenticeship and proficiency" (Blackler & McDonald, 2000, p. 841). Drawing on complexity theory, Mitleton-Kelly (2003) described this learning process as

> an emergent property in the sense that it arises from the interaction of individuals and is not just the sum of existing ideas, but could well be something quite new and possibly unexpected. Once the ideas are articulated they form part of the history of each individual and part of the shared history of the team...and these new ideas and new knowledge can be built upon to generate further new ideas and knowledge. (p. 42)

Four Approaches to Organizational Learning

Given its complex origins in dialogue, history, and shared and unique experiences, what can be expected as the outcome of organizational learning? The literature offers a variety of disciplinary perspectives, each with its own ontological and methodological framework and thus a distinctive view of its dynamics and inherent problems. Within these various approaches to organizational learning, Rifkin and Fulop (1997) identified four categories: the *learning organization* (LO), *organizational learning* (OL), the *learning environment* (LE), and the *learning space* (LS). The primary factors that distinguish these four themes are the degree to which they are prescriptive and the amount of managerial control over the learning process. We briefly outline the four categories, from most to least prescriptive.

At the most prescriptive end, the learning organization movement was spearheaded by Peter Senge's 1990 book, *The Fifth Discipline*. Senge's learning organization (LO) focused on structural concerns, teamwork, and concepts of "shared vision" that are presumed to help organizations meet predetermined, measurable learning goals (Rifkin & Fulop, 1997; Senge, 1990; Senge et al., 1999). Senge essentially viewed the organization as a system and applied the precepts of cybernetics and systems dynamics to the flow of knowledge and learning within the system across three levels of learning: individual, group or team, and organization. A highly multidisciplinary approach, the learning organization focused on action-oriented implementation (Easterby-Smith, 1997).

Since Senge's original writing, many others have criticized the notion of the LO. For example, Rifkin and Fulop (1997) argued that the LO takes a hegemonic approach to learning through its focus on teamwork and consensus, which serve as even stricter controls than those typically imposed by management through "participatory surveillance." Additional criticisms maintain that, although *The Fifth Discipline* claimed to refute modernist thought and scientific management, it instead assumed that certain policies, as developed by management and enacted by organizational members, will as a matter of course lead to the desired outcome. In contrast, Senge's critics have argued that learning is not something imposed on an organization by management but is indeed the default condition of any social system. For example, Appelbaum and Goransson (1997) argued that learning processes "take place continuously in the organization regardless of whether they are recognized and legitimized as organizational learning or not. These are the processes that lead to continuous change of the cognitive structures of the organization" (p. 119).

A less top-down approach than that of Senge (1990), the second approach to group learning is organizational learning (OL). This approach examines ways in which managers can implement and measure learning processes at both individual and organizational levels. Its primary concern is "understanding learning processes within organizational settings, without necessarily trying to change those processes" (Easterby-Smith, 1997, p. 1086). It is therefore an approach best suited to descriptive or preliminary research or simple monitoring.

The third approach to group learning, the learning environment (LE), seeks to create "an arena, rather than a bounded set of individuals or practices, that supports learning" (Rifkin & Fulop, 1997). The manager's role here is limited to helping "create conditions that might open up the LE, but he/she can neither totally determine nor mandate these conditions nor make them emerge through conventional OL strategies" (Rifkin & Fulop, 1997, p. 137). Instead, managerial prescriptions are limited to facilitating and sensemaking about concepts, actions, and events within the organizational context. These loosely structured approaches that attempt to create the proper habitat for learning are sometimes referred to as *holographic designs,* because they serve to break down perceived boundaries (such as those between the organization and its external environment) and because they do not focus simply on the component parts of organizations but rather on the organization as a whole (Mirvis, 1996). In short, they treat organizations as complex systems with permeable boundaries and learning as an emergent phenomenon whose history is an essential component of understanding.

The learning space (LS) is the least structured of the four approaches. Within this framework, "managers are meant to reflect on and engage in practices that are not controlling" and to encourage learning by providing the space for it to take place (Rifkin & Fulop, 1997, p. 137). In this case *space* refers both to physical areas in which organizational members may gather and talk freely and to broader interpretations that include providing the time to engage in nonproductive activity and the freedom to question organizational practices, policies, and power structures without inhibition (Rifkin & Fulop, 1997, p. 137). In this spirit, Gherardi (1999) pointed out that learning is not necessarily a purposeful activity undertaken by an individual or group but may also be a passive process whose locus of control remains outside of the individual. Along the same lines, Heiss (2006) observed that the various interlocking knowledge networks in organizations "mainly exist as ephemeral instantiations in the minds of interacting organizational agents" (p. 3) and that these cognitive maps are both idiosyncratic and dynamic. In this model, learning is an ongoing experiential process. In other words, sometimes learning "just happens," whether we seek it out or not.

The last two approaches to group learning, and especially the LS approach, parallel recommendations made by organizational theorists who draw on complexity. For example, Lewin and Regine (2003) applied complexity theory to a case study of a London advertising agency that was structured around a number of nontraditional properties. Ownership of the firm was equally distributed among employees; rather than individual offices, there were common spaces for work; and clients and agency staff worked simultaneously on campaigns rather than following the traditional linear process of passing the work from specialist to specialist. This naturalistic learning proved highly effective in a pragmatic business setting, even though its unconventionality made some employees uncomfortable. In fact, the agency became so successful that it had to stop taking clients even after it tripled in size.

As this case study indicates, the LE, and especially the LS, take an emergent view of learning in terms of the natural patterns that result from interaction at the local level. Rather than prescribing top-down, outcome-oriented models that seek to meet goals set by management, they prefer to relax controls and let learning determine its own course. As Lewin and Regine (2003) pointed out, such processes mirror some of the fundamental concepts of the complexity sciences: nonlinearity, emergence, and local interaction. The paradox that "freedom is essential to order" (Mirvis, 1996, p. 25) is taken here as a motivation to break down what are perceived to be structural and social barriers to learning.

Modes of Learning: Facts, Worldviews, and Large-Scale Patterns

The view of organizations as "systems that learn" is now well established in the literature. However, there are many different types of organizational learning, some more efficacious in crisis situations than others, and there are barriers that prevent effective learning entirely.

Cognitive psychologist Jean Piaget (1950) described two basic types of learning: assimilation and accommodation. Assimilation involves absorbing facts and sorting and interpreting them based on previously acquired schemas or worldviews. Accommodation involves changing one's worldview based on experiences in a symbiotic interrelationship with others and the environment, which leads to the adaptive behavior that helps organizations succeed (De Geus, 1997).

Piaget's (1950) assimilation/accommodation dichotomy is further enriched by the concept of learning loops, which help to preserve the status quo or foster adaptive change. The image of "loops," such as those found in electrical circuitry, is widely used in the literature on organizational learning. Rooted in systems theory and cybernetics, the metaphor gained currency through an influential article in which Argyris (1977) described two modes of learning found in organizations. The simplest mode, single-loop learning, involves finding and correcting factors that prevent the organization from meeting its objectives. Argyris compared this mode to a thermostat set to a particular temperature: It receives information about the external temperature and takes the necessary corrective action to maintain its setting. From a systems perspective, this type of learning loop provides negative feedback; it has a stabilizing influence on the system. In terms of organizational crises, single-loop learning is analogous to the mindset that Bechler (2004) argued is dominant in crisis research: the "homeostatic perspective" (p. 70) that crisis comes from outside and needs to be resolved so that the organization can return to normal.

Double-loop learning, on the other hand, would require the thermostat to be able to question the unspoken assumptions behind the setting. Why was that particular temperature chosen? Is it truly the most appropriate for the room and its purpose? Therefore double-loop learning is a reflexive process that can potentially effect internal, as well as formal, change (Argyris, 1977). Whereas single-loop learning has a stabilizing effect, double-loop learning has an amplifying effect. Like positive feedback in a complex system, it describes a process by which conclusions from one stage of deliberation can become input for the next stage. In terms of crisis, Bechler (2004) captured the same view of double-loop learning and change when he noted that "when the crisis is perceived as an important and potentially beneficial corrective, change within the organization becomes an expectation" (p. 70).

There is also a third level of learning, alternately defined as deutero learning or triple-loop learning (Romme & van Witteloostuijn, 1999; Senge et al., 1999). This mode increases "the fullness and deepness of learning about the diversity of issues and dilemmas faced, by linking together all local units of learning in one overall learning infrastructure as well as developing the competencies and skills to use this infrastructure" (Romme & van Witteloostuijn, 1999, p. 440). Triple-loop learning is analogous to expert knowledge. It focuses on structural patterns, both at the cognitive level of mental maps and at the organizational level, as it attempts to discern configurations and organizational designs that will facilitate higher-level learning.

Insistence on a rational approach that ignores the larger patterns of deutero learning can aggravate the disadvantages of having only a narrow range of available knowledge, as in the case of a complex system without effective distributed cognition. If all actors make individual rational choices without regard for the big picture, the consequences may be "unit practices on the organizational level" (Marion, 1999). That type of rational decision making without regard to context may have led to the 1986 tragedy of the gas leak at Union Carbide's Bhopal plant. In that instance, according to Weick (1988), Union Carbide's senior management viewed the Bhopal plant as unimportant and therefore allocated limited resources to run it. That decision set off a corresponding vicious cycle in which worker indifference and management cost-cutting became mutually reinforcing. Those attitudes in turn caused plant conditions to deteriorate dangerously, not only because of decreased maintenance but also due to "increased inattention, indifference, turnover, low cost improvisation, and working-to-rule, all of which remove slack, lower the threshold at which a crisis will escalate, and increase the number of separate places at which a crisis could start" (Weick, 1988, p. 312). Weick commented: "The point is, this scenario starts with top management perceptions that set in motion enactments that confirm the perceptions....Strategy [in Bhopal's case] became an inadvertent source of crisis through its effects on realities constructed by disheartened workers" (1988, p. 314).

Some authors have linked triple-loop learning to the principles of nonlinear science, pointing out that this mode "is governed by the types of dynamics which one might associate with strange or chaotic attractors" (Daneke, 1997, p. 256). Just as such attractors create parameters beyond which a complex system cannot stray, organizations are underlain and shaped by cultural patterns that constrain the varieties of behaviors they display. Triple-loop learning is the process of discovering these hidden constraints or attractors. In terms of crises, a triple-loop perspective argues that "for real change to occur the whole must be analyzed and accounted for rather than just a singular part," looking for the "interrelationship between the corrective role of crisis and the organizational whole (or the overarching organizational culture and history)" (Bechler, 2004, p. 70). Table 6.1 summarizes the basic characteristics and objectives of the three types of learning.

Other scholars of organizational learning have affirmed these three basic levels of learning: assimilation of facts (single loop), change in worldview (double loop), and the ability to see larger patterns (triple loop). Like Piaget (1950) and Argyris (1977), they envisioned learning along a continuum anchored at one end by maintenance of the status quo and at the other end by initiation of profound change. For example, Cope and Watts (2000) examined learning in natural environments, or "learning by doing," in which they described three distinct levels of learning. Level 1 involves "surface learning," assimilating data, facts, and routine tasks that do not have long-term developmental consequences. It is comparable to Piaget's concept of learning as assimilation of information. Level 2 learning refers to acquiring knowledge that is context-specific, such as a skill, but that also affects some aspect of the learner's worldview. For

Table 6.1. Three Types of Learning Loops

	Single-Loop Learning	Double-Loop Learning	Triple-Loop (deutero) Learning
Level of learning	Assimilation of facts	Change in worldview	Ability to see larger patterns
Description of learning process	Identifying and correcting factors that shift the organization from its stated or preferred course	Questioning assumptions behind the status quo	Linking together individual and collective learning units to identify patterns
Type of change	Negative feedback	Positive feedback	Emergence and innovation, including complete systemic change
Objective	Homeostasis, return to "normal" steady state	Questioning assumptions behind status quo procedures	Discovering hidden patterns (attractors) and developing expertise
Type of system	Closed system	Open system	Complex system

example, studying a foreign language involves level 2 learning because it offers insights into other cultures and provides a new outlook on one's own language and culture. Level 3 learning is the mode that comes closest to Argyris's (1977) double-loop mode, as it stimulates profound change by questioning deep, unexpressed assumptions and increasing the learner's self-awareness. This is also the mode most commonly found to result from "learning by doing" through active knowing, or experience. In addition, it describes the profound change experienced by people who have undergone crisis—in Weick's (1993) terms, the *cosmology episode* in which all customary beliefs and opinions are open to question. During a cosmology episode, "people suddenly and deeply feel that the universe is no longer a rational, orderly system" (p. 633). Recovering from a cosmology episode requires an intense learning process.

Experience is one of the most effective platforms for organizational learning, as it leads to successful adaptation. Hence Megginson (1996) argued that the most effective learning may be achieved by a combination of informal, action-based learning and deliberate reflexivity. Action-based learning leads to what he called "emergent" learning, in which the responsibility for the process rests with the individual learner rather than with an authoritative instructor or other knowledge gatekeeper; reflexivity makes it possible for the learner to take utmost advantage of the learning potential of various experiences. Cope and Watts (2000) advocated using this combination of experience and reflection during "critical incidents," or episodes of discontinuity that may offer occasions for profound change. Organizational crises demand this combination of emergent learning and reflection as they offer critical occasions to reassess culture, goals, and relationships with publics.

This combination of learning in response to stimuli from the environment and collaborative inquiry is referred to as "adaptive learning." Such an approach often characterizes learning in organizational settings and involves changes to both behavioral performance and cognitive understanding (Fiol & Lyles, 1985). Adaptive learning is situated learning: It is firmly grounded in particular surroundings, both physical and social, that define both opportunities for learning and constraints on what may be learned and in what manner. Adaptive learning also emphasizes the role of action and interaction, a way of "learning by doing." The process is analogous to the micro interactions between agents in a complex system, highly local exchanges that lead to new patterns in the larger culture.

Learning from Experience

Given most researchers' emphasis on action as a key component of knowledge, it is not surprising that many people particularly value learning from experience. Such learning is often presumed to be more "authentic" than reflexive processes. However, nonreflective action does present drawbacks; as Benjamin Franklin (1743) said, "experience keeps a dear school, but fools will learn in no other."

In organizational terms, learning purely by direct experience has numerous disadvantages (De Geus, 1997). It takes longer to see the final effects of one's actions, and its high level of public commitment also involves a high degree of risk for both the organization and the decision maker. Thus, in Piaget's (1950) terms, assimilation (which stays at the level of information) becomes a more attractive alternative to accommodation (which involves reflection), because it does not require the decision maker—organization or individual—to effect any profound change. Psychological security can be derived from repeating past formulas and routine processes. Boisot (2003) observed, "*pace* Tom Peters, [firms] do not thrive on chaos if they can possibly help it....More often than not, they also seek to escape from the complex regime into the stability and security of the ordered regime, of simple and predictable routines, and of uncomplicated, hierarchical relationships" (p. 197). Nonetheless, this security can be deceptive: as De Geus (1997) warned: "History does, in fact, repeat itself—but never in quite the same way" (p. 80), so that adaptation is usually essential to success in the longer haul.

Given this ambiguity, it can be hard to decide which experiences offer the best bases for learning. For example, Nidumolu et al. (2001)

pointed out that even though failures may provide more useful learning experiences than successes, they are underrepresented in the literature. However, past successes alone make for incomplete learning, biased toward "notions of competence" and fostering "incremental refinement rather than innovative problem solving" (Nidumolu et al., 2001, p. 117). In addition, exemplars of success may not be generalizable, especially in the turbulent environment of corporate exigencies such as crises. In these "complex and dynamic contexts, the generalizability of prior lessons is often ambiguous and normal learning processes can lead organizations into unexpected states when failures occur" (Nidumolu et al., 2001, p. 117). Therefore, the emulation of successes should be balanced with instances of failures in which managers can learn from an organization's shortcomings. In fact, Bazerman and Watkins (2004) devoted an entire volume to "predictable surprises," many of which could have been avoided by learning from past failures.

The crisis literature has generally managed to maintain a balance between learning from success and learning from failure, as indicated by cautionary case studies of such notable failures as the Exxon Valdez and the Challenger and Columbia disasters. Nonetheless, conflicting lessons have been drawn from all crises. For example, some argue that Exxon did the most it could to contain the Valdez leak, given the circumstances (Lukaszewski, 1993), whereas others say that it failed miserably (Small, 1991). Similarly, some claim that NASA successfully applied what it had learned about crisis communication from its Challenger disaster to the Columbia tragedy (Martin & Boynton, 2005), whereas others say that its crisis communication continued to reflect "serious problems with its organizational culture" (Kauffman, 2005, p. 264).

In addition to ambiguous lessons, another problem with learning from experience in real-world settings is that feedback cues are not always detected, not always unambiguous, and not always correctly interpreted. As an example, numerous commentators have discussed the self-delusion that took hold at Enron and thwarted management awareness of the company's impending collapse. According to Seeger and Ulmer (2003), Enron's prevailing culture of "no bad news" led to

> self-censorship and self-persuasion. Weick (1988) described these conditions as a kind of unwitting collusion or stunted enactment, whereby followers can neither recognize nor attend to certain kinds of information....Even as the evidence of inevitable failure became increasingly clear, employees still repeated the Enron mantra and bought more company stock. The interpretation that Enron was a model of business success and innovation so dominated that any information inconsistent with this was simply ignored. (p. 74)

To observers standing outside Enron's culture, this self-delusion was so clear that many described it skeptically as a kind of organizational psychosis. Yet this self-imposed blindness is not uncommon in the lead-up to crisis; it is part of problems with learning that make organizations prone to exigencies. The following sections describe two such learning patterns that pose particular hazards: neurotic learning and superstitious learning.

Neurotic Learning

A neurotic symptom is defined by persistence in an action that is no longer appropriate in given circumstances (Watzlawick, 1976). By examining the outcomes of our past choices, we decide which have been successful and thus which behaviors to reinforce (Gavetti & Levinthal, 2000). However, these decisions are by no means clear. As van Ginneken (2003) noted, "social actions are nested in moving patterns of relevant context. That is to say, no two situations are entirely identical, and one should be careful in trusting 'eternal laws.' The fact that certain things have in the past always turned out in a certain way does not in itself guarantee that will hold in the future" (p. 24). Neurotic learning is closely related to probabilistic ignorance (Harvey et al., 2001), discussed in the previous chapter: Our natural desire to identify and follow rules and principles can sometimes blind us to change.

Psychologists are well aware that we do not always consider changing circumstances when repeating the behavior. For example, Watzlawick (1976) described an experiment in which a horse received a mild electric shock under one hoof whenever a bell rang. The horse learned to lift its hoof each time it heard the bell, even after the experimenters ceased to deliver the shock. Each time the horse lifted its hoof and failed to feel the shock, the behavior was reinforced as "correct" in the horse's mind because it avoided the undesired consequences, although the horse had no way of knowing that it was no longer necessary.

Applying the concept of neurotic learning to crisis, a similar type of persistent, dysfunctional learning underlay the mercury poisoning crisis in Minimata, Japan. Sickened by chemical residues in the local fish, townspeople treated their ill health by consuming ever-greater quantities of the contaminated fish that were making them ill (Lagadec, 1993). Centuries of tradition had indicated that eating fish increased health; it proved extremely difficult for the community to "unlearn" this expectation, and their misinterpretation only sickened more people and deepened the crisis.

Ulmer et al. (2007) also discussed the importance of being able to "unlearn" outdated crisis response behavior. They noted that willingness to give up allegiance to procedures that worked in the past—what we term *neurotic learning*—enables organizations to expand their options. Willingness to experiment even with behaviors with unknown consequences can increase blind variation in organizations (Romanelli, 1999). In complexity terms, such unlearning allows organizations to increase the "requisite variety" of actions to meet the unpredictable challenges in their surrounding context.

Superstitious Learning

It is also possible to learn compulsive superstitious behavior, a particularly insidious problem for organizations wedded to a culture of careful planning and control (Kersten, 2005; Kets de Vries & Miller, 1984). In general, superstitions are efforts to impose order and control on one's environment, and they often reflect a deeply rooted belief in the direct causality of one's actions (Watzlawick, 1976; Weick, 2001). For example, Watzlawick (1976) released a laboratory rat into a bounded area containing a food tray at the opposite end. Food was automatically released 10 seconds after the rat entered the area, but not if the rat had already reached the food tray and was waiting. Because it took the rat only about 2 seconds to travel the distance to the tray, it felt compelled to find alternate behaviors to delay its arrival at the tray. The delay acquired what Watzlawick called a "pseudocausal significance": The rat came to believe that whatever it did in that time interval was the action that produced the desired outcome. These actions were often quite elaborate, with a certain number of steps to the right or left, jumps and pirouettes, turns and twists of the tail. Each time the rat repeated the action, reached the food tray at the appropriate time, and received its food, the conviction that the behavior was correct was reinforced.

Other, similar experiments have found that people will tend to generate superstitious rules to guide their behavior in uncertain situations, even when outcomes are entirely noncontingent (Rudski, Lischner, & Albert, 1999). Most organizational exigencies display a high level of ambiguity, often with loose coupling between outcomes and causal events, and therefore neurotic or superstitious inferences may occur more frequently than managers realize. As Weick (2001) noted, in situations in which ambiguity is high:

> superstitious learning is probable as it is more difficult to attach specific outcomes to specific prior causal action, communications will be delayed and distorted, people may find it difficult to learn because feedback is delayed beyond the point at which someone is able to understand precisely what prior action is relevant to the feedback, and there may be a high incidence of giving up and resignation when systems are not responsive to demands. (p. 44)

As Weick's description suggests, superstitions are often related to the illusion of control. The pre-Challenger NASA offers an example of superstitious learning as a cause of crisis. Having long lived in a culture of "acceptable risk" without severe consequences, NASA's management had developed a "fantasy of NASA's infallibility subject to the following of its forms and rituals. If the forms were followed, success was assured" (Schwartz, 1987, pp. 65–66). This mind-set led to "the most remarkable aspect of the public testimony concerning the disaster—NASA management's apparent belief that they made the right decision" simply because they had held a formal discussion between managers and engineers before launching the Challenger. According to Schwartz, "The only way this belief can be maintained is by supposing that making the right decision means making the decision in the right way, regardless of consequences" (1987, p. 66). Yet it was clear to anyone who was not within NASA that, in the words of one Marshall Space Center manager, "the shuttle blew up and you had pieces falling from the sky....How could [the decision] not be flawed?" (Schwartz, 1987, p. 66).

Kersten and Sidky (2005) argued that "traditional crisis management tends to take a rationalistic approach to the organization and its functioning"; however, dysfunctional organizations—those most prone to crises—"often lack rationality, or, more precisely, they use an alternative rationality that is created by systemic psychodynamic dysfunctions" (2005, pp. 472–73). This dysfunctionality is amply illustrated by neuroses and superstitions—a result of learning the wrong lessons from experience. In addition, sociopolitical and psychodynamic barriers may prevent people from learning anything of value.

Sociopolitical Barriers

Double- and triple-loop learning, which involve changes in viewpoints or behavior, are not common in organizations for a number of reasons. Such learning is a difficult and potentially painful process that requires the ability to recognize, and willingness to correct, one's own flaws and mistaken decisions. Furthermore, it may require going against deeply ingrained societal and organizational norms. Finally, the politics of organizational hierarchy make it difficult for anyone within the organization to "rock the boat" and set the learning process in motion.

Again, NASA's culture before the 1986 Challenger tragedy shows how sociopolitical barriers lay the groundwork for crisis. During a prelaunch conference between NASA and Morton Thiokol, the maker of the problematic O-rings, the "management" aspects of a launch decision were separated from the "engineering" aspects of shuttle safety. As a result, once Morton Thiokol senior management "announced that a 'management decision' would have to be made, the issue was already decided and further disagreement on engineering grounds became irrelevant" (Schwartz, 1987, p. 65). Sociopolitical barriers thus constrained decision making and created blind spots that led directly to the shuttle tragedy.

In addition to silencing dissenters, barriers to double-loop learning can place employees in a double bind of deception. For example, Argyris (1977, p. 116) described an organizational culture in which, when "employees adhere to a norm that says 'hide errors,' they know they are violating another norm that says 'reveal errors'." Yet if they reveal the error, they may expose "a whole network of camouflage and deception." In response to this double bind, employees may "begin to conceive of the error hiding, deception, and games as part of normal and organizational life"; however, "the moment individuals reach this state, they may also lose their ability to see the errors" (Argyris, 1977, p. 116).

Attempts to mitigate this type of double bind explain a number of crises that have ethical aspects, such as the reluctance of Enron's financial managers to blow the whistle on the accounting malfeasance of their top management. In fact, this inability to engage in double-loop learning precisely describes the disintegrating ethical climate that led Enron to crisis. As Seeger and Ulmer (2003) observed, "Enron executives created...[a] culture of secrecy and 'no bad news.'... Any hint of negative information was quickly squelched....Employees described an unwitting collusion that developed as people learned to acknowledge publicly only the positive" (p. 74). The effect of this culture was to continually reinforce only certain patterns of cognition, a kind of positive feedback that became increasingly extreme. That positive feedback was further augmented by hands-off management that did not regulate the increasingly exaggerated patterns of risk and secrecy. From a complexity standpoint, Enron's collapse involved more than being caught making illegal accounting maneuvers; it involved out-of-control reiteration of cultural patterns in which the same attitudes and behaviors were constantly reinforced and embellished until the system broke down.

Because of deeply ingrained social norms that make people reluctant to upset others, especially their superiors, it is extremely difficult to overcome these obstacles to learning. The cycle of error and cover-up is especially insidious within organizations—such as NASA—that revere the rational model that "presumes that actions based on knowledge and undertaken with skill are supposed to turn out right" (Mirvis, 1996, p. 20). This rationale leads naturally to the deduction that, if something goes wrong, either knowledge or skill, or both, are at fault, and therefore one or more persons are to blame. In truth, as Perrow (1984) noted, accidents are "normal" events when operating in a tightly coupled technological society. Yet widespread belief in the rightness of a rational approach leads many employees working in such a context to become socialized to covering up not only their own errors but also those of others as a way to avoid blame.

Psychodynamic Barriers

Some scholars have argued that organizations fail to learn from experience because of individual and group defenses enacted to protect self-esteem. This self-protective behavior may work in the short term, but it carries two significant risks. First, organizations that suffer from excessively high self-esteem will have correspondingly strong ego defenses, inhibiting their ability to notice and assess potential threats. Second, at the other extreme, organizations with low self-esteem and low defenses will be open to fears and anxieties that interfere with members' spirit of initiative and thus impede learning activities. At various points along the self-esteem continuum, ego defenses may inhibit learning "through their influence on (1) the external search for information, (2) the interpretation of information, (3) the use of information, (4) the storage of information, and (5) the internal recall of information" (Brown & Starkey, 2000, p. 105).

In response, organizations may enact a variety of ego defenses. First, they may engage in denial, a means of negating knowledge and responsibility for events that affect the organization. Second, they may try rationalization, a process of making unacceptable thoughts, behaviors, and perceptions tolerable. Third, they may use idealization, which divests people and entities of negative characteristics. Fourth, they may try fantasy, or unrealistic visions of people, groups, systems, or events. Finally, they may employ symbolization, a form of self-deception that restricts people's ability to examine the reality behind the symbols (Brown & Starkey, 2000).

This series of learning difficulties sounds much like the roster of 31 perceptual dysfunctions that Pauchant and Mitroff (1992) identified as making an organization crisis prone, including perceptions that size renders the company dominant and therefore immune from threats, beliefs that the company is liked by all its stakeholders, and excessive reliance on technology. They commented: "Crisis-prone organizations and crisis-prone managers seem to have this characteristic in common: the inability to imagine and feel that the world is different from themselves" (1992, p. 102). As Brown and Starkey (2000, p. 103) suggested, "the processes by which organizations preserve their identities are, in many ways, analogous to the methods that individuals employ in defense of their own self-concepts." Therefore, any information that threatens this self-concept is "ignored, rejected, reinterpreted, hidden, or lost" (2000, p. 103).

This idealization sounds very much like the syndrome that affected NASA and led to the Challenger disaster. According to Schwartz (1987), in its early days NASA was widely perceived as a "can't fail" venture. However, this belief led to "an organization that had abandoned reality and chosen to live in fantasy," whereby "the business of NASA had become the creation of the image of American society's perfection" (pp. 60, 61). As a result, NASA managers ignored discussion of the defective O-rings, thereby "reinforcing the drama of perfection by dramatizing to their superior that everything was just fine and that NASA was moving along in its inexorably perfect way" (Schwartz, 1987, p. 63).

A final factor that can distort experiential lessons is causal attribution, also known as attribution bias. Coombs and Holladay (2001) applied attribution theory to explain how stakeholders process organizational crises, assigning greater or lesser weight based on the organization's past performance record, perceived degree of organizational responsibility for the crisis, and relationship history with stakeholders. Attribution bias exists within organizations as well, indicating that decision makers "attribute good outcomes to their own actions and qualities while attributing poor outcomes to external factors such as environmental events and bad luck" (Schwenk, 1995, p. 476). On an organizational level, it is often not clear whether these biased attributions are deliberate manipulations of the truth to reassure stakeholders or truthful reflections of managers' beliefs. For example, Italian multinational Parmalat issued a number of press releases in the period leading up to its dramatic financial collapse in 2003. The company sought to shape the media narrative surrounding its crisis, emphasizing its financial successes as a sign of control, while assigning responsibility to external factors—from seasonal market slowdowns to alleged false rumors spread by competitors—for its troubles (Gilpin, in press).

Organizations can avoid falling into these dysfunctional learning patterns. In the next chapter, we describe a form of organizational knowing, a synthesis of adaptive learning techniques that can most effectively cope with crises when they occur and may even help to prevent crises altogether.

7

Sorting Out the Complex World

Sensemaking and Decision Making

The preceding chapter discussed ways in which information and knowledge can become dysfunctional, actually preserving ignorance and shaping bad decisions. However, at its best, knowledge leads to a state of knowing, a dynamic learning interaction between individuals and their environments, and to expertise, the ability to intuit patterns and make connections when information is incomplete or uncertain. In turn, both knowing and expertise are fundamental to the collective process of understanding known as sensemaking.

In this chapter, we show how sensemaking and group learning lead to flexible, expert decision making. We culminate with the concept of the "expert organization" that can regroup effectively to both anticipate and deal with a crisis. Our concept of the expert organization has affinities with Choo's (2001) "knowing organization": one that synthesizes sensemaking, knowledge, and decision making in a cycle that leads to effective learning and adaptation. Although the emphasis here is on theories of organizational learning, we place these themes in the context of complex systems and crisis management.

Following Weick (1995), Choo (2001) defined sensemaking as a process that organizational members use to "negotiate beliefs and interpretations to construct shared meanings and common goals." The shared meanings and purpose that emerge from sensemaking "constitute the framework for explaining observed reality, and for determining saliency and appropriateness" (p. 200).

Sensemaking is prompted by changes in environmental conditions that arouse notice within the ongoing flow of events in an organization (Choo, 2001; Weick, 1995). The sensemaking process involves first noticing these changes—in the form of surprise, discrepancies, or incongruencies—as differences from expectations based on past experience. To make sense of the current situation, an individual speculates on plausible explanations for the noticed cues. At the group or organizational level, these speculations are typically exchanged and discussed with others in an attempt to reach a collectively accepted meaning, which then becomes part of the shared environment and experience. The agreed-on version produces an enacted environment that is "meaningful in providing a cause-and-effect explanation of what is taking place. In retention, the organization stores the products of successful sensemaking (enacted or meaningful interpretations) so that they may be retrieved in the future" (Choo, 2001, pp. 197–98).

Rooted in cognitive dissonance theory (Festinger, 1957; Street, Robertson, & Geiger, 1997; Weick, 1995), sensemaking is concerned with reducing uncertainty, generally after a decision has been made. In addition, because sensemaking involves problem framing, it is also a pre-decision framework. In this respect, sensemaking is not the same as interpretation, which generally assumes that a problem is already framed and awaiting such exposition. Instead, sensemaking advances the notion that practitioners must also construct the problem from a situation of uncertainty, things that make no sense. Thus Weick (1995) emphasized that the key distinction between interpretation and sensemaking is that "sensemaking is about the ways people generate what they interpret" (p. 13). This framing of the problem sets boundaries and narrows our view of the situation and its context, thereby limiting our range of actions. Using Giddens's (1984) structuration theory, Thiétart and Forgues (1997) summarized the process thus:

> System behaviour is the consequence of deterministic rules which originate from the actions of the organizational actors themselves. Causality, though, runs in both directions. System behavior elicits actions and actions shape system behaviour. Recursive relationships take place between cause and effect. Effect becomes the cause, end becomes the origin, actions create structure and structure determines actions. (p. 120)

As this view suggests, sensemaking depends on perspectives from inside the system rather than an objective analysis from outside. The "sensemaker" is a self-conscious being who reflexively questions the meaning of his or her surroundings and events, using this reflection to shape his or her opinions and general worldview. Sensemaking is also firmly attached to history, because it is retrospective in nature. If time is seen as an ongoing stream, then the tendency to divide the past into discrete "experiences" rather than the singular holistic "experience" seems inappropriate.

This attentiveness to past experience led Weick (1995) to reach four conclusions. First, meaning comes from paying attention to what has already occurred. Second, what is occurring at the moment will influence what we notice when looking backward. Third, because this retrospection means we are dealing with memories, anything that affects memories will affect the sensemaking process. Fourth and finally, often the "stimulus-response" sequence is actually "response" followed by "stimulus definition." Because experience is ongoing, we cannot locate the beginning until events have already begun; only then can we look for antecedents. Both the identification of the stimulus and the definition of the action depend largely on what is salient in the present situation.

This retrospective view of stimulus captures the essence of complex responsive processes discussed earlier, in which meaning is said to emerge in the living present while remaining firmly grounded in the past. The point is not that past experience leads inevitably to the present situation. Rather, many possibilities exist at any one time; a group of people may consider possible interpretations and act on one particular choice or follow one particular path. In turn, those choices favor a new set of circumstances and more choices of direction. Just as Weick's (1995) sensemaking is set in motion by a problematic circumstance, complex systems respond to a break in normal patterns by experimenting and then selecting a new path to follow. Crises are the pattern breakers that often set this type of course correction in motion.

Enactment and the Enacted Environment

A recurring concept in the sensemaking literature is *enactment*, which emphasizes that "when people act, they bring events and structures into existence and set them in motion" (Weick, 2001, p. 225). The first step in this process of enactment entails filtering experience to decide what to focus on, a framing of the situation based on existing knowledge and preconceptions. People then act within these self-imposed constraints. The enacted environment is thus the result of changes to the environment caused by enactment. In the same way, Mitleton-Kelly (2003) described individual life choices as a complex adaptive system: "It is the series of critical decisions each individual takes from several possible alternatives that may determine a particular life path for that individual.... The emergent behaviour of the person is not a matter of 'chance' but is the result of a person's selection among a finite set of perceived choices as well as the past choices made (the history) that have shaped that person's life path" (p. 34).

We might see enactment as another way of looking at chapter 5's knowledge/knowing dichotomy, in which action leads to understanding. To use the bicycle example described earlier, the act of riding contributes to our understanding because we are immediately able to observe the effects of our actions—the enacted environment—by seeing how the bicycle reacts to shifts in weight, movements of the handlebars, and so on.

Sensemaking is also a social process in which others' behavior shapes our own, whether or not they are physically present. The social process incorporates both anticipated reactions of others and face-to-face interaction. Particularly in organizations, there is constant negotiation of positions, most of which takes the form of face-to-face interaction. There is no clearly identifiable moment at which sensemaking begins, because "people are always in the middle of things, which become things, only when those same people focus on the past from some point beyond it" (Weick, 1995, p. 43). The implication of this conceptualization is that people are "thrown into" situations and are then obliged to somehow make sense of them. Holder (2004) pointed out that this process describes organizations' optimal response to crises. Although they can anticipate the kinds of crises they may face, "most companies cannot accurately anticipate what will actually happen"; she therefore invoked a Weickian perspective and argued, "the important thing may be *to simply act or be quick to respond*" (Holder, 2004, p. 54, italics in original). In other words, organizations define and control crises through cultural structures that inform spontaneous enactment rather than through advance planning.

The sensemaking process focuses on, and is in turn focused by, cues extracted from the environment. What happens to the cue once it has managed to arouse the sensemaker depends on context, as "context affects what is extracted as a cue in the first place" (Weick, 1995, p. 51). The subsequent interpretation of cues is also context dependent. Thus the final aim of sensemaking is not perfect accuracy—that is impossible in a rapidly changing, complex context—but plausibility, an explanation that "makes sense." This perspective highlights the pragmatic nature of sensemaking:

> Even if accuracy were important, executives seldom produce it. From the standpoint of sensemaking, that is no big problem. The strength of sensemaking as a perspective derives from the fact that it does not rely on accuracy and its model is not object perception. Instead, sensemaking is about plausibility, pragmatics, coherence, reasonableness, creation, invention, and instrumentality. (Weick, 1995, p. 57)

The sensemaker settles for what Weick (1995) called "circumscribed accuracy," a term that draws attention to the situated nature and relative validity of perceptions. According to Weick, "in a rapidly changing ongoing stream of activity, circumscribed accuracy seems to be the most one can hope for" (1995, p. 58). This constraint especially holds true for social perceptions rooted in identity and subjectivity rather than objective reality. Therefore, from Weick's perspective, it is not the crisis plan itself but rather "the reflective process of planning" that preceded it that enables organizations to respond effectively to crises, regardless of specific "lists of do's and don't's or lessons learned" in the plan itself (Weick, 1995, p. 52).

Making sense of reality involves integrating knowledge—of the particulars of which one is "subsidiarily" aware—with the features of a focal objective (Tsoukas & Vladimirou, 2001). In other words, one must match one's experience with the situation at hand and apply personal judgment based on both. Past experiences also color how information is enacted in the present. As a result, "action options are perforce limited by what sense people have made of what went on in the past and what they can foresee happening in the future" (Mirvis, 1996, p. 17). Due to this reflexive nature, sensemaking may be regarded as a "higher-order form of experiential learning" (Gavetti & Levinthal, 2000, p. 114).

Certain occasions or conditions act as special triggers for sensemaking activity because of their particular characteristics (Weick, 1995). For crisis management, three of the most significant occasions are situations of high information load, complexity, and turbulence. As *information load* increases, people neglect large portions of it. They adopt a variety of strategies to reduce the pressure, and these strategies affect what information is then available for sensemaking. As Weick put it, information load "is an occasion for sensemaking because it forces cues out of an ongoing flow" (1995, p. 87). Along these lines, Boisot (2003) used the image of the bond trader to show one management strategy of coping with information load by reducing phenomena to bits of information that can be rapidly distributed.

Increased *complexity* tends to lead to narrow specialization and thus self-censoring of cues, or filtering of how those cues are interpreted. As an example, Lagadec (1993) recounted a close call on an airplane crash that resulted from both information overload and increased complexity. Told by the control tower that his landing gear was not down, the pilot responded, "I'm not receiving you clearly, there's a siren blowing in my ears," and landed the plane without checking the reason for the warning siren (p. 47). The 1996 mad cow disease scare in Britain is another instance of how complexity affects crisis decision making. In that instance, too many contingencies—about causes, latency, safety precautions—made it impossible for either scientists or government officials to make decisions based on facts; the boycotts, bans, cattle slaughter, and other actions were based on public emotions driving political exigencies.

Finally, *turbulence* may be defined as "a combination of instability (frequency of change) and randomness (frequency and direction of change)" (Weick, 1995, p. 88). Both instability and randomness characterize crisis situations, in which an organization has poor control over crisis instigators, especially in the initial stages. Thus Weick's three triggers for sensemaking—information load, complexity, and turbulence—make this form of collective learning a central feature of crisis management in which managers must enact rapid decisions in the face of uncertain and changeable circumstances.

Group Sensemaking

From a sensemaking standpoint, groups do not so much share the same mental models as coordinate sensemaking among different but equivalent models held by individual members. Weick and Roberts (1993) called this coordination process "heedful interrelating," an ability that emerges through iterative, purposive interaction.

The construction of shared understandings among the members of a group does not imply the absence of individual differences or friction. Weick (1995) acknowledged that conflict is an essential factor in human interaction. Similarly, Choo (2001) noted that although shared meanings and purpose are constructed through sensemaking, this does not mean that organizational members necessarily share a common viewpoint. In fact, polyvocality and encouragement of internal dissent can generate the kind of comprehensive and creative thinking that wards off crises to begin with (see Christensen, 2007; Holtzhausen, 2000; Tyler, 2005). For example, among cockpit crews handling airborne crises, members of the most successful crews have the liberty to challenge decisions and make alternative suggestions—a literally lifesaving license during this kind of crisis (McKinney, Barker, Davis, & Smith, 2005). Even when lives are not at stake, the ability to handle multiple perspectives does not obscure the "collective recognition that these issues are salient to the organization" (Choo, 2001, p. 200). This type of heedful interrelating offers one means by which organizations can navigate complex, ambiguous, and equivocal circumstances "by supplying assumptions and expectations to fill in the voids" (Choo, 2001, p. 200) in the style of experts.

According to Daft and Weick (2001), organizations interpret events in a three-stage process. The first stage involves scanning the environment, a process familiar to issues managers. This environmental scanning is followed by interpretation itself, defined as "the process of translating events and developing shared understanding and conceptual schemes among members of upper management" (Daft & Weick, 2001, p. 244). The final stage in the process is learning, which occurs concomitantly with action, thereby making action a firmly embedded component of the learning process rather than its product or precursor. As we discuss in the next section, action is also a key component of decision making.

Decision Making

In Choo's (2001) conceptualization of knowledge, decision making plays the role most directly related to action, serving to filter the information received from the knowledge and sensemaking functions—which already contain an action component—and structure it into further courses of action. Here we consider two models for decision making that are especially germane to crisis situations: rational choice and naturalistic approaches. The first emphasizes logic, the consideration of carefully delineated alternatives. The second emphasizes context and action.

Rational-Choice Decision Making

Crisis management planning is traditionally based on the assumption of rationality. According to the rationalist model of decision making, managers list all available alternative courses of action, project the potential outcomes, and evaluate them according to their effectiveness in attaining the maximum payoff in relation to a known goal (Choo, 2001). Showing its roots in economic theories of rationality, this decision-theory approach draws on expected utility theory, multiattribute utility theory, decision analysis, behavioral decision theory, and similar models of preference-driven choice (Smith, 1997).

This type of analysis has an important place in decision making about major events with a long time horizon for planning. Rational analysis, therefore, would be the method of choice for the construction of a new plant or the introduction of a new product. However, in most crisis situations, it is not possible for the decision maker to know all of the possible range of options or to determine the causal links involved in predicting possible outcomes; and the time horizon is short. Hence Hayek's (1945) skeptical view of the rationalist approach describes its limitations for crises: "*If* we possess all the relevant information, *if* we can start out from a given system of preferences and *if* we command complete knowledge of available means, the problem which remains is purely one of logic. That is, the answer to the question of what is the best use of the available means is implicit in our assumptions" (p. 519; italics in original).

In addition, the large number of variables and the complex relationships among them necessitate decision making based on a simplified representation of reality. Particularly in the rapidly changing, equivocal environment of crises, the more schematic the simplification of reality, the less reliable it can be in predicting the actual outcome of any given decision alternative (Gavetti & Levinthal, 2000). In fact, the limitations of the rationalist model may stem from its origins in laboratory experiments with severely restricted options. These studies emphasized the role of bias and error, and problems were generally stated as a matter of choosing among a finite set of alternatives defined by the researcher (Canon-Bowers et al., 1996). Despite widespread acceptance of this model, it has limited applicability in most real-world conditions, because its "information gathering and information processing requirements are beyond the capabilities of any organization or any individual" (Choo, 2001, p. 199).

Given these shortcomings of rationalist decision making in crisis situations, managers may have to tolerate some degree of uncertainty in their judgment processes. Choo (2001) identified four decision-making modes—*boundedly rational, process, political,* and *anarchic*—all of which incorporate a certain degree of uncertainty. This uncertainty may be present in either or both of two dimensions: uncertainty about the desired final outcome or uncertainty regarding the possible and pre-ferred methods and means for pursuing this outcome. The *boundedly rational* mode (Simon, 1976) is characterized by relatively low uncer-tainty in both dimensions, and the decision-making process is usually simplified by the use of standardized procedures for executing organiza-tional routines in scanning and evaluating information. Clear goals but uncertain methods define the *process* mode, in which alternatives are sought or developed and then a choice is made based on an evaluation of available options. When different groups have clear but conflicting objectives, the *political* mode is used to negotiate a solution among the players. Finally, there is *anarchic* mode, in which:

> goal and procedural uncertainty are both high, decision situations consist of relatively independent streams of problems, solutions, participants, and choice opportunities. A decision happens through chance and timing, when problems, solutions, participants, and choices coincide; and when solutions are attached to problems, and problems to choices by participants who have the time and energy to do so. (Choo, 2001, p. 199)

The anarchic mode is the type of decision making most often encoun-tered in everyday situations in complex and turbulent contexts and is especially relevant to organizational crises. This type of mild disorder-liness is more common than the literature suggests. As Dörner (1996) remarked, only rarely are real-world decision processes documented. Published case studies tend to impose order and use hindsight bias to depict the decision-making process as more linear and rational than it often is. A more naturalistic style of decision making better reflects the high-uncertainty, high-stakes environment of organizational exigencies.

Naturalistic Decision Making

From its inception in the mid-1980s, naturalistic decision making has presented decisions as embedded in a situational context that helps to shape the decision maker's perceptions of the decision to be made, the decision itself, its objectives, and its outcomes. In many cases, within a naturalistic context it is difficult to identify exactly "*what* is being decided, by *whom,* and for *what* reason" (Schmitt, 1997, p. 94; italics in original). Naturalistic decision making (NDM) responds to this view of an unstable and uncertain context by examining how people bring their individual and group experience to bear on decisions made in a variety of natural contexts (Klein, 1998; Schmitt, 1997; Zsambok, 1997).

Poorly defined goals are of particular interest in NDM because they pose such difficulties in gauging success. As Klein (1998) remarked, "with an ill-defined goal, you are never sure if the decision was right" (p. 5). In talking about "wicked" decisions, Churchman (1967) could have been describing an NDM context: "a class of social system problems which are ill formulated, where the information is confusing, where there are many clients and decision makers with conflicting values, and where the ramifications in the whole system are thoroughly confusing" (p. B141). As Churchman made clear, some of the key factors in NDM are (1) ill-structured problems; (2) uncertain and dynamic environments; (3) shifting, ill-defined, or conflicting goals; (4) multiple event-feedback loops; (5) time constraints; (6) high stakes; (7) lack of decision-maker expertise; and (8) multiple players (Canon-Bowers et al., 1996; Klein, 1998). It is not necessary for all of these factors to be present in the extreme in order for a decision to be considered naturalistic, yet most of the time they are all present in crisis situations.

Canon-Bowers et al. (1996) narrowed the range of these key factors to the six shown in table 7.1. Concerning the first trait—a unique and dynamic decision environment—they argued that even though classic decision-making research has considered the role of uncertainty, it has typically been within the context of a static and controlled environment. In contrast, one of the chief identifying characteristics of NDM is its emphasis on studying changeable and changing circumstances.

A related trait of NDM is its interest in how the results of decisions affect both the environment and subsequent choices in an ongoing and

Table 7.1. Defining Traits of Naturalistic Decision Making (NDM) Research

Trait	Relative to	Comments
Unique and dynamic situational context	Decision environment	Defined by Canon-Bowers et al. (1996) as "perhaps the single most important feature of interest" (p. 198)
Multiple decision feedback loops	Decision task Decision environment	A by-product of the complexity of the environment and/or of the task, as well as their dynamic nature
Meaningful consequences	Decision environment Decision maker	"Meaningful" is subjectively defined by the decision maker and/ or the decision environment
Multiple goals	Decision task Decision environment	Stability, focus, and conflict among goals may vary
Decision complexity	Decision task	Has been studied by traditional decision researchers, but not within a dynamic framework
Knowledge richness	Decision task Decision environment	Density of information and knowledge from which the decision maker has to draw cues and inform actions

dynamic context, in turn becoming part of the decision problem. Canon-Bowers et al. (1996) described these multiplied impacts as decision feedback loops, the second trait of NDM. The description of these feedback loops comes close to Weick's (2001) previously quoted definition of the enacted environment and its role in the sensemaking process: "When people act, they bring events and structures into existence and set them in motion" (p. 225). Similarly, the way in which the effects of each decision shape the course of events so that it becomes part of the next decision context mirrors the sense of history in a complex system: "Once the decision is made, there is a historical dimension and subsequent evolution may depend on that critical choice" (Mitleton-Kelly, 2003, p. 34).

The third NDM trait, meaningful consequences, is clearly a subjective assessment. Moreover, the relative "meaningfulness" of a decision event and its consequences may be determined either internally, based on the decision maker's own goals and values, or externally by the environment itself or by other people or entities (Canon-Bowers et al., 1996).

The degree to which the goals of decision events are ill defined, poorly focused, or conflicting may vary within a naturalistic setting, but the common denominator is that such settings always involve multiple goals—the fourth NDM trait. Most published research regarding NDM has been carried out in fields in which both the stakes and time pressures were very high, such as military operations or among firefighters (Klein, 1998). Canon-Bowers et al. (1996) offered a military example of multiple goals in a high-stakes, rapidly changing crisis environment:

> A Navy ship commander may have as an overriding goal to protect the ship from hostile attack (which is clear and unchanging). Pursuant to this goal, however, are a series of subgoals and associated goals (e.g., conserve resources, maintain tactical advantage, follow rules of engagement, avoid unnecessary aggression); under each of these may be even finer proximal goals. (p. 199)

This type of disorderly situation might be studied by classical decision researchers, who might study the effects of cue interdependence or number of task elements. However, classical decision research does not consider the further complications imposed by a dynamic environment and multiple goals (Canon-Bowers et al., 1996).

The mad cow furor of the 1990s reflects another type of crisis in which multiple goals were linked in a high-stakes environment. In the 1970s, British authorities changed meat processing techniques in an effort to protect human workers from toxic chemicals. However, that decision is thought to have allowed the development of the current form of bovine spongiform encephalitis (BSE) that eventually caused human deaths. Those deaths in turn led to the slaughter of thousands of cattle, to multiple bankruptcies in the beef industry, and to strained relations between Great Britain and the European Union. Would it have been better to have kept the original level of risk for meat processing personnel and save the British beef industry, as well as the handful of humans who died from BSE-related causes later on? The tight linkage between multiple interests and conflicting goals makes such a policy question difficult to answer.

Finally, one important aspect of this complexity is the relative degree of knowledge richness, or the sheer amount of information from which decision makers need to elicit important cues and components for decision making. As Boisot (2003) described it, "corporate and business strategists are today expected to deal with ever more variables and ever more elusive non-linear interaction between the variables. What is worse, in a regime of 'time-based competition', they are expected to do it faster than ever before. This often amounts to a formidable increase in the objective complexity of a firm's strategic agenda" (p. 185). Along with this overload in exogenous complexity comes the subjectively experienced complexity that characterizes managers' experience and impairs their decision making during a crisis. As Kersten (2005) pointed out, "our ability to act rationally in a crisis is severely limited to begin with....But if we acknowledge that rationality is situated within a specific cultural context and shaped by that context, then we understand that a crisis is likely to *strengthen* rather than weaken those contextual influences" (p. 545; italics in original). The result is decision making that outsiders would see as distinctly irrational, such as deciding to fly the Challenger mission with flawed O-rings.

NDM shifts the focus away from decisions as a string of separate choices and toward the study of goal-oriented action. As a result, NDM expands the field of study to include the broader realm of situation assessment; it examines the role of decision-maker expertise in the decision-making process; it focuses on dynamically evolving decision-making contexts rather than static ones; and it includes both action and perception as integral components of the decision-making process (Canon-Bowers et al., 1996).

One of the findings of NDM research has been that decision makers with high levels of expertise are able to use a form of mental shorthand that matches patterns of context-specific domain knowledge to the situation at hand (Canon-Bowers & Bell, 1997; Klein, 1998). This process is known as recognitional pattern matching, or RPM, and is the primary component of the recognition-primed decision model (RPD). RPD is one way in which NDM researchers have characterized expert decision makers' ability to make rapid, accurate decisions under high-pressure conditions. When experts use the RPD model:

> they understand what types of *goals* make sense (so the priorities are set), which *cues* are important (so there is not an overload of information), what to *expect* next (so they can prepare themselves and notice surprises), and the *typical ways of responding* in a given situation. By recognizing a situation as typical, they also recognize a *course of action* likely to succeed. The recognition of goals, cues,

expectancies, and actions is part of what it means to recognize a situation. (Klein, 1998, p. 24, italics in original)

The RPD model of expertise has particular importance in the turbulent context of crisis, because few crisis decisions can be made in advance: They are context specific. A person capable of using RPD has acquired the knowledge and experience necessary to make these assessments on the spot. Based on this description, it is easy to see why NDM is sometimes referred to as the study of "how experts think" (Klein, 1998). Like expertise, RPD requires the ability to intuit patterns and fill in missing information.

Table 7.2 compares the basic steps involved in the traditional and naturalistic decision-making processes. The advantages and disadvantages of the two models are clear from the chart. The analytical model requires that decision makers gather a considerable amount of information before they reach a decision. It also assumes a relatively static, knowable context. However, field research indicates that even with the support of the formal heuristics offered by decision theory, decision makers who adopt it are no more likely to make successful decisions than those using less structured models. It may be that the heuristics are used as a crutch to make up for a lack of experience. For example, Klein (1998) found that analytical methods offer a "fallback for those without enough experience to know what to do" (p. 103). In contrast, the expert responds to the situation, takes action, and responds to the changes in the situation enacted as a result of the prior decision, all in a seamless process of which he himself may be unaware. The novice, on the other hand, will need to follow explicit instructions and will be unable to respond as promptly

Table 7.2. Comparison Chart of Analytical and Naturalistic Decision-Making Processes

Analytical Decision-Making Model	Naturalistic Decision-Making Model
Situation is static and clearly delineated, with unambiguous goals	Situation is dynamically evolving; it is not always certain that a decision is necessary, or what the desired outcome should be
Decision maker gathers as much information as possible about the situation in the time available	Decision maker consciously or subconsciously assesses the situation and notices familiar aspects
Brainstorming generates largest possible number of options	Assessment prompts limited range of appropriate options
Formal evaluation of the pros and cons of various alternatives	Mental simulation applying suitable options, one at a time; simulation also spots any weaknesses and allows changes to be made "online"
Comparison of all assessments to select the best available option	Select the first workable option without comparing to others

or effectively to variations in the context. Although a crisis plan might supply these instructions, it suffers from the faults of the traditional decision-making model, mainly assumptions about rationality, linearity, and factual certainties. Therefore, one task of crisis planners must be to develop expertise in key managers.

Team Decision Making

The crisis management team is one major venue in which key managers meet to share their expertise. Even though no one individual on the team has all the necessary knowledge, over time the group can create a unified vision of potential crises and responses. A significant role in team decision making (TDM) processes is thought to be played by shared mental models, what Eisenhardt (1989, 1999) called "shared intuition" and Klein (1998) called "team mind." These models are analogous to the concept of shared understanding in sensemaking. Like the "heedful interrelating" of sensemaking, the shared mental models of TDM are developed through frequent and regular collaborative interaction among group members (Eisenhardt, 1989, 1999; Klein, 1998; Zsambok, 1997).

In order to emphasize the significance of this team concept, we use the term *team decision making* rather than *group decision making,* which implies that any casual assembly of people will adopt a certain manner of making decisions. In contrast, teams are relatively stable groups that have frequent opportunities to cooperate, get to know each other, and develop certain kinds of routines and shorthand. Eisenhardt (1989, 1999) found that top management teams that met frequently and established a regular pattern of interaction developed a shared intuition that allowed them to make better decisions more quickly than less collaborative management teams. Klein (1998) noted that "a team that has much experience working together can outperform a newly assembled team" (p. 219), because even if a new team is made up of individual experts, it is missing the repeated communications that make for superior performance. Any sports coach would certainly agree with this assessment.

Numerous studies over the years have examined how groups cooperate to make decisions and have identified processes and factors that differentiate successful decision-making groups from their less successful counterparts. Primarily, research shows that

> good teams monitor their performance and self-correct; offer feedback; maintain awareness of roles and functions and take action consistent with that knowledge; adapt to changes in the task or the team; communicate effectively; converge on a shared understanding of their situation and course of action; anticipate each other's actions or needs; and coordinate their actions. (Zsambok, 1997, p. 112)

This description sounds very much like the self-organizing behavior that underlies complex adaptive systems. For example, Cilliers (1998) identified several principles of self-organization in complex systems: These include a movement toward change and differentiation resulting from mutual feedback; cooperation among various agents; and reinforcement that eventually leads the system to form coherent patterns (entrainment).

More specifically, successful teams in NDM settings typically include four traits: (1) competencies, (2) identity, (3) cognitive skills, and (4) metacognition (Klein, 1998). *Competencies* are important because a crew of novices cannot hope to become an expert team without being able to rely on experienced individuals. Indeed, even an assembly of experts may constitute a novice team until they have had some practice working together. The second element of successful teams, *identity*, refers to a sense of one's own role within the team, of others' roles, and of the team's overall status and aims. The third element, *cognitive skills,* is important because, in order to function efficiently and effectively, the team as a whole must also be capable of assessing the situation, understanding what needs to be done, and dealing with uncertainty and ambiguity. Finally, a team with a strong identity and well-developed cognitive skills is also capable of *metacognition*, the ability to juggle ideas and assess multiple perspectives in order to take advantage of any opportunities that may arise. Klein (1998) described the strength of such a team as the ability to "create new and unexpected solutions, options, and interpretations, drawing on the experience of all the team members to generate products that are beyond the capabilities of any of the individuals" (p. 245). Metacognition also involves the team's ability to assess its own performance on the fly and to make any necessary adjustments. The dynamic nature of metacognition allies it with the team learning process described in the following section as part of the "expert organization."

The Expert Organization

The literature on knowledge and learning displays a wide variety of disciplinary approaches, theoretical foundations, and methodologies, but it is unified by certain specific themes. First, it distinguishes between information, knowledge, and learning. Second, it distinguishes between different types and levels of learning, particularly focusing on the role of learning in bringing about organizational change rather than mere mastery of facts. Third, it distinguishes between conceptual and experiential learning, emphasizing the importance of holistic awareness and learning by doing. Fourth, it is concerned about whether and how knowledge can be transmitted to others, particularly how individual expertise can contribute in a team setting.

These lessons are especially valuable for organizations in the turbulent context of crises because the learning literature addresses precisely these skills needed in crises: adaptation, action, collaboration, and sensitivity to underlying causes of organizational behavior. In turn, all these qualities come into play to create Choo's (2001) model of the knowing organization with which this chapter began. Choo's model combined sensemaking, knowledge, and decision making in an ongoing learning process: "By marshalling the skills and expertise of its members, [the knowing organization] is able to engage in continuous learning and innovation. By applying learned decision rules and routines, it is primed to take timely, purposive action" (p. 197). Choo placed great emphasis on the management of information processes that would enable organizational learning and sensemaking.

We propose an augmented version of Choo's (2001) model, one that puts less emphasis on learned decision rules and more on intuition or expertise as an essential component of organizational learning. In this model, shown in figure 7.1, explicit knowledge is essentially information,

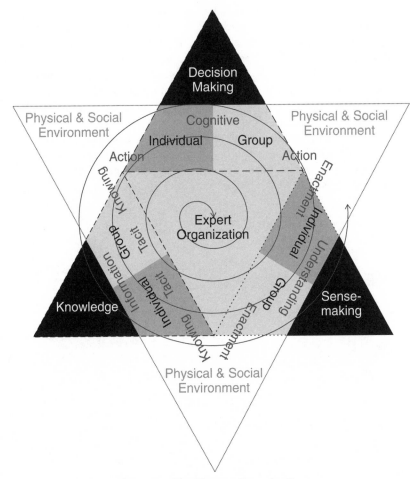

Figure 7.1. The Expert Organization

and tacit knowledge is an intrinsic component that both shapes and ensues from the act of knowing. However, our model is designed not to adapt to a perceived external environment, as Choo intended it, but instead to *enact* the environment in the sense that Weick (2001, p. 225) used the term. In other words, the expert organization model describes actions that shape and launch other actions, all of which are impelled by people's shared conceptions of a situation. As a result of continued reflexive enactment, the organization engages in an ongoing process of learning. Because of the strong component of teamwork, learning here takes the form of "collective accomplishment," as suggested by Gherardi (1999).

This model incorporates knowledge, knowing, sensemaking, and decision making at both the group and individual levels. Through reflexive, recursive interaction among individuals and groups, among themselves and in relation to contextual factors, the organization represented in the model engages in continuous learning while simultaneously enacting its knowledge. This approach cultivates a dynamic, emergent character in organizations that helps them operate as complex systems, constantly self-organizing and evolving. The model can be said to represent the "expert organization," because it synthesizes all of the components of organizational learning discussed previously: tacit and explicit knowledge, team collaboration, sensemaking and enactment, and expertise as the ability to intuit hidden patterns.

Although the expert organization model appears as an abstraction in this context, it is intended to be a pragmatic model for practical application in organizations. The remaining chapters argue that such a model is uniquely suited to the context of crisis management.

Part III

RECONFIGURING THE DOMINANT
PARADIGM

Case History

Nonlinear Diffusion

China and Food Contamination

It started with a handful of sick pets and ended in the execution of a high-level Chinese official. On March 17, 2007, Menu Foods, a Toronto-based manufacturer of premium pet food, announced the recall of 60 million units of wet pet food that had been marketed under the labels of 88 separate brands. The recall, affecting cat and dog food sold in North America between December 3, 2006, and March 6, 2007, was described by a corporate spokesperson as "precautionary" (Perkel, 2007), despite the suspected link between Menu Foods products and the deaths of at least 10 household pets in the United States and Canada that had precipitated the recall. The company had supplied store-brand pet food to 17 major U.S. chain stores and several popular pet food companies, and the recall quickly snowballed. Within weeks the contamination would be implicated in the illnesses of thousands of cats and dogs, with the Food and Drug Administration reporting 8,500 unconfirmed claims of pet deaths caused by the recalled products (Goldman & Lee, 2007). What had begun as a relatively straightforward product recall would reverberate across several countries and industries, affecting Fortune 500 companies, government regulatory agencies, and U.S. trade relations with foreign nations.

Within a week of the recall, investigators at Cornell University's New York State Food Laboratory announced that they had found aminopterin, a type of rat poison not approved for use in the United States, in samples of pet food (Zezima, 2007), and reports of poisoning quickly circulated. The U.S. Food and Drug Administration (FDA), unable to replicate those findings, attributed the contamination instead to wheat gluten and rice protein concentrate tainted with the industrial product melamine, which is sometimes used to artificially inflate protein levels in food products. The contaminated products were traced to two different Chinese companies. The Chinese government vehemently denied that Chinese exports had been responsible for pet illnesses.

Nonetheless, the United States put a hold on all wheat gluten imports from China.

In response to the recall, pet owners scrambled to find the safest alternatives to feed their animals. Wayne Pacelle, president and chief executive officer of the Humane Society of the United States, observed that "the kind of drumbeat, day after day, of recalls has shaken consumers' confidence in the pet food industry's adherence to food safety standards" (Bridges, 2007). A poll conducted soon after the recall found that only half of those pet owners whose brand of pet food had been recalled planned to return to their original brand, even after the recall was lifted. "It's made me so wary and skeptical of all dog food," noted one pet owner. "It's all mass produced" (Weiss & Trejos, 2007). Some consumers turned to small pet boutique food brands that promised local and organic ingredients (Baca, 2007). Sales of pet food cookbooks increased dramatically in response to the recall (Rosenthal, 2007).

In the weeks following the recall, the Internet became a key source of information for the more than 56% of U.S. households with pets (Weise, 2007). Web sites and blogs geared toward pet owners became hubs for finding up-to-date information on details regarding the recall. The Web site Pet Connection, run by a veterinarian and a former newspaper copy editor, created an online searchable database to which pet owners could submit data on pets that were thought to have been sickened or killed by the contamination. Pet Connection also provided live transcripts of FDA press conferences conducted via telephone, providing concerned citizens with a means to obtain actionable information from the federal agency nearly as quickly as the journalists themselves received it. "We've been accused of feeding people's emotion," noted Gina Spadafori, one of the site's owners, "but there's a lot of stuff here that's just flat-out good reporting" (in Weise, 2007).

Beyond its emotional impact on people whose pets had been endangered, the recall also became a touchstone for broader anxieties about the safety of the human food supply. In mid-April came news that the FDA had quarantined 1,500 hogs in northern California because some of them had been fed melamine-contaminated feed imported from China (Henderson, 2007). Soon after, the FDA announced that feed farms in Indiana had provided melamine-contaminated feed to chickens (Lopes, 2007). Though the FDA indicated that the potential threat to humans caused by the livestock feed contamination was low, many remained skeptical (Henderson, 2007).

The spinach outbreak of *E. coli* had occurred just 6 months earlier; soon after, another *E. coli* outbreak was attributed to green onions used in Taco Bell salsa (Burros, 2006b). The spinach recall and the Taco Bell contamination together represented "'a signal event' in the public's perception of food safety" (Lorin, 2007). A survey conducted by the advertising agency JWT one week after the pet food recall suggested that many Americans were concerned about the possibility of a terror-ist attack on the food supply ("Americans Doubtful," 2007; "Americans Doubt Safety," 2007). Almost half of the nearly 1,200 respondents expressed doubt that the U.S. government would be able to respond appropriately to an attack on the American food or water supply. Sixty percent of respondents agreed with the statement, "I'm starting to believe that the food supply in the U.S. isn't as safe as it used to be."

As more reports emerged about pet illnesses and deaths that might be attributed to tainted pet foods, consumers, politicians, and the press scrambled to ascribe blame for the contamination. The activist organi-zation People for the Ethical Treatment of Animals (PETA) called for criminal investigation into the pet food-related animal deaths (Bell, 2007). Class action suits were filed against Menu Foods in both the United States and Canada (Bell, 2007; Sullivan, 2007). The U.S. FDA came under fire from both citizens and members of Congress seeking answers regarding the extent to which the agency had lapsed in allow-ing the tainted gluten to be imported. In response to criticism of the FDA's role in overseeing the safety of the U.S. food supply, President Bush created the post of Assistant Commissioner for Food Protection, colloquially dubbed the "food safety czar," to help the FDA adapt to the changing landscape of the global food system (Lopes, 2007).

Prior to the recall, the American public had shown little awareness of, or interest in, the issue of the safety of Chinese food exports, even though it has been said that "the list of Chinese food exports rejected at American ports reads like a chef's nightmare: pesticide-laden pea pods, drug-laced catfish, filthy plums and crawfish contaminated with salmonella" (Bodeen, 2007). Two months before the pet food recall, an Asian Development Bank report had called attention to the issue of food contamination in China, claiming that over 300 million Chinese citizens were affected yearly by tainted food. The pet food contamina-tion sparked large-scale concern over the regulation of U.S. imports of food products, particularly from China (Phuong, 2007). In a letter to the editor of his local paper, one Florida man demanded that "the whole country should rise up in outrage and anger at the infection of our society by filthy and sometimes deadly Chinese food imports," a prob-lem he attributed to the "parasitic relationship between corporations and elected officials" (Stephens, 2007).

The international outcry over the tainted pet food further impli-cated Zheng Xiaoyu, the former head of the Chinese State Food and Drug Administration, who was already facing corruption charges stemming from his reported acceptance of $832,000 in bribes. Just 10 weeks after Menu Foods' initial recall of contaminated pet food, Zheng was sentenced to the death penalty, an unusually harsh sentence for someone at such an elevated position in the Chinese government. He was executed on July 10, 2007 ("China executes food safety chief for bribery," 2007; Magnier, 2007). Although he had been fired in 2005 and had been implicated in dozens of deaths related to subpar food and drugs, Zheng's sentence appeared to be part of a larger public relations strategy to diffuse international anger at China's careless business practices. But the damage had already been done.

8

Complexity, Crisis, and the Expert Organization

Reconfiguring the Dominant Paradigm

As we have described it so far, the conceptual foundation of crisis communication includes three main components: the crisis literature itself, theories of complex adaptive systems, and theories of organizational learning. Chapter 2 traced the evolution of mainstream crisis communication studies during the past 20 years. It showed that an early focus on the tactics of information dissemination later expanded to include strategy. Currently, crisis management has started to consider the permeability of boundaries between an organization and its publics, the uncertainties of crisis planning, and the possibility of multiple outcomes. Chapters 3 and 4 laid out the basic premises of complexity theory and showed their relevance to crisis situations, especially the growing interest in multiple goals and audiences, social context, and uncertain outcomes. Chapters 5 and 6 examined ways in which organizations learn, both competently and dysfunctionally, and Chapter 7 proposed the concept of the "expert organization" as an effective approach to volatile and unpredictable crisis situations. In this section, we bring together these three streams of thought—crisis literature, complexity, and organizational learning—showing how their combination extends our thinking about crisis communication.

Table 8.1 summarizes the key assumptions that inform most mainstream approaches to crisis communication. They are divided into four general categories, arranged along a continuum from a broad perspective to those assumptions that relate more narrowly to crises (see also Gilpin & Murphy, 2005). *Philosophical assumptions* imply a certain general outlook on "how things work," whereas *assumptions about organizations* suggest a specific approach to organizations and their characteristics. *Assumptions about knowledge* describe concepts that govern how information, knowledge, decision making, and learning are viewed, and finally, *assumptions about crisis management* deal specifically with organizational crises and how best to prevent and manage them.

Table 8.1. Reframing the Assumptions of the Dominant Crisis Management Paradigm

Dominant Paradigm	Reframed for Complexity
Philosophical assumptions	
The future is, at least to some extent, predictable.	The future is unknowable yet recognizable, the product of everyday micro interaction among people, entities, and the environment.
It is possible to control events and/or perceptions of events by directly influencing the system at large.	It is not possible to fully control the perceptions of events in a crisis, or many events themselves, as they depend on too many exogenous factors and complex interactions. The organization can control only its own behavior and ability to develop new patterns of interaction.
Ambiguity and uncertainty are undesirable states that should be overcome through communication and action strategies.	Ambiguity and uncertainty are unavoidable states that should be accepted and embraced through communication and action patterns that allow the organization to both enact and adapt to changing circumstances.
Stability is a desirable and attainable state, and the preferred outcome of a crisis situation.	Stability is possible only in an inert (dead) system and hence is an undesirable state. Even apparent stability in a social system is actually dynamically changing through patterns of micro interaction.
Assumptions about organizations	
The organization may be likened to a mechanical system.	The organization is a complex entity that demonstrates emergent behavior, quite unlike a mechanical system.
There are clear boundaries between the organization and its external environment, including stakeholders. The organization should learn as much as possible about this environment in order to adapt appropriately.	The organization is defined by fluid, changing, socially constructed boundaries that form a tenuous separation between the organization, its stakeholders, and the environment. Members of the organization should actively engage with this environment so as to enact and be part of changes.
Organizational culture is an identifiable, measurable variable that may be manipulated as needed, also as a means of overcoming (silencing) conflict and dissent.	Organizational culture is a paradoxically identifiable yet dynamic trait that is perpetually in flux, a blend of multiple conflicting voices that is constantly produced and reproduced through micro interaction and everyday behavior, inside and outside the organization, as well as across organizational "boundaries."

(continued)

Table 8.1. (*Continued*)

Dominant Paradigm	Reframed for Complexity
Assumptions about knowledge	
The most effective means of creating, developing and transferring knowledge within the organization is an institutionalized, trackable system for gathering, evaluating, and distributing information (focus on explicit knowledge).	The most effective means for learning at the individual and organizational levels is a combination of real-time information, knowledge and knowing (gained by daily interactions throughout the organization and its environment), the authority to enact decisions, and conscious efforts to make sense of ongoing events (focus on acquiring expertise).
The best way to make a decision is the analytical method, considering all possible alternatives and selecting the "optimum" one.	The best way to make a quick, effective decision in changing circumstances is to develop "expertise" by combining information and acquired knowledge with sensemaking and decision-making skills.
Assumptions about crisis management	
The primary aim of crisis management is to avoid or limit the loss of organizational assets and to maintain or restore organizational legitimacy in the eyes of key stakeholders as quickly as possible.	The primary aim of crisis management is to avoid or limit the loss of organizational assets and to maintain long-term organizational legitimacy in the eyes of key stakeholders by engaging in double-loop learning that may require internal change.
The best response by an organization in crisis is to centralize information and decision-making procedures around a designated crisis management team whose members convene and work together solely and specifically on crisis-related matters.	The best response by an organization in crisis is that produced by an experienced team whose members possess the necessary expertise and authority to take immediate action, recognize their limitations, and know where to find other information they realize they need.
The best way to handle time-sensitive, critically important situations is to follow a detailed procedure previously prepared using analytical decision-making techniques.	The best way to handle time-sensitive, critically important situations is to develop the expertise necessary for skilful bricolage/improvisation.
An organization will learn the necessary lessons from a crisis if the crisis team examines the data gathered during the crisis containment stage to identify any mistakes that may have been made and updates the crisis plan accordingly.	An organization will learn the necessary lessons from a crisis if it takes the time to reflexively examine the multiple, complex causes behind the situation, to engage in double-loop learning, and to make the necessary changes to ensure long-term legitimacy.

An earlier version of this table appeared in Gilpin and Murphy (2005), pp. 382–83.

The philosophical assumptions summarized in table 8.1 provide a starting point for combining traditional crisis communication approaches with complexity and learning theories. At the broadest level of philosophical assumptions, most crisis writing views the future as being both predictable and controllable, at least to some extent, by influencing current conditions. Crisis managers make an effort to avoid ambiguity and uncertainty and to establish clear goals and messages. Crisis experts also generally assume that stability is a desirable characteristic and, therefore, that successful crisis management will either return the organization to the status quo or improve on the status quo (Roux-Dufort, 2000). Hence, when asked to define the goal of crisis management, a typical practitioner response is "to get back to business as usual and get the whole issue off the table" (Bechler, 2004, p. 67).

On these broad foundations the crisis literature builds specific views about organizations. Assumptions about control often imply a view of the organization as a machine-like system that can be fine-tuned and optimized. In addition, although they encourage extensive interaction between organizations and their environments, most crisis authorities assume clear boundaries between organizations and their external context, including stakeholders.

Fundamental assumptions about control, predictability, and stability also steer most crisis experts toward restricted views of knowledge and learning. Generally, crisis experts treat knowledge as explicit, with defined and circumscribed channels for gathering and distributing information around the organization. Favoring control and predictability means that traditional social science methods, based on rational analysis of alternatives, are the primary bases for decision making. The same fundamental philosophical assumptions apply to crisis management. Most experts manage the problem of uncertainty and the sense of being overwhelmed by dividing the crisis into smaller, more comprehensible parts. Hence the dominant crisis management paradigm deliberately takes a reductionist approach. Advocates of this approach focus on the parts of the organization, view its environment objectively as a discrete entity that can also be apportioned (by audience, by threat level and type), and break down the crisis management process into parts. They reason that such partitioning allows less-than-optimal crisis responses to be analyzed and fine-tuned to work better in subsequent crises.

This approach is both practically feasible and psychologically comforting. However, perspectives from complexity theory and organizational learning suggest other ways in which organizations can improve their performance during crises. As previously explained, traditional crisis communication recommendations deliberately seek to eliminate or control ambiguity, paradox, and uncertainty. In contrast, complexity-based thinking posits a recognizable but unknowable future and the absence of permanent stability in any but inert systems. Learning theory supports a complexity perspective, adding that certain frequently prescribed crisis management techniques may constrain learning at both individual and organizational levels and can prevent organizations from using the variety of responses they need in fast-moving, unstable crisis situations. Centralized responsibility for planning and messages also may not work for every crisis situation. For all these reasons, crises require an approach that complements efforts to manage uncertainty and exert control on the one hand with complexity-based thinking and theories of organizational learning that help to develop agile, improvisational responses to crises on the other hand.

Nowhere is the contrast between the two approaches plainer than in the assumptions that drive crisis planning. The remainder of this section looks at crisis communication before, during, and after a crisis event. In particular, it looks at six areas of crisis planning in which assumptions made by most crisis experts and assumptions based on complexity and learning theories are apt to be different. These six areas are (1) the goals of crisis planning, (2) assumptions about relationships, (3) assumptions about the environment, (4) assumptions about planning processes themselves, (5) heuristics for decision making, and (6) the role of organizational culture. In each case we look first at the major principles of the mainstream crisis communication literature, then we consider the same principles from the standpoint of complexity and learning theories.

9

Expecting the Unexpected

Challenging Precrisis Assumptions

Most experts agree with Heath (2004) that "a crisis is a predictable event that occurs at an unexpected time....It challenges the ability of the organization to enact the narrative of continuity through constructive change to control the organization's destiny" (p. 167). Most experts also agree that crises threaten two of the most important assets that organizations possess: their relationships with constituencies and their appearance of legitimacy. These assets are intertwined, as breaches of constituent trust can lead to scrutiny of an organization that strips away its legitimacy. The result often takes the form of sanctions—legal, financial, or public opinion—that constrain its ability to do business.

In comparison, complexity and learning theories take a somewhat broader view of crisis, focusing on characteristics both within the organization and in its relationship with the environment that may be causing crises to occur. From this standpoint, an appropriate goal for surviving a crisis is organizational transformation rather than a return to, or improvement in, the status quo. Indeed, crises may not reflect accidents or random misfortunes so much as they express "the outcome of the normal functioning of a dysfunctional system" (Kersten & Sidky, 2005, p. 472) in which corrective measures are seriously overdue.

These goals—complexity theory's transformation or mainstream crisis management's return to the status quo—are not mutually exclusive, but they do emphasize different aspects of crises and planning. For example, whereas most crisis literature divides the communication planning process into discrete steps, complexity theory looks at the whole; whereas mainstream crisis experts advocate precisely quantified and systematized scanning and measurement, complexity and learning theories generally tolerate—even encourage—ambiguity and contingency. At times complementary and at times conflicting, these approaches offer useful correctives to each other and encourage critical thinking about the assumptions people make concerning crisis communication.

Apart from overall goals, most crisis experts agree that there are two essential areas that an organization must address before a crisis strikes. First, the organization needs to cultivate and maintain good relationships with important constituencies such as employees, the community, suppliers, customers, stockholders, and media. Second, the organization needs to monitor its environment to ensure that it becomes aware of emerging problems and resolves them before they reach crisis proportions. Next, we consider each of these two efforts, showing how a complexity perspective enhances mainstream crisis management thinking.

Relationships and Legitimacy

Above all, crises threaten an organization's legitimacy, the general perception that its actions are "desirable, proper or appropriate within some socially constructed system of norms, values, beliefs and definitions" (Suchman, 1995, p. 574). Threats to legitimacy also constitute threats to an organization's ability to conduct its business. If a company cannot take care of its constituents, then other entities will step in to do that job—regulatory bodies, activist groups, shareholders, lawyers, and unions. Therefore, maintaining the organization's legitimacy is fundamental to maintaining its autonomy. Although legitimacy theory was originally the province of political science, it now involves all organizational audiences, not just regulatory or legal bodies. Organizations can survive only if they can continuously maintain involvement with a web of legitimating internal and external stakeholders (Boyd, 2000; Palenchar, 2001).

Two major forms of organizational legitimacy emerge from the literature: strategic and institutional. Crisis management literature has focused primarily on *institutional* legitimacy, as organizations look to stakeholders to confirm that they are "responsible and useful" (Boyd, 2000, p. 343). Essentially, stakeholders concede the organization's right to continued existence. This approach "focuses attention on the cultural environment in which organizations exist and on the pressure that this environment exerts on organizations to engage in expected, normative behaviors" (Massey, 2001, p. 155). As a complement to institutional legitimacy, some authors have addressed *actional* (or strategic) legitimacy as the foundation on which close organization-stakeholder relationships are established. Actional legitimacy focuses on the "assumption that the actions of an entity are desirable, or appropriate within some socially constructed system of norms, values, beliefs, and definitions" (Suchman, 1995, p. 574). From a crisis management perspective, Boyd (2000) observed that "although not all corporations will face crises requiring institutional legitimation, almost all will introduce on occasion new or controversial policies that require actional legitimation" (p. 342)—that is, they will do something that their constituencies dislike, whether they are generally considered to be good corporate citizens or not.

One major factor that complicates organizations' efforts to improve their legitimacy is the heterogeneity of organizational stakeholders (Massey, 2001; Suchman, 1995). Stakeholders have conflicting, changing needs and desires, requiring the organization to continually re-earn its legitimacy. Fortunately, unanimous legitimacy is not necessary; generally, an organization need only achieve a "critical mass" of legitimacy conceded by its network of stakeholders (Boyd, 2000). However, achieving that critical mass is difficult because relationships are constantly changing as priorities, values, attitudes, and players shift and give way to others. This instability becomes a particular problem "in contexts where multiple institutions place conflicting demands on organizations and their members" (Wicks, 2001, p. 666). For example, Morton Thiokol, the manufacturer of the Challenger space shuttle's faulty O-rings, had an outstanding financial performance in 1986, the year that the shuttle exploded. In its annual report it had to balance regret for the devastating consequences of the O-rings against applauding its outstanding results for shareholders. In situations such as the pet food contamination issue recounted at the beginning of this section, a single organization's success is overshadowed by pervasive industry-wide threats that must be addressed in stakeholder communications.

Organizations that are trying to gain, maintain, or reacquire legitimacy from their stakeholders can select from several strategies. First, they can effect change within themselves to better meet their audiences' criteria, a viewpoint espoused by J. Grunig's (2001) symmetry theory. Second, they can try to alter their audiences' ideas of legitimacy to be more congenial to their own organization's ideas through issues management and advocacy campaigns (Heath, 1997). Third, they can "identify with symbols, values, and institutions that already possess strong social legitimacy" (Boyd, 2000, p. 345). Rhetoricians call this approach "transcendence," as when Union Carbide attempted to set the Bhopal accident in the context of issues in the chemical industry overall (Ice, 1991) or when President Bush, unable to justify the Iraq war on the basis of weapons of mass destruction, placed it in the context of fostering democracy in the Middle East.

Relationships and interdependencies also lie at the core of complexity-based thinking. However, a complexity approach to relationships differs from the assumptions of mainstream crisis writing in three significant ways. First, complexity does not assume clear boundaries between the organization and its environment, including stakeholders, so there is no sense of "us" versus "them." Second, complexity theories posit that relationships are never entirely static, but constantly changing. These changes may be incremental, or a relationship may be pulled unexpectedly into a radically different attractor basin at a bifurcation point, often represented by the crisis situation itself. These dynamic changes emerge from local, repeated interaction between mutually influencing individuals or entities.

A third way in which complexity-based thinking differs from mainstream crisis strategy is that, because it is open-ended and nonlinear, a complexity approach does not lend itself to quantified audience and relationship measurement of the kind recommended by many crisis experts. Most mainstream crisis management models recommend rating stakeholders and their concerns with methods such as decision trees, stakeholder surveys, or response testing (Coombs, 2007; Ferguson, 1994; Lindenmann, 1998; Pearson & Clair, 1998; Ulmer et al., 2007). This view sees relationships as sufficiently constant to be measured and sufficiently linear to extrapolate origins from consequences. It also suggests that the crisis is external to the organization—a function of audience perceptions—and divorced from the context of internal problems that may have caused or worsened the crisis in the first place (Bechler, 2004). For example, Millar and Beck (2004, p. 162) found that one of the most common metaphors for crisis was the container, to "distinguish what is 'inside' from what is 'outside.'" Therefore "crises happen when either: (a) an 'outside' agent or event damages the container's boundaries... or (b) an 'inside' dynamic or agent implodes the contents beyond their distinguishing boundaries" (p. 162). Yet, as we have seen, in complexity-based thinking the boundaries between various agents in the system are permeable and influence is mutual, so that measurement and control are imperfect at best: "Information from the environment has a direct, though non-determinate, influence on the system: it *causes* certain changes in the system, but it does not fully *determine* the nature of these changes," in a nonlinear relationship with an interpenetrating environment (Cilliers, 1998, p. 125; italics in original).

Furthermore, from a complexity perspective, measurements of relationships in terms of variables and numbers do not capture other, equally important, contextual factors that may emerge unexpectedly. For example, the use of corporate social reporting indicators as a standard crisis preparation tactic does not take into account the unexpected power of certain issues or minor groups to seize the attention and support of large publics. One classic illustration is the case of the Brent Spar oil rig that Royal Dutch-Shell planned to sink in the North Sea. The company was prevented from carrying out the project because the environmental activist group Greenpeace rallied support against the venture through an intensive information campaign (Elliott, Smith, & McGuinness, 2000; van Ginneken, 2003). Ranking issues and stakeholders assumes an objectively measurable environment with limited room for the sudden emergence of unforeseeable matters or groups that form spontaneously around an issue without prior warning (Stauber & Rampton, 1995). From a complexity perspective, measuring and ranking relationships is an attempt to impose order and control onto a complex and changing world that resists such categorization.

Credibility and trust are additional areas that feature prominently in crisis managers' concerns about audience relationships. Like legitimacy, credibility and trust can be gained and lost based on an organization's behavior (Coombs, 2007; Massey, 2001). Like legitimacy, credibility is not something the organization can construct alone; it must be earned from stakeholders on a continuing basis.

Organizations are interested in achieving "terminal" credibility, public confidence based on both general behavior and responses in specific situations (Coombs, 2007). However, from a complexity point of view, it is very difficult for an organization to plan and carry out targeted credibility efforts. In part, credibility is problematical because complex systems do not represent linear relationships between actions and responses; instead, multiple factors may affect the context. In public relations, this type of multifaceted and overdetermined judgment has been examined in terms of contingency theory. For example, Cameron and his associates identified more than 80 variables as "candidate factors" that affect the stance of an organization (Cancel et al., 1997, p. 33; Cancel et al., 1999).

Credibility is thus situational and subjective, dependent on some factors over which the organization has little control, such as attitudes toward businesses in general or toward a certain industry. People tend to distrust corporations as a rule, and certain industries have a lower baseline credibility than others (Petrick, Scherer, Brodzinski, Quinn, & Ainina, 1999; Stevens, 1999). Even a crisis suffered by a competitor can affect an uninvolved organization's reputation and, thus, credibility. For example, a series of well-publicized frauds by U.K. lenders in the early 1990s led to widespread public mistrust of the credit and banking industry, sparking a government investigation (Knights, Noble, Vurdubakis, & Willmott, 2001). Similarly, in 2002, the mega-accounting firm Arthur Andersen made an effort to salvage its credibility by separating itself from the auditing debacle at its client Enron, splitting off its consulting business and giving it the connotation-free name "Accenture." Furthermore, in a global environment, loss of credibility in one locale spreads rapidly throughout the global network. Therefore, when bad publicity about ill-tasting Coca-Cola spread throughout Europe in 1999, the company needed to be concerned about its sales on every continent.

The pet food contamination issue is another example of how credibility crises can traverse national, industry, and issue boundaries. The crisis began as a suspected case of product tampering, an instance of rat poison added to a particular batch of pet food ingredients. As a result of the ensuing investigations and media coverage, the issue expanded to include questions of U.S. food safety policy in general, trade regulations for human and animal food imports, fears associated with "anonymous" mass-produced food products, fraudulent practices in the international trade arena, and doubts regarding the viability of a global supply system that evades national controls. The resulting credibility deficit affected pet food suppliers and, indeed, any food manufacturer known to import ingredients from China, importers and distributors, Chinese businesses trading with the United States in various industries, legislators, and policy makers.

Like credibility, trust—another vital component of stakeholder relationships—is viewed somewhat differently in the literature of crisis communication and complexity theory. Few organizations attempt to actively manage trust as a valuable stakeholder asset, in part because the concept of trust is elusive (Elliott et al., 2000). Like other aspects of the organization-stakeholder interaction, trust is subjective and situational. As Williams and Olaniran (1998) observed with respect to the Exxon Valdez, "the opposing sides of the issue are judged with differing standards by the general public in regard to what is trustworthy" (p. 392). For example, the 2002 sex abuse scandal involving Catholic priests was seen in very different ways by the Church and by the lay community. Whereas the latter was concerned with the victims, to the Church the problem was far more multifaceted: "a sociological, psychological, legal, theological, and ethical issue framed as much by anti-Catholicism and ideological disagreements with Catholic doctrine as by legitimate concerns over the safety of children" (Maier, 2005, p. 220). The lay establishment wanted immediate punishment of the breach of trust committed by priests who had abused children, but the Church establishment defined the traditional Church hierarchy as the primary repository of trust. Therefore, it first reaffirmed that hierarchy by dismissing challenges from radical reformists and then turned its attention to punishing the abusive priests (Dixon, 2004).

Although it is difficult to manage, trust is often called for in the ambiguous and contingent circumstances of a crisis. Aspects of crisis planning that attempt to overcome ambiguities and establish control and prediction are seeking to replace trust with confidence. According to Seligman (1998), "confidence is what you have when you know what to expect in a situation: trust is what you need to maintain interaction if you do not" (p. 391). Confidence requires some degree of knowledge about the status, terms, or consequences of a relationship, as the following example indicates:

> When I say that I "trust" the doctor, I am not quite correct. Rather, I mean that I have confidence in her abilities, in the system that awarded her the degree on the wall (and I may have greater confidence if the degree is from Cornell University and less from a west-coast mail order address), as well as in the epistemological assumptions of American medicine. Of course I may also lack such confidence and take my daughter to Lourdes instead, or I may trust (have faith in) the Lord if, for instance, I am a Christian Scientist. (Seligman, 1998, pp. 391–92)

Trust comes into play when there is no way of knowing whether our confidence is well placed, "when the other is unknowable, when behavior cannot be imputed or predicted" (Seligman, 1998, p. 393). Conceptualized in this way, trust is an intangible and dynamic attribute of relationships.

Most crisis experts instead tend to see trust as confidence and try to manage it in terms of information and control. If the organization appears to be in control of a critical situation—having information that shows it knows what is wrong—audiences are more inclined to trust it. They have confidence that the organization knows what to do to resolve the crisis. However, complexity views trust somewhat differently, more in keeping with Seligman's (1998) approach to trust as a response to the unknowable, unpredictable, and unstable. In contemporary organizations, when relationships go beyond contractual or other formal agreements, trust must be continually negotiated between individuals based on various elements of the relational history. Trust is a relative trait that varies dynamically and cannot be controlled by either party; rather, it emerges as a result of everyday interaction. Trust is inherent in complex social systems because "the very differentiation and complexity of the system makes it impossible to predict the nature of the alter's role performance" (Seligman, 1998, p. 399). From a complexity standpoint, in a crisis trust exists at the system limits, as a feature of the so-called "edge of chaos," an unstable and swiftly changing state in which customary controls no longer govern events in ways that can be anticipated.

Mainstream crisis literature diverges from the complexity and learning literature on the degree to which organizations can control what audiences say and think about them. One way in which organizations try to influence relationships is through mutual interaction with audiences. Many models for building favorable relationships point to the description of "excellent" two-way communication, originally developed by James Grunig and his colleagues, that calls for ongoing two-way communication between the organization and its key stakeholders (Dozier, Grunig, & Grunig, 1995; Fearn-Banks, 2007). According to this model, communication with stakeholders is not a matter of sending persuasive messages to a passive receiver; rather, it means sharing impressions and ideas on an even footing. Coombs (2007) noted that this ongoing interaction to develop mutual understanding also doubles as a means of signal detection because an organization will become aware of problems more quickly when it is engaged in active, continuous dialogue with its stakeholders. The same mutual understanding helps contribute to an organization's reputation and may enhance credibility as well.

Although both mainstream crisis literature and complexity theory emphasize mutual interaction between an organization and its audiences, their different attitudes toward influence and control cause them to view that interaction differently. From the standpoint of traditional crisis management, questions of influence and control lie at the root of trust and legitimacy issues. Organizations do not want their audiences to constrain their ways of doing business; crises are threats in part because they are occasions on which the organization has lost control; the organization hopes to gain enough trust from its constituents so that it may influence them to interpret crises in ways that minimize damage to the organization's legitimacy.

Unlike this traditional viewpoint, a complexity-based viewpoint sees relationships less in terms of "managing communication" than in terms of "communication as a tool for negotiating relationships" (Kent & Taylor, 2002, p. 23). Botan (1997) referred to the difference between the two communication modes as monologic and dialogic. The dialogic view sees audience-organization interaction as "a two-way process, suggesting an active receiver involved in the creation of shared meaning" (Massey, 2001, p. 156). Although a symmetrical point of view (Dozier et al., 1995) seeks feedback from audiences and is willing to implement organizational change to accommodate audience needs, it is still similar to systems theory in its focus on soliciting feedback from a discrete environment in an effort to respond to external expectations. In contrast, dialogue is the product of an ongoing communicative relationship with less structure and more left to chance: It is "unrehearsed and spontaneous. Dialogic exchanges are not scripted, nor are they predictable. This spontaneity emerges in the interaction of participants and their individual beliefs, values and attitudes. Indeed, it is the presence of an interpersonal relationship...between participants that facilitates dialogue" (Kent & Taylor, 2002, p. 28). Because of its emphasis on interdependencies and its view that relationships are mutually defined through ongoing micro interaction, the dialogic approach is especially compatible with the theory of complex adaptive processes. For example, Kent and Taylor (2002) also emphasized that there is a temporal dimension to dialogue, as it looks beyond the present toward "a continued and shared future for all participants" (p. 26). In terms of adaptive systems, dialogue involves trust as an emergent phenomenon whose character evolves over time.

In contrast, many mainstream crisis experts envision a symmetrical, rather than dialogic, approach to managing stakeholder relationships in relation to organizational crises. The symmetrical approach advocates the use of regular, two-way communication to help an organization determine stakeholders' expectations. Through such communication, the organization can learn what expectations the stakeholders have about the organization, and the organization can inform stakeholders about how it is meeting those expectations. During that process, stakeholder expectations may themselves be shaped to conform better with the organization's views, as stakeholders are "convinced that the expectations are unrealistic and need to be modified" (Coombs, 2007, p. 60).

However, if a crisis truly does violate stakeholder expectations, most crisis experts suggest some version of the image repair process developed by Benoit (1997). Using this monologic process, the organization determines which message—based on relational history, crisis history, and locus of control—can restore legitimacy as quickly and effectively as possible; it attempts to "repair" stakeholder relations in order to reestablish stability and reputational status quo. This monologic approach is quite different from the mutual influence that occurs within a complex adaptive system, which views legitimacy as a dialogic process, part of the overall organization-stakeholder relationship (Massey, 2001). The perception of legitimacy originates in the stakeholders themselves and cannot be imposed or claimed by organizations; it emerges over time from the interaction of multiple, often conflicting, internal and contextual factors.

Indeed, one of the important factors in an organization's relationship with its stakeholders is the influence of history. Coombs and Holladay (2001) found a correlation between negative relational history and postcrisis organizational reputation. An organization's negative reputation prior to a crisis shows a "Velcro effect": "It attracts and snags additional reputational damage" (p. 335) regardless of efforts to control the immediate news event. The objective of building strong stakeholder relationships is therefore to forge a strong reputation with individuals and groups that contributes to the organization's success and can help it to prevent or weather a crisis more effectively. A crisis becomes a single incident within the larger context of the organization-stakeholder relationship over time or of the relational history between them (Coombs, 2000; Coombs & Holladay, 2001).

From this standpoint, reputation is a sort of bank account into which organizations must make regular and consistent deposits in order to have "funds" available for withdrawal in case of need (Caponigro, 2000; Coombs, 2007; Coombs & Holladay, 2001; Veysey, 2000). Organizations with a positive reputation can count on stakeholders discounting bad news about the organization—or at least temporarily withholding judgment—thanks to the positive "account balance" that has accumulated over time. This suspension of judgment holds true even in preventing negative speculation, the uninformed rumor-mongering that often occurs immediately following a crisis and before the facts emerge (Coombs, 2007). A solid reputation should help protect the organization from the worst of such speculation and give it an opportunity to present its explanation of the incident.

Like mainstream crisis management, complexity-based thinking also emphasizes the relational history and the necessity for an organization to constantly build its reputation. However, it places more emphasis on the instability of reputation and views the organization's prediction and control abilities as highly imperfect. Within a complex system, a corporate reputation is not "a static element that can only be influenced and hence managed through...well planned formal communication activities" (Gotsi & Wilson, 2001, p. 29). Rather, reputations are "dynamic constructs, which influence and are influenced by all the ways in which a company projects its images: its behavior, communication and symbolism" (Gotsi & Wilson, 2001, p. 29). In a complex system, reputation is inherently unstable and only partially controlled by its possessor. Thus organizational image making is a shifting, repeated process whereby "one image can emerge as strong at one moment in time, and another, contrasting image can emerge as dominant at a different moment in time because of the multiple and contradictory factors involved" in the audience's processing of organizational traits (Williams & Moffitt, 1997, p. 241). From a complex-system standpoint, reputation building becomes a shifting, recurrent process whereby an organization and its publics negotiate meaning through dynamic exchange; there are multifarious influences on image and dynamic negotiation over meaning that neither sender nor receiver can fully control.

In sum, even before a crisis occurs, complexity theory-based thinking presents complementary and, to some extent, corrective differences from mainstream crisis planning. First, it emphasizes that relationships are never static; all aspects of relationships are dynamic, emergent, and developed through dialogue between an organization and its publics. Second, it does not assume that an organization has good control over its environment, nor does it assume that the organization and its environment are definably separate so that one side can "operate on" the other. Third, it views past history as causing change within an organization without creating a predictable path for specific changes. Fourth, it views the goal of crisis management as organizational transformation rather than a return to the status quo. These philosophical differences between the perspectives of complexity-based thinking and mainstream crisis advisors also affect views about issues management.

Environmental Boundaries and Scanning

Clearly, the most acceptable organizational crisis is one that never happens. Most people agree that crises are best avoided by recognizing the warning signs in time to allow the organization to take appropriate action (Coombs, 2007; Fearn-Banks, 2007; Gonzalez-Herrero & Pratt, 1995; Kash & Darling, 1998; Mitroff et al., 1996). Even when the crisis cannot be averted, organizations have a considerable advantage if they know about it before their publics hear about it, particularly before media coverage begins. In fact, Mitroff and Anagnos (2001, p. 102) claimed that there should be no surprises at all, because "all crises send out a repeated train of early warning signals," although these signals can often be "weak and filled with noise." Therefore, most crisis management efforts begin with issues management and environmental scanning, processes that help the organization to sift out genuine signals of crisis from the general background noise in which they are embedded.

An organizational issue is "a trend, dilemma, or development that affects an organization's position and performance" (Thomas, Shankster, & Mathieu, 1994, p. 1253), and issues management consists of "systematic procedures designed to influence the issue's resolution in a manner favorable to the organization" (Coombs, 2007, p. 51). As described in mainstream crisis management literature, the process is linear and systematic, involving three stages: source identification, information gathering, and signal evaluation.

At the *source identification* stage, managers decide where to find the information that can help in signal detection. Most experts advise a highly structured and systematic approach to *information gathering*, the second stage of signal detection. For example, sources can be approached unobtrusively using coded content analysis of items that reveal public opinion, such as published or broadcast materials, and statistically coded records of customer complaints and worker safety violations. These techniques produce quantitative data that can be used for measurable comparisons over time. Whatever the source of information, many experts emphasize the need to record data systematically. Seat-of-the-pants approaches, such as simply reading a variety of trade and general interest publications or having a broad network of contacts inside and outside the company, industry, and community, are less highly regarded than methodically recorded material that can be analyzed systematically.

Once sources have been identified in the first stage of signal detection, and once preliminary information has been gathered on a variety of potential crises in the second stage, it is time for the third stage of signal detection. That is *signal evaluation*, or assessing the relative probability and presumed impact of each issue. Methods for quantified assessment are nearly as numerous as crisis experts themselves. Most suggest multiplying certain impact and probability ratings—for instance, on a scale of 1 to 10—to yield a "crisis coefficient" for each crisis type. The resulting coefficients form the basis for a ranked list of issues and risks that should be monitored closely (Barton, 1993; Coombs, 2007; Fearn-Banks, 2007; Fink, 1986; Regester & Larkin, 2005).

Perhaps the most systematic treatment of this issues management process was described by Mitroff and Anagnos (2001) in terms of a metaphorical signal detection machine. Once a signal is picked up, it must cross an "intensity threshold" in order to be recognized, and every signal detector must be "calibrated" in order to indicate developments that clearly belong in the "danger" or "potential danger" region, after which "an alarm must go off" (p. 108). The metaphor recalls the feedback processes described in chapter 3, in which complex systems can be governed by negative feedback in order to maintain stability or by positive feedback that encourages pattern breaking and loss of control. Envisioning issues management in terms of negative feedback supports most crisis experts' goal of maintaining or restoring the status quo. In traditional terms, positive feedback leading to an out-of-control system would be the least desired approach because it hastens an organization toward crisis.

In addition to systematic scanning and evaluation techniques, traditional crisis management also recommends that there should also be systematic procedures to get the relevant information to those who monitor the environment in search of crisis-related signals. Most authors agree that it is important to have people assigned specifically to crisis monitoring, although this may not be their full-time occupation (Caponigro, 2000; Regester & Larkin, 1997). The importance of this function was underscored by Mitroff and Anagnos (2001, p. 109), who noted that "signals go off all the time in organizations, but because there is no one there to recognize them, record them, or attend to them, then for all practical reasons the signals are 'not heard.'" This deficiency was noted many years earlier by Henry Kissinger, who observed that:

> after every crisis there surfaces in the press some obscure intelligence report...purporting to have predicted it, only to have been foolishly ignored by the policymakers. What these claims omit to mention is that when warnings become too routine they lose all significance; when reports are not called specifically to the attention of the leadership they are lost in bureaucratic background noise. (as cited in Lagadec, 1993, p. 62)

Managers from organizations as diverse as NASA, Enron, and the Catholic Church have made similar complaints to explain why they did not act sooner to forestall crises. For example, with respect to the decision processes of NASA management prior to the Challenger disaster, Vaughan (1996) remarked that instead of an "irrefutable signal" that the shuttle should not fly, managers received "weak and missing signals incapable of altering the scientific paradigm supporting the belief in acceptable risk" (p. 398). Naturally, after the Challenger disaster, "outsiders perceived that continuing to fly under the circumstances that existed at NASA was deviant; yet as the problem unfolded, insiders saw their behavior as acceptable and nondeviant" (p. 406) because they had performed correctly according to the tenets of their homogenous engineering culture.

Generally, monitoring responsibilities go to the crisis management team, or CMT, consisting of individuals who form the center of a crisis-sensing mechanism that stretches across the organization. Despite this wide network, Mitroff and Anagnos (2001) warned that usually "there is at least one person in every organization who knows about an impending crisis. The problem is that those who often know most about it are the ones who have the least power to bring it to the attention of the organization" (p. 102). After the fact, these knowledgeable employees can appear as whistleblowers who suffer discrimination: Roger Boisjoly, an engineer at NASA; Sherron Watkins, who warned Enron's CEO about deceptive accounting practices; or FBI agent Sibel Edmonds, who urged superiors to arrest 9/11 hijacker Zacarias Moussaoui before the attacks. Therefore, most experts advise crisis teams to ferret out these internal sources and also to develop precise definitions for signal evaluation so that the evaluation criteria are applied consistently. Finally, the entire signal detection system should be tested for accuracy and effectiveness, perhaps by sending control information to be tracked through the system (Coombs, 2007).

As can be seen from this overview, most crisis experts recommend a linear, systematized precrisis intelligence gathering process whose overriding goal is to diminish ambiguity, uncertainty, and inconsistency while enhancing predictability and control. At its most stark, the organization becomes a mechanical system, with the crisis management team at the center of a web of information consisting mainly of explicit knowledge—quantified, formatted, and rated for importance.

These techniques have clear value as decision aids that permit managers from widely different backgrounds to share information. They enable the crisis management team to distribute knowledge in the manner of Boisot's (2003) bond traders, "from screen to screen instantaneously and on a global scale" (p. 189). Furthermore, the extensive use of codification ensures that the necessary tasks of environmental scanning have been identified and acknowledged as important. However, as organizations grow more accustomed to precrisis monitoring, they may temper their approach with the more open-ended perspective of complex adaptive systems.

When considering the topic of environmental scanning, most crisis management experts assume clear boundaries between the organization and its external environment. However, from a complexity standpoint, experience is much more blurred; organization-environment boundaries appear "fluid, dynamic, and constantly evolving" (Sutcliffe, 2001, p. 203). This lack of clear distinctions manifests itself especially with stakeholders. For example, employees, customers, and suppliers are generally also members of the community, and they and their families may be part of special-interest groups affected by or involved with the organization in another capacity. Friends and family members may work for competitors, banks, local authorities, regulatory groups, or the media. Contractors and temporary employees could be viewed as either internal or external stakeholders (Williams & Moffitt, 1997; see also Cheney & Christensen, 2001). Therefore, by making a distinction between internal and external, crisis planners run the risk of overlooking multiple stakeholder roles that may sway both the type of information received and how it is interpreted.

In a larger sense, as well, organizations' attitudes toward environmental scanning and information gathering are influenced by the degree to which they see the environment as either a wholly discrete and objective entity or as a projection of themselves. How an organization views its environment substantially determines both crisis strategy and tactics. For example, Daft and Weick (2001) pointed out that:

> if an organization assumes that the external environment is concrete, that events and processes are hard, measurable, and

determinant, then it will play the traditional game to discover the "correct" interpretation. The key for this organization is discovery through intelligence gathering, rational analysis, vigilance, and accurate measurement. This organization will utilize linear thinking and logic and will seek clear data and solutions. (p. 246)

In terms of crisis management, an organization of this type may put most emphasis on step-by-step planning, checklists, prewritten news releases, and phone trees.

This linear thinking contrasts with that of an enacting organization, which views the external environment as "unanalyzable" and complex. An enacting organization may cocreate its external context: "The key is to construct, coerce, or enact a reasonable interpretation that makes previous action sensible and suggests some next steps....The interpretation process is more personal, less linear, more ad hoc and improvisational than for other organizations" (Daft & Weick, 2001, p. 246). For such an organization, the outcome may include "the ability to deal with equivocality...to invent an environment and be part of the invention" (Daft & Weick, 2001, p. 246). This type of environment has clear affinities with the complex systems described in chapter 3, in which the micro interactions between local agents build into macro-scale social patterns, through a process of mutual influence that gets modulated by other agents or attractors along the way.

Further differences between linear and enacting organizations can be seen in their approaches to information. Sutcliffe (2001) examined the relationship between information processing and perceived organizational environments, identifying three key perspectives about the environment: objectivist, perceptual/interpretivist, and enactment. The *objective environment approach* sees the world outside the organization as consisting of stakeholders and other resources that place discernible constraints and demands on the organization. This conceptualization of environments as "objective, concrete, external, or tangible" also implies that attributes and processes are "hard, measurable, and determinant" (Sutcliffe, 2001, p. 200). Such an outlook views environmental information as a "thing 'out there' to be discovered...independent from the meanings ascribed by organizational members" (Sutcliffe, 2001, p. 201). This certainty-seeking approach characterizes most organizations' traditional issues management efforts.

The *perceptual approach,* or information-processing perspective, conceives of the environment as a source of information and focuses attention on the processes by which the organization notices, receives, and interprets this information. This view maintains the boundary between the organization and its environment but does not necessarily assume that information about the environment is accurate. Rather, this information-processing approach examines how executives cope with uncertainty in the environment and how this uncertainty affects their perceptions. This perceptual approach is seldom considered in crisis communication literature (see Kersten, 2005; Tyler, 2005). However, it is an important component when organizations are considered as complex systems operating in exigencies that take them far from established norms, where the heuristic power of custom, experience, and training can be considerably diluted. For example, the British government found itself mired in a quandary reflecting the perceptual approach when it attempted to make decisions about mad cow disease by juggling decision criteria on risk, disease latency, and economic and political impacts with few or no precedents or scientific certainties.

The *enactment perspective* is familiar from chapter 7's discussion of sensemaking, in which organizations help to shape their environments and are in turn influenced by them. From this perspective, environmental scanning is the first stage of a process, followed by interpretation and learning. The boundaries between these stages are blurred because the process involves mutual influences among multiple factors and players (Daft & Weick, 2001). In addition, the "environment" itself is an ambiguous concept, although it strongly affects behavior within the organization. This perspective emphasizes the contingent nature of decision makers' standpoints; enactment allows the social construction of environment rather than assuming a constant and objectively given environment. As Sutcliffe (2001, p. 201) explained, from this view "decision makers pay attention to certain aspects of their environments as a consequence of attentional processes," which may be biased, inaccurate, or eccentric.

The enactment perspective helps to explain what otherwise appears to be an implausible degree of management obliviousness to a crisis environment. Although the phenomenon is hardly rare, it figured especially prominently in crises such as the 2001 collapse of Enron or the 2002 Catholic Church sex abuse scandal in Boston. With regard to the Church, commentators expressed amazement and disbelief that the head of the Boston Diocese, Cardinal Law, simply moved abusive priests around from parish to parish while assuring parishioners that he was taking care of the problem. However, Cardinal Law's failure to act can be understood as enacting the worldview of the Catholic Church, which had achieved success for centuries through a highly hierarchical culture in which cardinals and bishops, like secular senior management, determined what was true and what mattered, so that other voices, such as those of abuse victims, simply were not heard. As Tyler (2005) argued with respect to postmodern public relations:

> The power elite within the organization usually determine whose truths count as true....If the power elite is particularly successful at suppressing other truths, those executives within the elite then become particularly vulnerable should those truths erupt into public attention—in part because the executives' very success at suppression means that they are probably unacquainted with the suppressed stories within and about their own organization. (p. 568)

Reacting to "an increasingly secular and aggressive media culture" (Maier, 2005, p. 222), Law's hierarchical and authoritarian worldview exerted control by repressing unpleasant facts both within its own ranks and in the public domain.

These different approaches to the crisis environment are important because they shape the kinds of advance warning an organization perceives. For example, Sutcliffe (2001) urged the same distinction between signal detection and signal interpretation identified by Coombs (2007), but she argued that "scanning" as a coordinated and proactive effort is rare. Although formalized scanning structures operate in some organizations and are prescribed by most crisis management and issues management authorities, the information environment necessarily filters the kinds of material that may be actively sought. Sutcliffe, therefore, preferred the term *noticing* to describe how managers become aware of certain environmental factors—a process that is formal or informal, voluntary or involuntary, tactical or strategic. Similarly, an issues manager interviewed by Thomsen (1995) described a process of "getting into the market": "I'm sure it is the same kind of process that advertisers look to when they run a Chevrolet commercial. They're aiming that commercial to someone who is in the market for a car. They don't know who that is. But I find that when I'm in the market for something, suddenly I'm just magically aware of all of the commercials that have to do with that.... Your attention is automatically drawn to them" (p. 109).

In addition to perceptual filters, signal detection may be swayed by a characteristic of complex systems: Knowledge is local, so that any single element in the system cannot have knowledge of the entire system as a whole. If knowledge and information flow freely and effectively within the organization, this problem of partial vision may diminish somewhat. Nonetheless, context will always be represented incompletely so that managers must cultivate their ability to make decisions based on incomplete information, while being able to grasp the potential range of outcomes and understand long-term consequences of actions (Dörner, 1996). Indeed, as described in chapter 5, one of the essential components of expertise is the ability to distinguish key features of the landscape. A comparable illustration of the expert's ability to extract key features appears in the Sherlock Holmes story, "Silver Blaze" (Conan Doyle, 1894). Holmes solved that mystery by noticing that the family dog did not bark to signal the presence of an intruder, and therefore he deduced that the culprit was someone known to the dog. Like Sherlock Holmes, organizational experts will notice features that nonexperts will not, including elements that are missing (Klein, 1998). In this way, local knowledge may fill in for holistic, detailed, or proven knowledge about a troubling situation.

Smallman and Weir (1999) noted the importance of expert hunches in detecting incipient crisis situations, defining them as "shorthand for a complex and inter-related set of judgments about a multiplicity of factors;

none of them is perhaps individually significant but taken together justify a cautious view that something is wrong" (p. 37). In the wake of 9/11 it was learned that the hijackers had not bought return tickets; since then an airline clerk might consider a passenger's request for a one-way ticket as a warning signal. However, most organizations, like the 9/11 airline clerks, figure out the significance of something missing only after the fact. If crisis signal detection were simply a matter of knowing what to look for, then it would be possible to prepare an explicit procedure to guide information-gathering efforts. But knowing to look for what is *not* there involves highly complex processes and encompasses too vast a range of possibilities for experts themselves to master, or even to explain fully how they read a situation so others can be trained.

Attempts to render explicit these complex ways of understanding have achieved only limited success, and this shortfall has led to "radical uncertainty" because firms "do not, they cannot, know what they need to know" (Tsoukas, 2005, p. 110). The same radical uncertainty is one of the identifying features of being in a crisis; it was described by Hayek (1945) more than half a century ago: "Which of the events which happen beyond the horizon of his immediate knowledge are of relevance to his immediate decision, and how much of them need he know? There is hardly anything that happens anywhere in the world that might not have an effect on the decision he ought to make" (p. 525). Given these dramatically multiplicative possibilities, it is not surprising that firms have sought to codify and simplify information-gathering procedures in order to bring information to heel—nor that these procedures have not worked to everyone's satisfaction.

Planning and Decision Making

One reason for the deficiencies of environmental scanning is that the systematic discovery process recommended in crisis planning presumes rational decision-making skills. It requires that organizations make advance decisions about where to look for information and what sort of information to look for. This prescription assumes that important phenomena may be defined before the specific decision problem has arisen. Essentially, it asks organizations to assign meaning and value to information a priori and to make strategic decisions on this basis. This process usually works well for some types of high-probability crises such as communications about hurricanes or other natural events (despite its failure in the South Asian tsunami of December 2004).

However, organizations are not as well served by these rationalist assumptions when the situation involves low-probability, high-consequence events such as mad cow disease, 9/11, or the Challenger tragedy. The same might be said for crises with decentered and uncertain points of origin, such as the spinach *E. coli* outbreak or pet food contamination.

It is a complicated task for an organization involved in such a diffused crisis situation to identify reliable sources of information, track issue processes, and monitor stakeholder reactions. As Weick (2001) noted, "The complaint is not that rationality is ill-conceived but, rather, that the conditions under which it works best are relatively rare in organizations" (p. 34). More typical are the feelings evoked by crisis that Millar and Beck (2004) described: "Imagine yourself at a dead end on a country road where you can only turn left or right and you do not know whether either path will get you back on the desired direction. You are in an equivocal situation, at a turning-point that evokes dis-ease [sic]—uneasiness, anxiety, discomfort, and confusion" (p. 153).

The role of senior executives is often characterized as that of providing meaningful interpretations to guide the organization's overall direction (Daft & Weick, 2001; Haeckel, 1999; Thomas et al., 1993). Issues themselves are complex, emergent, and broad, meaning that they are also ill structured and open to a range of interpretations. Therefore, "strategic issues are not 'prepackaged'; rather, decision makers identify and formulate them by selectively attending to some aspects of their environment while ignoring others" (Thomas et al., 1994, p. 1253). At the simplest level, this behavior means that two organizations may act in radically different ways in response to the same information, based on varying interpretations and other factors affecting the decision (Sutcliffe, 2001; Thomas et al., 1993). Therefore, the provision of consistent information is no guarantee of consistent decision making at the other end of the process.

Rather than looking for ways to overcome this multiplicity, executives may use it to their advantage. For example, in addition to using the expert's pattern-seeking mode of knowledge, executives in highly successful firms frequently update their mental models (D'Aveni & Macmillan, 1990; Sutcliffe, 2001). In some studies, this characteristic correlates negatively with systematic scanning and planning functions and instead functions as trial-and-error action (Sutcliffe, 2001; Thomas et al., 1993). In other words, formalized strategic planning and information-gathering systems may produce executives who are less aware of the current state of affairs compared with those who engage in active sensemaking: scanning through informal processes, interpretation, and action. This evidence is also supported by the view of knowledge advanced in chapter 5: Knowledge must be enacted in order to become "knowing," which leads to genuine learning. Therefore, although no one would suggest the abandonment of issues management methods, it would be equally impractical to limit organizational learning to highly circumscribed signal detection procedures.

Plan Dependency

Another disadvantage of the standard information-gathering approaches is a limited horizon for interpreting that information. Crisis planning—with its scores, decision trees, and procedural notebooks—encourages crisis managers to select important features, decide on a course of action, and then adhere to the plan. This prescription is a useful way to help managers preserve a clear view of their goals amid the "fog of war," the confusion about information, analysis, and choices that descends during a crisis. However, it does not necessarily encourage the crisis management team to remain open to feedback and adjust plans rapidly as needed.

More conceptually, the importance of flexibility was demonstrated in a computer simulation game used by Dörner (1996) to study management decision making. Participants were placed in charge of an imaginary African country named Tanaland and could take any measures they deemed desirable and necessary to ensure its well-being. Their range of powers was virtually unlimited, from enacting legislation to introducing new technologies or infrastructures. Participants had six sessions in the game, during which they were given any information they needed and could make all the decisions they wished. Dörner found that most participants failed to consider the interrelated consequences of their actions—for instance, that improving medical care and agricultural practices would lead not only to a healthier, longer-lived population but also to increased birth rates and resource consumption levels. Most were surprised when famine set in a few years after the improvements were implemented.

Such reasoning errors among top managers often resulted from excessive planning up front, coupled with insufficient adjustment to changing circumstances over time. Early on, most players gave considerable time to devising strategies and planning how to solve the country's various problems. However, they spent later sessions almost exclusively carrying out those early plans. Despite the availability of feedback, participants showed less interest in gathering and reviewing information during subsequent sessions and preferred instead to focus on implementing planned actions. Furthermore, as the situation progressively worsened, participants suffered from "learned helplessness" (Karniol & Ross, 1996; Sitkin & Weingart, 1995) and grew apathetic in their responses. The consequences were generally catastrophic. As shown in table 9.1, these

Table 9.1. Decision-Making Errors in Complex Circumstances Encountered by Dörner (1996)

- Taking action without understanding the current situation
- Failing to take complexity into consideration (ignoring potential side effects and long-term outcomes)
- Basing assessments of success on the absence of immediately apparent negative outcomes
- Becoming sidetracked by "pet projects" instead of paying attention to emerging needs and changes in the situation
- Becoming cynical and apathetic as negative outcomes emerged

managers primarily displayed an orientation toward immediate results and an inability to move beyond original plans. Dörner (1996) argued that these behavioral flaws characterize real-world decision makers.

A similar experiment found that good decision makers—those who successfully improved Dörner's (1996) simulated environment—made more decisions than their less successful colleagues; they also viewed their decisions as hypotheses to be tested rather than final conclusions. This attitude comes close to that of enacting organizations, which engage in a significant amount of experimentation as a means of making sense of and shaping a complex and unpredictable environment (Daft & Weick, 2001). In contrast, Dörner observed that the unsuccessful participants took the opposite approach: "For them, to propose a hypothesis was to understand reality; testing that hypothesis was unnecessary. Instead of generating hypotheses, they generated 'truths'" (1996, pp. 23–24).

Good decision makers were also more interested in mastering not just facts but also the causal links within their simulated world, leading them to ask more "why?" questions. This attitude extended to their own behavior, as well, rendering them significantly more reflexive and open to considering alternatives. As a result, the decisions made by successful participants also showed a high degree of innovation overall, indicating that they were not inflexibly committed to any particular course of action but willing to make decisions in a wide range of areas, even in contrasting directions within the same area if the situation warranted it. Tests showed that the discriminating factor between successful and unsuccessful decision makers was a tolerance for ambiguity. The poor decision makers avoided difficult problems and self-reflection and instead showed "a tendency to seek refuge in certainty and security" (Dörner, 1996, p. 28). It appears, then, that decisional open-endedness and the ability to change course in midstream can be important attributes in good crisis management.

Structural Inertia as a Barrier to Managing Issues

Sometimes people become aware of situations that require attention, but in a highly proceduralized environment they may not know what action to take in consequence. For example, Mitroff and Anagnos (2001) observed that "if a signal does not relate to any of the daily, standard operating procedures of an organization, then even though it may be loud enough to be observed by many people, they may not know what to do about it. If it falls outside of the repertoire of known or expected behaviors, then people are at a loss what to do" (p. 110). Like many crisis experts, they recommended better procedures that more clearly specified "to what potential problem a signal might relate, and further, if a signal is noted, what is to be done about it" (p. 110). However, such an overdetermined approach may be counterproductive, as it limits flexibility and fosters structural inertia.

Structural inertia refers to the tendency of organizations to proce-duralize interaction, thereby making them less responsive on an every-day basis and decreasing their ability to maintain long-term legitimacy (Massey, 2001). In particular, behaviors that generate initial success encourage inertia in the longer term. As a result, organizations "run the risk of embedding false assumptions within their decision making. This becomes part of the organization's core paradigm and is, therefore, difficult to change," inhibiting effective learning (Elliott et al., 2000, p. 21). At its most extreme, the routinization of false assumptions and worthless procedures also characterizes superstitious learning, and the drive to proceduralize may also become a factor in probabilistic igno-rance. As seen in chapter 5, such a syndrome inhibits the development of nonlinear thinking skills while encouraging escalating commitment to false premises (Harvey et al., 2001). Hence Weick (1995) advocated an interpersonal approach to scanning because it "facilitates perception of complex events and the invention of innovations to manage the com-plexity" (p. 73). Gathering information through face-to-face interaction with people who come into direct contact with a variety of stakeholders and real or potential issues provides a number of contextual cues, offers greater flexibility in terms of information format and dialogic exchange, and can both strengthen and expand social ties within and beyond the organization. In contrast, when interactions are mediated by paperwork and computers, "relatively mindless routines" ensue; "control drives out innovation, organization becomes synonymous with control, and generic subjectivity becomes sealed off from any chance for reframing, learning, or comprehension of that which seems incomprehensible" (Weick, 1995, p. 73).

Thus overzealous efforts to systematize information gathering may work against crisis effectiveness in several ways. First, they intensify organizational members' reliance on formalized procedures and can thereby desensitize people to factors not covered by the guidelines. In turn, that desensitization diminishes the capacities to learn fast and to think on one's feet that are essential to crisis response.

Heuristic Errors: The Fallacy of Centrality

Overreliance on rules and routines may also damage issues management efforts by contributing to the fallacy of centrality. This heuristic error occurs when people, especially those in positions of power, overestimate the likelihood that they would surely know about a given phenomenon if it actually were taking place (Weick, 1995). The more tightly coupled a network is, the more likely the fallacy of centrality becomes, as peo-ple lose sight of nonhabitual information and unaccustomed points of view. The fallacy of centrality is particularly encouraged by heavy use of advanced technology, as the responsibility for finding and retrieving information gets delegated to the system. In fact, the more advanced the technology is, the more credibility it is assumed to have, so that people mistrust information that does not come through it. Thus, paradoxically, "the better the information system, the less sensitive it is to novel events" (Weick, 1995, p. 3).

If unrestrained, the fallacy of centrality can actually contribute to lack of vigilance. When everyone believes that information flows freely and efficiently, people are less likely to pay close attention to their surroundings, assuming that anything important has already been discovered. Crises such as 9/11 show the danger of such unvigilant overconfidence. Among contributing factors to that tragedy, the 9/11 Commission named government agencies' "tendency to match capabilities to mission by defining away the hardest part of their job. They are often passive, accepting what are viewed as givens, including that efforts to identify and fix glaring vulnerabilities to dangerous threats would be too costly, too controversial, or too disruptive" (National Commission on Terrorist Attacks upon the United States, 2004, p. 352). Thus the fallacy of centrality is one further way in which rules and procedures meant to streamline an organization's precrisis scanning actually render it less agile and less perceptive.

In sum, before a crisis, the two most important areas are relationships with constituencies and issues tracking. Within those areas, most crisis literature emphasizes the importance of maintaining organizational legitimacy in the eyes of audiences by cultivating trust and a good reputation. One way in which relationships can be stabilized at a positive phase is by identifying and dealing with emergent issues before they become crises. Most crisis literature recommends that these priorities can be managed using highly systematized techniques. Complexity and learning theories also put an emphasis on relationships. However, they give more primacy to unintended or uncontrollable factors in relationships, to the history of relationships as a whole, and to the ways in which entities in a relationship both affect what the other entity does and are shaped by it in return.

These differences in worldview also affect managers' views about the goals of crisis planning. For most crisis experts, the main goal is averting a crisis altogether—or, if a crisis does occur, restoring the organization's control as soon as possible and reverting to the status quo or to an improved form of status quo. In contrast, complexity theory views stability as transient, perhaps unattainable. In other words, crises will occur, and they present opportunities for organizational transformation rather than reversion to a prior state. Similar concerns and discrepancies characterize how each worldview approaches managers' behavior during a crisis.

10

Adapting to a Complex World

Challenging Assumptions During a Crisis

When crisis hits, an organization's two most important assets are its team of leaders and its preparation for the crisis. Neither emerges on the scene fully prepared; the question then becomes how to make both leaders and groundwork most useful. In the preceding chapter, we looked at the early warning systems that many organizations put in place. We saw that mainstream crisis planners favor formalized and systematic forms of information gathering and data analysis, whereas a complexity approach favors pattern recognition and expert intuition. Like the previous chapter, this chapter adopts two perspectives to examine major assumptions about developing teams and carrying out crisis plans. It looks first at assumptions made by mainstream crisis management and then at how those assumptions are modified and extended by theories of complexity and organizational learning.

Assumptions About Teamwork

Traditionally, crisis plans are the product of two components. First, the content comes from a vast body of information collected in the signal detection stage, and, second, the supervising intelligence comes from a crisis management team drawn from across the organization. Most experts recommend group management as opposed to assigning all responsibilities to a single crisis management leader because effective teams usually produce more positive outcomes than the aggregate of individual members acting on their own (Pearson & Clair, 1998).

The crisis management team (CMT) is therefore the nerve center of the crisis management process. Because of that central role, crisis experts often detail the individual and group skills that CMT members should possess. In the discussion that follows, we rely most heavily on the recommendations by Coombs (2007), who devotes more attention to CMT attributes than most other experts do.

First, and foremost among these qualities, is the ability to work as part of a group toward shared goals. Second, in order to carry out the crisis management plan, CMT members need both functional knowledge and the ability to deal effectively with the pressure and ambiguity inherent in crisis situations. Third, in order to handle unforeseen circumstances, CMT members must be able to understand critical decision making, especially how to analyze problems, evaluate alternatives, and balance the positive and negative aspects of alternatives. Fourth, they need good listening skills. Together, these qualities add up to what Coombs (2007) termed "vigilance," a form of critical thinking that combines knowledge, skills, and personal traits. Although CMT members should have the necessary inherent traits, the knowledge and skills involved in crisis management can also be honed through practice and training.

A group that masters all these qualities is very rare. For that reason, it can be useful to temper aspirations for team composition with more limited views of group behavior and organizational learning that account for bounded rationality, blind spots, and faulty heuristics. As Coombs (1999) pointed out, "any Dilbert cartoon will remind us that the organizational world does not run on pure logic" (p. 94).

Coombs (2007) addressed five interpretation problems that he believed crisis managers should be aware of: serial reproduction errors, the MUM effect, message overload, information acquisition bias, and group decision-making errors. *Serial reproduction errors* are the distortions that occur when information is handled by numerous people, as in the children's game "telephone." The *MUM effect* is the tendency people in organizations have to withhold or improve negative information, generally to protect themselves or others. *Message overload* is a serious problem for crisis teams attempting to make sense of a mountain of data and extract relevant information.

Information acquisition biases constitute more elaborate issues, as they refer to cognitive tricks the mind may play on crisis managers. Mainly these tricks take the form of selective perception, filtering out information that does not meet preconceived ideas. For crisis management, Coombs (2007) defined the main risk as focusing only on information that confirms a crisis manager's initial impression of the situation. As we saw earlier with Dörner's (1996) Tanaland simulation, such a commitment to original conceptions stifles necessary adjustments later on. Perhaps more dangerously, managers may rely too heavily on experience with a past crisis that resembled the present one in some way. If the fit is poor, the CMT will apply "the wrong template" and attempt to manage "the wrong crisis" (Coombs, 2007, p. 118). Finally, Coombs (2007) warned that groups may be prone to errors when making decisions related to a crisis. This syndrome may arise from either a group form of selective perception or failure to exercise critical thinking in examining alternative solutions.

The need for a formalized set of procedures—a crisis management plan—is one point on which virtually all crisis experts agree. They give many reasons for preparing such a plan. First, it improves response times after a crisis breaks by collecting information in advance, assigning task responsibilities, and identifying priorities (Coombs, 2007; Dyer, 1995; Fearn-Banks, 2007; Kash & Darling, 1998; Ramée, 1987). Second, a plan ensures an efficient and effective response by allowing CMTs to develop strategies and make decisions without the time pressure and stress of an actual crisis situation (Coombs, 1999; Fearn-Banks, 2007; Kash & Darling, 1998). Finally, a plan allows an organization to take proactive control of the crisis situation rather than being forced to passively react to events as they occur (Coombs, 2007; Kash & Darling, 1998).

For all these reasons, crisis plans have traditionally formed the centerpiece of crisis management as presented by scholars and practitioners. However, complexity and learning theories suggest that difficulties may be hidden in this ostensibly smooth script for success. In fact, the crisis plan itself raises concerns about the hazards of overdetermination, even as it provides the security that most eventualities have been foreseen and appropriate strategies devised. In addition, irrationality, faulty heuristics, and blind spots may render a crisis management group less than effective when it designs its plan in the first place.

Planning and the Rational Actor

One problem with traditional crisis planning is that CMTs rarely possess all the necessary information. From this perspective, Hayek (1945) took issue with the assumption that planners and decision makers are always in possession of a complete and reliable set of facts. Rather, he argued that "there is something fundamentally wrong with an approach which habitually disregards an essential part of the phenomena with which we have to deal: the unavoidable imperfection of man's knowledge and the consequent need for a process by which knowledge is constantly communicated and acquired" (p. 530). If planning is "the complex of interrelated decisions about the allocation of our available resources" (Hayek, 1945, p. 520), then such planning must be based on the knowledge available, which is necessarily limited. As we discussed in chapter 5, knowledge is locally situated, and organizational actors have access only to contextually constrained and filtered information.

In addition, there is no way to judge the effects of this limited knowledge on the planning process. Hayek (1945) particularly disagreed with the more extreme forms of rationality, stating that "much of mathematical economics with its simultaneous equations, which in effect starts from the assumption that people's knowledge corresponds with the objective facts of the situation, systematically leaves out what it is our main task to explain" (p. 530). Thus the impoverishment of content that comes with reduction of knowledge to models and quantifiable variables can actually exacerbate a crisis. For example, engineering models that predicted that New Orleans levees would hold through a category 3 hurricane failed to consider the devastating flooding brought by 2005's category 4 storm, Hurricane Katrina.

Another miscalculation related to reductionism started a controversy that emerged from the federal government's attempt to help homeless people by donating wool blankets to shelters. In 1992, after donations to some 2,000 shelters, it came to light that the blankets were treated with small amounts of DDT, a pesticide widely used to suppress moths in military cloth. Although DDT was banned in 1972, when the U.S. Environmental Protection Agency found that it could cause cancer, military experts considered homeless people's immediate risk of freezing to death to be far more serious than the infinitesimal risk of eventual DDT-incited illness. Therefore, the ensuing public outcry took government decision makers by surprise ("Discard tainted blankets," 1992). The experts' view of DDT's "negligible risk" based on reliable mathematical models held no more persuasive power with the homeless than the British government's assurances about the negligible risk of contracting mad cow disease in 1996. Instead, the well-meaning gesture caused shelter operators to "wonder how the government could dump illegal carcinogenic material on society's most vulnerable population" ("Blankets with DDT spur outcry," 1992, p. A27). Amid analogies to prior practices, such as giving native populations smallpox-infested blankets, the military found it necessary to hold news conferences, to establish a toll-free number for advice on disposing of the blankets, and to assure the public that the blankets had not been given to disaster survivors elsewhere. What had appeared to be flawless planning and a win-win situation was sunk by the assumption that knowledge about statistical risk would prevail with the public as it had with the scientists.

What appears to be a flawless crisis management plan can also fail once it confronts a flawed reality unless it has clear, positive goals. As discussed earlier, classic analytical decision making and planning models involve setting goals, deciding on courses of action, taking action, reviewing feedback, and making corrective adjustments. However, crisis situations often pose an obstacle to this model, as the primary aim in managing them is less to attain a certain objective than to avoid undesirable consequences—that is, not to have a crisis in the first place. This is known as a *negative goal*. Negative goals tend to be vague, based mainly on the realization that things cannot remain as they stand, and therefore they often create problems up front in designing a strategy. As Dörner observed, "a 'nonstove' or 'nonchair' is more difficult to define than a 'stove' or 'chair'" (1996, p. 50). Returning to a noncrisis time of status quo—the goal of most crisis planning—can be nearly as difficult as defining as a "nonstove," as crises tend to radically and permanently transform an organization's status in the world. Furthermore, lack of

clear, positive goals also complicates evaluation, because crises normally do not yield "a criterion by which we can decide with certainty
whether the goal has been achieved" (Dörner, 1996, p. 50). In addition,
crisis goals are often multiple: Resolving a crisis may mean having to
satisfy various stakeholders, to take corrective action, to limit negative
media coverage, and so on—a complex brew of objectives that makes
evaluation hard.

The variables involved in a crisis situation may also be linked in
a variety of complex ways that become apparent only as the situation
unfolds—or even long after the crisis appears to be over. This problem surfaces most readily with respect to unforeseen vagaries of public
opinion, as shown by the U.S. government's problem with distributing
DDT-impregnated blankets to homeless shelters. Crisis plans seldom
deal with these unanticipated or unintended consequences, but it is not
unusual for such unforeseen problems to surface. In the case of the military blankets, the government had anticipated neither the association
with smallpox-infested blankets given to Native Americans nor public
resistance to statistical risk projections. This combination of incomplete
information, conflicting goals, and unintended consequences considerably complicates a traditional crisis plan. Instead, crisis planners are
faced with the need to develop procedures to meet complex multiple,
unclear, negative goals in relation to an event that has not yet occurred.
Seen in this light, planning is primarily an attempt to reduce ambiguity
and assert control. By reducing the uncertainty of the circumstances to
a set of rules and steps, the perceived risk is decreased, and the world
appears more controllable (Dörner, 1996).

When planners face complex and shifting threats, many assume that
even an incomplete plan is better than no plan at all. The reason is
not that the plan contents are useful in themselves. In fact, "it is the
reflective glance, not the plan per se, that permits [crisis response] to be
accomplished in an orderly way" (Holder, 2004, p. 52). Indeed, in some
cases, "actions guided by highly complex plans may undermine the ultimate communicative effectiveness of those who use them" (Berger, 1997,
p. 42). Most authors acknowledge that a plan cannot be expected to cover
all situations. Penrose (2000), for instance, reflected on the complexity
of organizations and their environments and observed that "the infinite
number of possible crisis scenarios has prevented the adoption or implementation of a universally accepted planning strategy. Indeed, there are
times when a plan may not be as relevant to a crisis as planners might
have envisioned" (p. 157). Similarly, Marra (1998) concluded that having
a crisis plan is a "poor predictor of excellent crisis communications," as
field research demonstrates a low correlation between the presence of
a crisis plan and successful crisis management. He argued instead that
an organization's culture ranks among the most reliable variables that
predict crisis outcomes, concluding that "crisis communication plans
simply aren't as valuable as many practitioners believe" (p. 471).

Despite these shortcomings of planning, the process is too deeply embedded in many organizational cultures to curtail its use. Hence Weick (1995) observed with regard to strategic planning: "Managers keep forgetting that it is what they do, not what they plan, that explains their success. They keep giving credit to the wrong thing—namely, the plan—and having made this error, they then spend more time planning and less time acting. They are astonished when more planning improves nothing" (p. 55).

Threat Rigidity

In certain respects, a little planning may be a dangerous thing—that is, the crisis planning process may mask dysfunctional aspects of organizational culture or even cause managers to make less good decisions. Kersten (2005) warned, "we still think that rational crisis training, crisis preparedness, and a good plan will save us. What needs to be acknowledged is that 'irrationality' may not be random, incidental, or even correctable but could be systemic" (p. 546). This sense of complacency can be further reinforced if organizations overcome various problems with minimal preparation. Such a pattern can create a "comfort zone, leading executives and managers to lose any fears of problems and to become (over)confident of their own actions and decisions" (Pearson & Clair, 1998, p. 70). As we saw earlier, that description characterizes such organizations as the pre-Challenger NASA, which had for years pushed the limits of technological flaws until its management began to believe they were impervious to errors and unknowns. Corporations such as Enron and Parmalat also partially owe their ultimate financial collapse to overconfident executives whose repeated risk-taking behavior reinforced a false sense of invulnerability.

Despite this evidence that crisis plans may inhibit effectiveness, few crisis experts question the need for a plan. More typically, experts value plans for their heuristic and training merits, not as step-by-step instructions for behavior. In fact, the sheer number of intervening variables in any real-world crisis makes it difficult to determine the extent to which a crisis plan was responsible for a successful crisis outcome. Many researchers recognize this fact and include warnings about the need for crisis teams to remain flexible. For example, Pearson and Clair (1998, p. 70) cautioned that "no matter how many preparations an organization makes, victims' and other organizational stakeholders' responses to crisis will involve individual and collective cognitive, emotional, and behavioral reactions." Therefore, organizations must "develop ad hoc responses in the face of unexpected occurrences. These reactions, both expected and unexpected and planned and ad hoc, will most directly influence the degree of success and failure outcomes" (Pearson & Clair, 1998, p. 70).

Regardless of these warnings, evidence suggests that crisis plans may encourage inflexibility in management. As Dörner (1996) noted, "If we expect the unexpected, we are better equipped to cope with it than if we lay extensive plans and believe that we have eliminated the unexpected" (p. 165). Yet many executives believe the opposite, according crisis plans a nearly talismanic value. For example, one Nestlé executive advocated crisis planning because "a series of checklists or a template can help a company go into auto-pilot...communicating proper information to internal and external audiences, including government authorities, company executives, brokers, employees and consumers" (Thayer, 1998, p. 12). This approach does not describe flexible reactions to the fluidly changing circumstances that characterize most crises.

Studies of threat-rigidity responses also suggest that meticulous planning may be counterproductive. Numerous researchers have noted organizations' tendency to react to a threat by adopting a defensive pose, causing them to self-limit information-gathering and processing capacity and narrow their decision options as a means of reducing uncertainty (Barnett & Pratt, 2000; D'Aveni & Macmillan, 1990; Penrose, 2000). If an organization has limited its options a priori by specifying a fixed set of procedures, it may fail to absorb information or to consider decisions that fall outside this predetermined range of options (Pfeffer & Sutton, 1999). Managers who prefer to allow the company to "go into auto-pilot" (Thayer, 1998) willingly adopt this mind-set as a means to reduce confusing stimuli.

Institutionalization

One form that managerial rigidity may take is described by institutional theory. This approach to organizational behavior stands in contrast to other styles that focus on efficiency, rational actors, and adaptation to definable environmental conditions. Rather, institutional theory posits that organizations participate in the construction of the same environment in which they operate. Institutionalization is generally reflected in the formal and accepted (including unspoken and taken-for-granted) structures of an organization, which develop and change over time as a result of recursive everyday interaction.

However, institutionalized processes tend to favor stasis over change. Although some natural variation occurs as habitual actions are repeated, institutions gradually come to represent real or perceived constraints on behavioral alternatives for members of the organization (Barley & Tolbert, 1997; Stacey et al., 2000). Thus institutions evolve into "socially constructed templates for action"; through repeated interactions, certain "patterned relations and actions...gradually acquire the moral and ontological status of taken-for-granted facts which, in turn, shape future interactions and negotiations" (Barley & Tolbert, 1997, p. 94). For the most part, individuals' ability to influence institutions requires a reflexive attitude—a willingness to engage in double-loop learning that is rare in organizations. More typical is the move toward institutionalization described by Burke (2000): "It is virtually inevitable that institutions will sooner or later congeal and become obstacles to further innovation. They become the seats of vested interests, populated by groups who have invested in the system and fear to lose their intellectual capital" (p. 51).

Once institutionalization has taken hold, inflexible attitudes often make an organization more crisis-prone than it had been in an earlier, more flexible state. In this connection, Wicks (2001) referenced the "three pillars of institutions": regulative (power/coercion), normative (social), and cognitive (individual). These three mainstays may be present in varying degrees in a given context; his research found them all to have contributed significantly to the 1992 Westray mine crisis. As a result of the punitive institutionalized rules and culture of the Westray mine in Nova Scotia, management grew neglectful of miner safety and denied workers even the most basic comforts, focusing solely on output productivity. Evidence of these factors can be found in incidents such as the 5-hour power outage that shut down equipment designed to pump out poisonous methane gas and ensure adequate air circulation underground; miners were ordered to continue working regardless. After the power was finally restored, "the men were groggy and disoriented from breathing the foul air" (Wicks, 2001, p. 671). No lavatories were provided in the lower levels of the mines, and those who ventured to complain were ridiculed and even sanctioned. The cumulative interaction effects of abusive power, disregard for safety, and a culture of helplessness eventually culminated in an explosion that killed 26 men.

Similarly, Weick (2001) found that institutionalized attitudes at Union Carbide set in motion the neglect that led to the tragedy at Bhopal: "A plant perceived as unimportant proceeds to act out, through turnover, sloppy procedures, inattention to details, and lower standards, the prophecy implied in top management's expectations. A vicious circle is created and conditions become increasingly dangerous.... Susceptibility to crisis varies as a function of top management assumptions about which units are important" (p. 232).

In addition to creating the conditions that may breed crises, institutionalization also inhibits double-loop learning, the mode of thought that stimulates profound change by bringing to light buried assumptions and increasing the learner's self-awareness. In contrast, by its very nature institutionalization renders procedures and assumptions invisible: "By creating taken-for-granted expectations about appropriate behavior, institutions often avoid direct scrutiny, because habit, history and/or tradition suggest they are proper" (Wicks, 2001, pp. 688–89). Institutionalized behaviors and attitudes are rarely questioned, which is precisely what makes them so insidious. They form an often-invisible part of an organization's culture, accounting for crises of management duplicity in corporate trading cultures such as Enron's or Parmalat's, crises of overconfidence at NASA, or crises of bureaucratic inertia surrounding intelligence that preceded the 9/11 attacks.

Crisis Plans Versus the Enacted Environment

Effective planning in a crisis is difficult in part because of the expo-
nentially expanding chain of events whereby initial decisions—right or
wrong—tend to drive subsequent decisions. As Weick (2001) noted, "the
assumptions that underlie the choice of that first response contribute to
enactment and the second stimulus. As action continues through more
cycles, the human responses which stimulate further action become
increasingly important components of the crisis" (p. 228). Researchers
have identified certain phenomena that may distort a course of action
when a crisis situation looms or when the first steps taken in the enactment process during a crisis meet with negative feedback, such as escalating commitment, self-fulfilling prophecy, and overrationality.

Escalating commitment is an insidious form of entrapment during the
public positioning forced by crisis situations. People caught in escalating commitment cling to previously made plans with increasing tenac-
ity, even when faced with evident failure (Edwards, 2001). Ross and Staw
(1993) identified five principal determinants of escalation. *Project determinants* are characteristics of the specific endeavor, such as expected
benefits, the estimated time frame for reaping those benefits, and the
economic and other resources invested in the endeavor. *Psychological
determinants* include self-justification and gratification seeking, as well
as decision-making errors and biases. They also comprise "reinforcement
traps" that lead executives to take positive outcomes for granted on the
basis of their prior history of success. Thus Edwards (2001) warned that
"strongly held beliefs in future success can bring about organizational
crisis through escalating commitment to a failing course of action" (pp.
344–45).

In addition, decision makers are subject to a variety of social *determinants*, which include pressures to meet collectively constructed standards of "strong" leadership, as well as the desire to preserve credibility
by justifying publicly made decisions. *Organizational determinants* result
from political pressure within the organization, secondary benefits to the
organization, and the extent to which the project or endeavor is woven
into the identity of the organization (and thus its degree of institutionalization). The fifth category of overcommitment comprises *contextual
determinants*, which take into account forces beyond the organization's
boundaries, such as wide-ranging social and economic issues, industry
trends, and even international events (Ross & Staw, 1993). Another component of escalating commitment not mentioned by Ross and Staw is
prospect theory (Kahneman & Tversky, 1979), or the tendency to adopt
risk-seeking behavior when faced with unexpected negative outcomes in
an attempt to recoup the losses incurred.

Certain personal characteristics, common in crisis situations, can
also indicate a propensity to overcommit. The first is *length of tenure* in
the same industry and, to a lesser degree, the same company; the second

is *successful past performance*; and the third is *centralized management* (Schwenk, 1995). Organizations that have enjoyed positive results under a leader with a tendency to centralize authority or a long-standing executive body therefore appear to be most susceptible to the effects of escalating commitment (Schwenk, 1995; Sutcliffe, 2001). In addition, as time passes, decision makers become more likely to choose unethical alternatives to preserve their commitments, even if the same decision makers would find such alternatives unacceptable in a nonescalating context (Street et al., 1997). One might describe escalating commitment as the opposite of learning in that it resists reflection about situations that could lead to insight and change. For example, such nonreflective commitment that goes well beyond legal and ethical limits helped to initiate crisis at Enron, as management sought to preserve a tottering financial structure through ever-riskier machinations. Parmalat's leadership continued to increase its debt load through bond issues while continuing to claim solvency in an increasingly desperate attempt to recoup losses and cover up its dubious transfers of funds through offshore financial entities (Malagutti, 2004).

Related to escalating commitment is the self-fulfilling prophecy, or expectations that are realized through actions by the holders of those expectations (Edwards, 2001; Weick, 1995). It may be tempting to hope that self-fulfilling prophecies will lead to successful outcomes, but the reinforcement traps just described illustrate the darker side of the power of positive thinking. The 1993 killing of Branch Davidian cult members at Waco, Texas, illustrates how escalating commitment and self-fulfilling prophecy can intertwine in a self-reinforcing loop and hide alternative choices, with disastrous consequences. In this instance, agents from the federal government's Bureau of Alcohol, Tobacco, and Firearms (BATF) attacked a sequestered group of religious cultists in the belief, against evidence, that the group's children were being abused and endangered. This belief resulted in a refusal to negotiate, a precipitous attack on the cult's compound, and the death of some 80 people, many of them the very children the BATF sought to rescue. Yet the decision to attack was explained by the BATF director as a logical, nearly inevitable, outcome, given his interpretation of information about the threat posed by religious groups.

Situations such as the Waco tragedy are aggravated by a high perception of behavioral control, in which the decision makers become convinced that they have the skills, tools, and willpower to overcome any potential obstacles to success. The conviction that they can control future outcomes "increases their tendency to forecast eventual success and escalate commitment even in the event of temporary failure" (Edwards, 2001, p. 352). Vaughan (1996) ascribed such cognitive self-delusions to NASA managers, leading up to the decision to launch the Challenger: "The boundaries defining acceptable behavior incrementally widened, incorporating incident after aberrant incident" (p. 407), until the managers were simply unable to see the extreme risks posed by launching the shuttle in freezing weather.

The Waco and NASA debacles provide further evidence of misplaced persistence on the part of leaders that makes serious crises even worse. However, less notorious crises can also be worsened if managers have excessive illusions of control. Indeed, rationalist management encourages a relatively high level of perceived control over circumstances, however complex they may be. As this philosophy underlies much of the dominant managerial discourse, we should not be surprised to find high perceptions of behavioral control among managers and executives (Cannon, 1999; Holtzhausen, 2000). This predisposition, along with social pressure to conform to models of strong, consistent, powerful leadership, represent warning flags about escalating commitment and the adverse effects of self-fulfilling prophecy.

Through strategic planning, managers attempt to rid the environment of uncertainty to the extent possible. However, crisis planning should not aggravate known risks, such as escalating commitment, by providing an institutionalized template for behavior that limits flexibility. An overly analytical plan can work against successful crisis resolution by fostering excess formalization, the illusion of predictability, and erroneous beliefs on the part of strategists and planners (Starbuck, 1992). In fact, overly formulized crisis planning can prevent an organization from learning and developing the kind of expertise that would allow it to be flexible and to enact behaviors that cope effectively with crises.

Argyris (1977) described these impediments as "Model I assumptions" underlying behaviors that run counter to double-loop learning: learning that questions basic worldviews. He summarized these Model I assumptions in four basic values: "(1) to define in their own terms the purpose of the situation in which they find themselves, (2) to win, (3) to suppress their own and others' feelings, and (4) to emphasize the intellectual and deemphasize the emotional aspects of problems" (1977, p. 118). The corresponding behaviors resemble the ways in which many organizations approach the uncertainties of crises:

> All of us design our behavior in order to remain in unilateral control, to maximize winning and minimize losing, to suppress negative feelings, and to be as rational as possible, by which we mean laying out clear-cut goals and then evaluating our own behavior on the basis of whether or not we've achieved them. The purpose of this strategy is to avoid vulnerability, risk, embarrassment, and the appearance of incompetence. In other words, it is a deeply defensive strategy and a recipe for ineffective learning. We might even call it a recipe for antilearning, because it helps us avoid reflecting on the counterproductive consequences of our own behavior. (Argyris, 1994, p. 80)

Despite their frequent inefficacy, most of these behaviors—control, winning, rationality, measuring up to goals—are advocated by most crisis planning approaches as a way to overcome uncertainty. Because crisis plans are necessarily based on current assumptions within the organization, the precautionary norms taken as a result may paradoxically express the very characteristics that predispose the organization to a crisis. Even where they do not underlie a crisis, defective norms and false assumptions are latent conditions that make it difficult for an organization to react to the emergent properties of a crisis (Elliott et al., 2000). Seen from the standpoint of complexity and learning theories, the crisis management process has the potential to be a self-perpetuating negative cycle leading to the institutionalization of solutions that appear to work without understanding their long-term effects. Double-loop learning, in which one's deep assumptions are challenged and changed, cannot take place because there is no motivation to look beyond the surface.

In order to avoid perpetuating false assumptions, complexity and learning theories diverge from most crisis planners' push to normalization and do not advocate returning to a stable state by quickly reestablishing apparent legitimacy. Learning theories view the push for normalization as a barrier to learning because it encourages managers to seek proximate and immediate fixes rather than to examine complexities, including institutionalized dysfunctions. Instead, learning theories encourage reflexive sensemaking and dynamic enactment of the environment. As part II of this book argued, learning theories encourage managers to question the norms within an organization that may lead to crises or interfere with their resolution. These theories envision the CMT as having the power to act immediately on decisions, an approach that encourages enactment and thus knowing and learning. Learning theories therefore favor the development of inherent expertise; they deemphasize reliance on prewritten procedures that may lead organizational members to ignore cues outside the prescribed framework.

In the chapter that follows, we look further at the search for certainty—this time, in terms of postcrisis evaluation—and we consider its effects on postcrisis learning.

11

Complex Recovery

Challenging Assumptions After a Crisis

As we argued earlier, assumptions about the organization's environment, including its audiences, influence the information collected before a crisis, as well as its interpretation and strategic use. Most experts take a strategic approach to relationships with constituencies. They advise organizations to seek audiences' input in order to be forewarned about impending problems and to adjust their behaviors accordingly. This consultation is symmetric but not fully dialogical in the sense that the organization and its constituents mutually define their situation through ongoing interaction. Complexity theory urges that organizations adopt a fully dialogic approach because it views relationships as reiterated local interactions that eventually establish larger patterns of meaning or behavior. Continuous mutual influence is central to that emergent pattern.

Even when they advocate a symmetrical approach, most mainstream crisis authorities view the external environment in which the organization operates as separate from the organization. However, for communication theorists in general, the boundaries between internal and external are becoming increasingly uncertain (Cheney & Christensen, 2001). From the standpoint of complex systems, boundaries between the organization and its context are particularly permeable and interactive. Complexity-based thinking views relationships as wholly in flux, being mutually constructed from moment to moment, so there is no linear sense of action-reaction as there generally is for most crisis experts. Instead, there are multiple contingent possibilities for responses to various factors in the environment.

Assumptions about separateness from and control over audiences and environment define most mainstream postcrisis assessments. A mainstream crisis team works hard to restore the status quo by following a detailed crisis plan. In contrast, a complexity-based approach accepts a certain amount of latitude; it avoids comprehensive and detailed planning that could lead to faulty decision making. Mainstream and complexity viewpoints apply different criteria to similar postcrisis questions: When is the crisis over? What constitutes success? What sort of information can establish how the organization weathered the ordeal? What can be learned from the outcome?

Information Gathering for Postcrisis Evaluation

Once the crisis itself has passed, most authorities propose some form of evaluation, primarily as a learning exercise to gain insight into the crisis management process, to fine-tune the crisis management plan, and to determine what skills may be lacking in the CMT or organization (Caponigro, 2000; Coombs, 2007; Mitroff et al., 1996). Evaluation is also used to calculate the impact of the crisis on the organization and thus to offer tangible evidence about the success of the crisis management effort.

One common denominator shared by these elements is their immediacy. As soon as a crisis seems to be over, the crisis team begins to review the accumulated documentation, gather the additional information necessary, and carry out the evaluation. Like precrisis information gathering, this stage is driven by an underlying assumption of objectivity: By bringing together hard data from a variety of sources, the evaluation process provides an unbiased overview of the crisis outcome.

A number of crisis experts look to the crisis management plan and the crisis team as primary indicators of crisis management success. Therefore, failure may be the fault of the plan, of the executors, or of both (Mitroff et al., 1996). One of the primary functions of evaluation is to determine where any problems lie and rectify them before the next crisis strikes. The documentation prepared during the course of the crisis constitutes the primary data source. Organizations may also survey internal and external stakeholders, including crisis team members, to gather opinions on how the crisis was handled. Finally, all media reports on the crisis are collected and studied.

Most crisis experts favor quantifiable forms of impact evaluation. For example, Coombs (2007) suggested that impact can be measured along a variety of dimensions, including financial, reputational, human factors, and media frames. The *financial* dimension is relatively straightforward, measured in terms of sales, stock prices, and other economic indicators, including long-term factors such as legal expenses and the cost of compliance with any new regulations or legislation implemented as a result of the crisis. The *reputational* dimension involves comparing reputation measures from before and after the crisis, stakeholder feedback, and media coverage. *Human factors* evaluation refers to deaths or injuries, environmental damage, community disruption caused by evacuations, or similar severe consequences of the crisis. Finally, the *media frames* dimension evaluates how successful the organization has been at presenting its side of the story through the media; it is assessed in terms of quantity (such as quotations from organization representatives in proportion to other points of view), accuracy, and the duration of media coverage. The aim is to keep the story in the media for as little time as possible, as all those involved in a crisis want to establish closure, whether that means reversion to the precise status quo or a "new normal" defined by changes in values and beliefs (Ulmer et al., 2007, p. 182). Just how successfully the crisis was managed can be determined by comparing the actual results with estimates of what the outcome would have been like without any crisis management efforts and with managers' desired outcome. The difference provides a measure of how successfully the crisis management program protected the organization and its assets, what factors played a role in the relative success or failure of the effort, and what areas require further adjustment (Coombs, 2007).

Because the goal of most mainstream crisis management is a return to the status quo, few experts consider actions beyond evaluation. Primarily, specific actions relating to the recently experienced crisis, as opposed to normal stakeholder relations and communication efforts, are those involving cooperation in any investigations, rebuilding projects, or other long-term effects of the crisis. In the mainstream "stage" model of crisis, this stage is often referred to as the "return to normalcy," the point at which the organization resumes business as usual (O'Rourke, 1996; Taback, 1991). For some experts (e.g., Fink, 1986), the achievement of normalcy means a return to the first stage of crisis planning, resuming environmental scanning as a regular part of the crisis management effort. Thus, for the most part, the "postcrisis" period overlaps the "precrisis" period.

Many of these mainstream assumptions are challenged by a complex systems standpoint. First, it is difficult to know when the crisis has come to an end, particularly if the goal is a return to the status quo. Complexity assumes that time is not reversible; that systems, once thrown out of order, cannot return to the same state of affairs in which they were before the crisis. Choices are not predetermined by the environment; nonetheless, once a given choice is made, other options recede and cannot be recreated (Briggs & Peat, 1989). Willingly or not, from the standpoint of complexity, organizational transformation is the outcome of crisis.

The difficulty of pinpointing the end of a crisis shapes the issue of lingering effects, particularly with regard to the media. For instance, a crisis that had a strong impact on the local community may be recalled through follow-up stories on the anniversary of its occurrence (Birch, 1994). Similar crises suffered by competitors may prompt comparisons, which involve at least a brief rehash of the details of the crisis. Mainstream media occasionally report on the crisis management industry itself, generally as an accompaniment to articles on high-profile crisis events. These will often review a variety of past crises for illustrative purposes. Finally, if the crisis response was particularly noteworthy, it may be elevated to "canonical" status and become one of the prototypes regularly held up as an example by practitioners and scholars of crisis management and communication. The effect is to perpetuate public memory of the crisis in such a way that an industry cannot return to "normal." When will Prince William Sound's main claim to fame cease to be the Valdez accident? When will the U.S. nuclear power industry overcome the images of Chernobyl and Three Mile Island sufficiently to build new reactors? When will FEMA regain its reputation as an effective resource for U.S. citizens and communities facing emergency situations?

Complexity theory makes it possible to deal with these kinds of questions because it sets a crisis in a broad historical context, including both the buildup to the event and its lingering effects. As discussed in chapter 3, complexity theory views organizations holistically, emphasizing that past history and the environment influence (though they do not determine) present and future identity. Thus the organization itself appears as a process and series of interactions, a recursively constructed entity. As a result, whereas mainstream crisis expertise assumes a definite end to a crisis, complexity theory sees crisis as part of the ongoing context of organizational evolution. It does not see a return to status quo.

Just as it is difficult to mark the end point of a crisis, from a complexity standpoint, the data available in the immediate aftermath of a crisis may incompletely reflect the outcome of the crisis. This incompleteness comes both from a view of organizational entities as perpetually under construction and from the irreducibility of a complex system, whereby a part cannot stand for the whole. This data shortage affects assessment of structural damage and financial indicators but is still more pronounced in relation to stakeholder attitudes and the effects of the crisis over time. Therefore, longitudinal monitoring of crisis effects should be an important part of the postcrisis management. As Massey (2001) noted, "crisis responses do not occur in a contextual vacuum; they are part of an ongoing dialogue between organizations and stakeholders" (p. 170). As a result, he emphasized that "complete understanding of the process of crisis management will not be achieved until duration is included as a part of the analysis" (p. 170). Nonetheless, longitudinal studies are relatively rare in most crisis follow-ups, in part because research methods still have problems addressing processual aspects of communication (Miller, 2001).

In fact, the use of statistical data at all is a mixed decision from a complexity standpoint. On the one hand, both the CMT and other stakeholders find it valuable to have quantitative data available for the purpose of comparison. Such information may also provide insight into previously unconsidered vulnerabilities that should be addressed to prevent future problems, and data gathered at intervals may help the organization gain a clearer understanding of how the situation evolved by providing a series of snapshots of the emergent patterns within the system. On the other hand, much as Alvesson and Deetz (2000) warned of "subjectivity masked as objectivity," (p. 140), complex thinking suggests that managers view the evaluation as interpretive. That standpoint keeps in mind that even in quantitative research, interpretation plays a role in selecting what is to be measured and in what manner.

Complexity theory would supplement these precise quantitative measurements with more free-form qualitative assessments, keeping in mind that complex systems tend toward organizational transformation, not a return to the status quo. Therefore, a complexity-based evaluation might ask to what extent the organization has been transformed by crisis in ways that might make it more successful—as a financial player, as an employer, as a designer of new products—than it was before the crisis. From this standpoint, Bechler (2004) observed that

> by focusing mainly on crisis containment and image management, researchers and practitioners may be encouraging change-resistant cultures to maintain patterns of behavior and communication that are damaging....Reframing the popular view of crisis so that it is also perceived as a necessary and important corrective...may also enable the organization to effectively respond to other problematic behaviors that have been embedded and protected within the organizational culture. (pp. 68–69)

This transformational approach represents a shift in emphasis from organization-centric evaluations to stakeholder perceptions, and it includes long-term impact.

Complexity theory also encourages organizations to be relative more than absolute when going through crisis evaluation. For example, Pearson and Clair (1998) suggested evaluating individual crisis management activities on a continuum of success, rather than defining an entire crisis event as a success or failure. They argued that "the novelty, magnitude, and frequency of decisions, actions, and interactions demanded by a crisis suggest that no organization will respond in a manner that is completely effective or completely ineffective" (p. 67). Whether an organization averts a crisis altogether or mishandles some aspects, there will always be elements of crisis management that it performed well or needed to improve, so a relativistic evaluation is appropriate and more accurate than an overall assessment. As Urry (2003, p. 14) noted, "social life is full of what we may term 'relative failure'"; it is not an aberration but rather a "necessary consequence of incompleteness" as a system evolves. Order and disorder, the intended and the unintentional, are always interconnected in complex systems.

Pearson and Clair (1998) also noted that the relative weight of evaluative factors might differ depending on the perspective of the person carrying out the evaluation. As an example, they argued that the Exxon

Valdez incident, held up as a notorious example of poor crisis communication, could be considered a success by financial analysts. That public might be satisfied by Exxon's ability to absorb the cost of the cleanup effort without undue hardship—and, indeed, by spending less than proactive crisis prevention efforts would have cost (Pearson & Clair, 1998). Marra (1998) also noted that, just a few years after the crisis, Exxon was the world's second most profitable corporation and observed that "Exxon's lack of an appropriate crisis plan to manage the 1989 Valdez oil spill certainly didn't affect its profit of $7.5 billion in 1996" (p. 464).

Learning, Debriefing, and Revising the Crisis Plan

Harking back to the Chinese conception of crisis as both "danger" and "opportunity," many authors believe that a crisis can provide an important learning experience for the organization. For example, Mitroff et al. (1996) asserted that effective crisis management requires us to understand and integrate the lessons that previous human-caused crises have taught. Ulmer et al. (2007) spoke of this understanding in terms of a "new normal" (p. 182). Although it is difficult to achieve in practice, without such learning we run the risk of repeating our mistakes. Coombs (2007) warned against remaining a captive of past events in order to avoid information acquisition bias, calling institutional memory of past crises "both a blessing and a curse" (p. 161).

Most mainstream crisis models include a postcrisis learning stage in which managers draw lessons from their own crisis experiences and those of other organizations to prevent future recurrences (Caponigro, 2000; Gonzalez-Herrero & Pratt, 1995; O'Rourke, 1996; Pearson & Clair, 1998). Learning theory supports this reliance on lived experience. According to sensemaking concepts, crises can trigger opportunities for learning outside the normal flow of events: "People frequently see things differently when they are shocked into attention, whether the shock is one of necessity, opportunity, or threat" (Weick, 1995, pp. 84–85). Yet many, perhaps most, organizations continue to fail to learn from these experiences (Elliott et al., 2000; Gilpin, 2005; O'Rourke, 1996; Roux-Dufort, 2000). If one accepts that the most successful form of crisis management is crisis prevention and agrees with Mitroff et al. (1996) that learning is a vital factor in preventing future crises, the failure to learn from crisis events is a significant flaw in current crisis management practice. One needs only to look at NASA's second shuttle disaster to see the human and institutional costs of failure to learn.

Lack of available and reliable data is one pragmatic reason that organizations do not learn from their crisis experiences (Elliott et al., 2000). However, more compelling explanations for the dearth of postcrisis learning may be cognitive limitations, such as recollection biases. Executives have been found to remember past strategies and outcomes

as more closely correlated to current positions than objective data demonstrate (Schwenk, 1995). They "may believe that they are reviewing the
mental equivalent of a videotape of what went wrong, when it is more
likely they are making up their own movie of the event, reconstructing
a story of what happened" (Cannon, 1999, p. 417).

Various forms of hindsight bias may negatively affect the value of
retrospective sensemaking and learning (Murphy, 1991). Hindsight bias
means that "once a person knows the outcome, the reasons for that outcome seem obvious and the person cannot imagine any other outcome"
(Weick, 2001, p. 37). Among other consequences, people's hindsight bias
"tends to exaggerate the consistency of experience with their prior conceptions" (Busby, 1999, p. 111). People also have a tendency to overestimate what they could have known or should have done at the time of an
event. Furthermore, their evaluations of behavior are likely to be influenced by outcomes (Busby, 1999; Weick, 2001). For example, if a rogue
cop in an action movie defies his superiors' orders and saves the day, the
positive outcome will result in his behavior being judged as courageous
and morally correct, and he is likely to be rewarded and celebrated as
an icon of courage and independent thinking. If the same behavior leads
to the death of innocent victims, it will be judged as reckless and criminal, and the offender is likely to be punished and scorned as evidence
of what can happen when individuals fail to follow the group wisdom.
People construct histories, then tend to see the actual outcome as inevitable. Thus "hindsight both tightens causal couplings and constructs
as coupled events a history that leads directly to the outcome" (Weick,
1995, p. 28).

These instances of biased sensemaking have substantial implications
for learning from crisis situations. In both successful and unsuccessful
circumstances, attempts to draw on behaviors and generalize them or
to formalize them into procedures based on the outcome of one situation may not provide a clear guide for future situations. The reason is
that ratiocination about prior actions "occurs in a very different context
than when the action was first initiated (e.g., the outcome is known),"
and, therefore, "the reasons singled out retrospectively are likely to be
of less help for the next prospective action because they underestimate
the vast amount of uncertainty that was present during the early stages
of acting" (Weick, 2001, p. 36). Biased sensemaking suggests a linear
cause-and-effect relationship that may not always pertain or may not
even have pertained in the original instance.

In postproject review meetings, retroactive sensemaking in small
groups can also be adversely affected by real-world factors such as organizational politics, the organization's unique history, payoff structures,
and time pressures. For example, Busby (1999) noted growing levels
of frustration experienced by group members during the sensemaking
process. The increase in overall information resulting from discussions naturally led to heightened ambiguity that violated participants'

expectations of coming to some sort of definitive conclusion about the project. Such effects may abbreviate the time spent discussing and trying to filter lessons from experiences, as team members grow frustrated at their inability to locate a simple cause.

However, Busby (1999) also found that strongly cognitive methodologies such as scenario building ("What would have happened if...?") and role playing were highly effective in both exploring alternatives and sidestepping potentially uncomfortable political and interpersonal situations. Improvisational approaches such as these focus on speculative outcomes rather than diagnosing actual errors. Indeed, he found that when participants in a discussion identified past mistakes, they always refrained from probing further to uncover the reasons behind the errors, presumably to avoid direct interpersonal conflict with coworkers. Busby concluded that "understanding experience is a matter not just of examining actual events but also of generating plausible, alternative events to examine" (1999, p. 122). In other words, outcomes need to be measured not only by what actually happened but also by what could have happened that was better or worse. Busby's (1999) conclusion reinforces the recognition, supported by complexity theory, that instigating actions can have multiple outcomes and that it is important to have requisite variety in imagining organizational responses.

The exceptional features that distinguish crises present additional challenges to crisis evaluation and organizational change. The apparent uniqueness of each crisis leads some managers to decide that crises are too unusual to make close examination and change worthwhile (Elliott et al., 2000; Roux-Dufort, 2000). This was the same logic followed by the supporters of the Shoreham nuclear power plant on Long Island, who pressed forward in the wake of the 1979 Three Mile Island nuclear accident and refused to engage in dialogue about possible risks to the community, claiming that such accidents were so rare as to be practically unique. There ensued the 1986 explosion at Chernobyl, which, along with skyrocketing costs and construction delays, caused the demise of the Shoreham project (Ross & Staw, 1993).

The reaction of Shoreham's management was not unique, however. As Roux-Dufort (2000) observed, most organizations "are very reluctant to learn from crises and even to consider them as learning opportunities. Organizations address crises as if they were too exceptional to justify a learning process. The organization's priority is to come back and maintain the status quo as soon as possible, rather than exploring the extent to which the crisis is a privileged moment during which to understand things differently" (p. 26). However, failure to debrief after a crisis represents a lost opportunity for sensemaking and learning, one that may cost the organization dearly if a similar situation arises in the future (Elliott et al., 2000). The fact that the identical crisis never happens twice makes it all the more necessary for managers to acquire skills of adaptation, improvisation, and tolerance for uncertainty.

Pressured by a need to reestablish the status quo, even managers who express willingness to learn may apply only peremptory, reductive problem-solving techniques that fail to get at the real causes underlying crisis situations. Roux-Dufort (2000) examined a number of barriers to organizational learning from crises. He identified as the main culprit the urge toward normalization, or a return to conditions as close as possible to those existing prior to the crisis situation. Indeed, the classic crisis paradigm sets this restoration as one of its primary goals. Yet, Roux-Dufort (2000) argued, this push does not leave the organization time to take advantage of the learning opportunities offered. Although many authors emphasize that crises have ambiguous, complex causes that require careful investigation of multiple interlinked dynamics, organizations hurry to identify the proximate, linear cause—nearly always "human error"—in an attempt to assign blame and take prompt, visible action as a message to stakeholders. Thus oversimplification of complex circumstances is one factor that inhibits learning from crises. A general inability to define problems clearly and a pervasive sense of complacency within many organizations are also at fault and, taken together, may lead to a hasty search for scapegoats rather than a deeper consideration of organizational change (Elliott et al., 2000).

According to Roux-Dufort (2000), three types of normalization pressures adversely affect an organization's response to a crisis. *Cognitive normalization* is a sort of sensemaking shorthand in which decision makers find and accept the first plausible explanation, quickly labeling the situation based on linear, cause-and-effect reasoning models. *Psychological and affective normalization* is the force that drives managers to resolve the ambiguity of the situation as quickly as possible; together with cognitive normalization, it provides the urge to seek out scapegoats to which to assign blame for the crisis. Psychological normalization also motivates managers to seek out consultants during a crisis. Although expert advice may be helpful, reliance on multiple consultants may fragment the crisis and divide responsibility, merely assuaging anxiety rather than solving the problem. Finally, *sociopolitical normalization* is the force that makes the crisis "socially, politically and symbolically acceptable" (Roux-Dufort, 2000, p. 28). This factor, in essence, is the equivalent of seeking legitimacy, because "a crisis is a sort of breach of trust regarding the expectation of the organizational stakeholders. They are thus expecting quick responses from the organization in terms of their need for explanation, compensation and comfort" (Roux-Dufort, 2000, p. 29).

In short, normalization favors restoring a perceived status quo over deeper, double-loop learning that leads to organizational change that, in turn, may solve the fundamental problems leading to crisis. The push to achieve normalization and reestablish legitimacy as quickly as possible may also become a platform to construct a reality in which "those in positions of power seek to (re)write history to serve their own short- and long-term interests" (Elliott et al., 2000, p. 21).

These normalization tactics aid organizational efforts to restore apparent legitimacy quickly. However, they may be counterproductive in the long run by encouraging a rush to a fallacious consensus based on an overly narrow interpretation of events. For example, Roux-Dufort (2000) reviewed managerial response to a 1987 ferry wreck in the English Channel. The ferry company cooperated with regulators, who imposed a series of post-hoc technical measures designed to improve safety, but this compliance was essentially a cosmetic change and a superficial adaptation to necessity. The company did not examine the fierce competition in the ferry industry that led to an institutionalized disregard for most safety practices, overloaded ferries, cost-cutting measures such as reduced manpower and limited safety precautions on board the ferries, crowded schedules that forced the limited number of ferry crew members to work long and tiring shifts, and other hidden factors. It was easier simply to find the nearest scapegoat and make the minimum effort necessary to regain legitimacy with stakeholders. Roux-Dufort (2000) observed, "rather than considering the crisis an opportunity to question managerial assumptions and to change, they simply viewed it as an excellent pretext to consolidate the very value system and managerial beliefs that had driven to the wreck. This is what we call a zero-learning process" (p. 26).

This substitution of superficial change for deeper transformation is a frequent response to wide-scale crises. For example, the aftermath of the 1986 Bhopal tragedy was clouded by recriminations between the Indian government and Union Carbide, none of which contributed to organizational change or proved helpful to the victims. In a similar fashion, Wicks's (2001) analysis of the 1992 Westray mine disaster in Nova Scotia found multiple signs of institutionalization that caused and deepened the crisis. On the one hand, there were easily identified proximate causes for the explosion, "a deadly combination of coal dust, methane gas and sparks" (p. 660). On the other hand, there were complex "organizational and contextual factors that contributed to the regularly occurring unsafe practices," consisting mainly of a "mindset of invulnerability" that gradually became institutionalized and eventually led to a catastrophic outcome (p. 660).

Scapegoating and superficial behavioral change are not merely barriers to learning from a single crisis; they may also prove counterproductive in the long run. When scapegoats are sought within the organization, members may feel vulnerable and respond by making great efforts to hide or cover mistakes. These behaviors increase the organization's chances of spiraling into crisis by covering direct causes; less directly, they "severely hinder the potential for effective communication, cultural change and, in turn, learning. In such a setting of non-trust, key managers and operators may not only contain potentially damaging information but may reconstruct their accounts of events to protect themselves from blame" (Elliot et al., 2000, p. 18). The "veneer of legitimacy" (Wicks, 2001, p. 674) that may have been gained with external stakeholders is lost with internal stakeholders, who, by changing their behavior to reflect a loss of mutual trust, substantially alter the essence of the organization. This type of dynamic was a significant cause of the Bhopal accident, as recalled by a project engineer: "The whole industrial culture of Union Carbide at Bhopal went down the drain.... Top management decided that saving money was more important than safety. Maintenance practices became poor, and things generally got sloppy. The plant didn't seem to have a future, and a lot of skilled people became depressed and left as a result" (Weick, 1988, p. 313).

Remembering that boundaries in complex systems are fluid, this mistrust cannot be expected to remain within the organization; it will also spread through a complex maze of micro interactions to negatively affect that very legitimacy that the organization originally sought to gain. That is why "the failure to learn lessons in the aftermath of one crisis incident provides fertile ground for the incubation of future crises" (Elliott et al., 2000, p. 21). Again, this warning is exemplified by NASA's failure to look beyond proximate causes or to apply double-loop learning to examine its cultural assumptions; the Columbia tragedy was one result.

Organizations have a critical choice to make after crises. On the one hand, they can discontinue crisis evaluation after finding proximate causes, a reductionist approach that can lead to worse crises in the future. On the other hand, theories of organizational learning and complexity argue that organizations can truly learn from crises only by taking a holistic approach, going back over the history of the system and looking for interrelationships, "elements of a system that interact to create properties that have previously been unforeseen" (Elliott et al., 2000, p. 18). This type of approach is obviously in line with a complexity-based understanding of the way organizations, their stakeholders, society, the environment, and other elements interact to mutually define emergent crisis situations.

The problem of learning from crises is a serious one, because, as the enactment approach makes clear, action, knowledge, and understanding are closely intertwined. These measures are not taken in a vacuum: Each step has short- and long-term consequences, with the potential to diminish or multiply future crises. As Weick (2001) suggested, "Action during crisis is not just an issue of control, it is an epistemological issue" (p. 225), in which each step taken both reflects organizational assumptions and sets up the parameters for the next step.

Throughout this book we have argued that crisis behaviors reflect underlying values of an organization, expressing its way of interacting with its environment and treating its stakeholders. These patterns of behavior are difficult to break, but change can be brought about if managers have the mind-set and the skills to facilitate it. With that in mind, in the final section we describe principles that an organization can adopt if it regards itself as a learning organization and sees its relationships as part of a complex adaptive system that changes through continuous interactions within itself and its context.

12

Conclusion

Reframing Crisis Management in a Complex World

Walter Lippmann (1922) began the last chapter of his landmark volume *Public Opinion* with the following admission:

> I have written, and then thrown away, several endings to this book. Over all of them there hung that fatality of last chapters, in which every idea seems to find its place, and all the mysteries, that the writer has not forgotten, are unraveled.... This last chapter is merely a place where the writer imagines that the polite reader has begun to look furtively at his watch. (p. 298)

In embarking on our own conclusion, we find ourselves with much sympathy for Lippmann's plight. Given their open-ended nature, theories of complexity do not lend themselves to tidy conclusions or neat summaries, nor can we expect to offer perfect prescriptions for dealing with uncertainty and ambiguity. What we can do, and hope we have done in this book, is present a new perspective on crises and organizational life that offers fertile ground for further research and practical exploration. Our intention has been to provide a theoretical grounding for practices that embrace uncertainty and change rather than resisting them, to work toward what we have called the *expert organization*. As we have repeatedly emphasized, the new viewpoint departs from traditional management approaches in significant respects.

A good portion of this book has described barriers to effective crisis management. Many of those barriers have been imposed by traditionally accepted management attitudes and practices; many could be removed by a complexity-directed approach. In this chapter, we summarize fundamental differences between the two approaches, and we derive some new, complexity-based management principles that, we argue, can mitigate crises better than current approaches.

It should be clear by now that the differences between mainstream crisis management and complexity-based crisis management involve far more than tactics; they involve fundamental differences in worldview.

We see major differences between the two in terms of four levels of beliefs: The first level of broad philosophical assumptions leads to the second level, beliefs about organizations. Those beliefs in turn lead to the third level, epistemological assumptions, which control the fourth level, approaches to crisis management. The two parallel sets of assumptions derived from mainstream and complexity theory were summarized earlier, in table 8.1.

At their most fundamental, traditional and complexity-based worldviews originate from beliefs about control and prediction. Mainstream management theories encourage broad philosophical assumptions that future events can be predicted and controlled, at least to some extent, and that certainty and stability are the desired outcomes of a crisis situation. These philosophical assumptions have channeled managers toward corollary beliefs that organizational entities are discrete from their environments; both can be systematically managed to produce planned outcomes. In turn, managers' assumptions about organizations restrict their thinking about preferred forms of organizational knowledge. These epistemological assumptions favor knowledge in the form of systematized information gathering and a rational, analytical approach to decision making. Finally, all three sets of assumptions—philosophical, organizational, and epistemological—lead to crisis management that emphasizes detailed planning, centralized responsibility in a crisis management team, and preserving the organization's assets, as well as restoring the status quo.

Parallel to these mainstream concepts is a set of assumptions derived from complexity theory. On the philosophical level, complexity-based thinking views the future as uncertain and unstable rather than predictable; it is amenable not to control but rather to influence through multiple interactions, both endogenous and exogenous to the organization. As for assumptions about organizations, complexity-based thinking views them as quite unlike mechanical systems, characterized instead by emergent behavior and constantly in flux. The same sense of flux also typifies the next level of epistemological assumptions, in which knowledge takes the form of action—but action that combines information with sensemaking. Finally, these complexity-based approaches create novel assumptions about crisis management itself. Here crises emerge as change agents necessary for the long-term legitimacy of the organization, and crisis preparation becomes a matter of improvisation, with choices among many possible actions, rather than highly defined or goal-oriented planning.

Building on this structure, this chapter concludes our argument that a complexity worldview can profoundly transform an organization's approach to crisis management. We consolidate the complexity and learning theories discussed in prior chapters into a model based on three related dimensions that we think are most central to the expert organization: knowledge/awareness, adaptability, and complexity absorption.

Table 12.1. Shifting Paradigms and Elaborating Practices

Complexity Aspect	Moving From:	Moving Toward:	Techniques, Strategies, Practices
Knowledge/ awareness			
Dense interconnectedness; arbitrary nature of boundaries (organization not seen as fixed, isolated entity); nonlinearity; irreducibility	Gathering information; analytical decision making	Working from a foundation of solid familiarity with the organization and its internal/ external constituents and environments; gathering more information and sharing it appropriately; situation assessment through carefully developed intuition (which relies on knowledge) and active sensemaking	Ongoing communication at all levels and with stakeholders; incorporation of communities of practice; issues management; environmental scanning
Adaptability			
Fractals; change through iterative microinteractions	Planning based on a static/control model	Sensitivity to changes in context and ability to make decisions rapidly (which relies on knowledge and awareness)	Scenario planning with focus on process rather than output; emphasis on developing teamwork skills at all levels of the organization through frequent simulations
Complexity absorption			
Unpredictability; self-organization; constant evolution	Seeking understanding through uncertainty reduction	Enactment through acceptance of ambiguity (possible only when the organization can rely on adaptability)	Flexible organization; ongoing practice; implementation of all of the above

Each dimension builds on the previous one, so that complexity absorption incorporates the preceding two. Table 12.1 summarizes the fundamentals of each dimension in complexity terms and shows what changes each introduces compared with the mainstream model. We explicate each dimension in depth in the following sections, and we suggest techniques and organizational practices that reflect these basic principles.

Knowledge/Awareness

In both mainstream and complexity-based approaches, crisis management begins with the acquisition of knowledge. In both approaches, relationships with various stakeholders are an important means of acquiring this knowledge, primarily because relationships create feedback loops that encourage organizational learning.

However, attitudes toward knowledge differ profoundly between mainstream and complexity-based approaches to crisis. Negative feedback loops prevail in traditional organizations, in which budgets, forecasts, reports, plans, and other written documents constrain change by reminding employees to stay close to explicit objectives (MacLean & MacIntosh, 2003; Mitleton-Kelly, 2003). In contrast, continuous learning in an adaptive organization relies on positive feedback loops. As discussed in chapter 3, positive feedback loops amplify change rather than dampen it, helping to diffuse constant adjustments around the organization.

In practical terms, positive feedback operates by focusing people's attention on the impacts their decisions have on both the environment and subsequent choices, thus ensuring that recent decisions enter into and influence the ongoing decision problem. The way in which each decision's effects become part of the next decision context reflects the sense of history in a complex system. In chapter 3, we explained the concept of fractals as an unfolding set of patterns, each of which arises out of the preceding pattern that it both resembles and transforms in subtle ways. Similarly, organizations that are conscious of decision processes as positive feedback can view their actions as a set of fractals that evolves over time, each decision reflecting the ones that came before.

In addition to preserving continuity, positive feedback loops have particular relevance to changeable environments, because such feedback works to keep options open, encourage innovation, and preserve adaptiveness. According to Lewin and Regine (2003), "when leaders are able to embrace small changes throughout their organizations, which propagate in an exponential manner, the organizations become highly adaptive and are able to evolve in a continually changing business environment" (p. 177).

Positive feedback fosters organizational change much like Kauffman's (2000) concept of the "adjacent possible." As discussed earlier, this concept regards change as gradually spreading out from localized interactions among individual agents. As the "adjacent possible" expands, large-scale changes diffuse throughout a complex adaptive system. In a similar way, Lewin and Regine (2003, pp. 175–76) viewed each change in an organization "like a drop of rain falling on a still pond," which "can create a ripple effect; that is, it replicates and spreads throughout the system," so that the new behavior is no longer localized but comes to characterize the entire organization. Alternatively, change can accumulate and then release suddenly, "like a grain of sand that falls on a sand pile, which sometimes causes large avalanches"; in this type of change, "something old collapses, and something new emerges."

Both of these types of change are relevant to crisis management. The first type—the gradual diffusion of local change—is something we might see in an organization that is not operating in crisis mode. It might reflect responses to patterns observed during the issues management process or scenarios brainstormed by members of a CMT. It reflects the type of positive feedback in which actions are taken in response to sensemaking observations and their impacts become part of the ongoing decision context. The second type of change—an avalanche of pent-up disturbance—more typifies the exigencies during crisis, in which an organization can be forced into radical self-transformation.

Networks and Dialogue

Regardless of its rate, the character of change is contingent on the network of relationships that form throughout an organization, reaching beyond its permeable boundaries into the environment in which it operates. As has been the case in nearly all aspects of crisis management, traditional and complexity-based approaches rely on different types of relationships to accomplish different goals and to coordinate their members in response to environments of varying uncertainty and turbulence. As we have seen, traditional organizations emphasize codified information and procedures, more than shared values and beliefs, to coordinate their members in a relatively impersonal manner. Such codification and impersonality efficiently coordinate large numbers of people and work best "in a world in which events are predictable and from which uncertainty has been banished" (Boisot & Child, 1999, p. 244). However, crises seldom occur in such a world.

An alternative approach replaces codified information with personal networks of face-to-face relationships in which people achieve coordination by sharing beliefs and values. This approach works particularly well when "the world is perceived as a discernible set of alternative possibilities that...require a repertoire of flexible responses" (Boisot & Child, 1999, p. 244). Such groups require more maintenance—more time and social resources—than traditional management approaches. However, they lend themselves to adaptation and improvisation in ways that more rigid approaches do not.

Despite the instability and inefficiencies of managing by personal, face-to-face networks, the adaptiveness and requisite variety built into this approach make it highly effective for crisis preparedness. Such groups are characterized not only by reliance on face-to-face relationships but also by a variety of actions typical of an enacting organization: a nonhierarchical approach in which members define goals through an ongoing process of negotiation (Boisot & Child, 1999). This approach requires a participative and networked organizational community whose members have the authority to initiate actions with the knowledge that these reflect organizational identity in a larger sense.

What would such information associations look like, in practical terms? Complexity-oriented thinkers suggest replacing formalized scanning procedures with human "boundary spanners" (Daft & Weick, 1984) to get "a greater diversity of people interacting at any one time" (Lewin & Regine, 2003, p. 179), and "reducing internal communication barriers" (Thomas, Clark & Gioia, 1993, p. 258). These actions suggest that crisis team members need to spend time with rank-and-file employees whose observations can make all the difference in implementing needed change before a crisis forces change on the organization. Experts who have studied efforts to operate organizations as complex systems have noted the importance of replacing hierarchy with networks that feature diversity in both knowledge arenas and job levels (Boisot & Child, 1999; Lewin & Regine, 2003). In such an organization, knowledge can be fluently diffused throughout the network. Along similar lines, the ideally designed CMT would follow the same logic as the communicative theory of the firm described by Kuhn and Ashcraft (2003) in terms of self-organizing, networked "communities of practice" that constitute organizations composed of "interconnected elements situated in a social and historical context" (p. 42).

Although democratic at the core, crisis preparation works best with intensive interactions among a relatively small group of people. Therefore, the CMT must remain at the center of the crisis response process. In practical terms, that means the various key organizational functions should be represented as they are in traditional planning; but in terms of learning and adaptation, this small team can coordinate more easily and cultivate such essential elements as shared identity and intuition (Eisenhardt, 1989; Klein, 1998; Weick, 1995). Pragmatically, those who are responsible for taking action during a crisis should be the first to gain the necessary awareness and abilities.

Most important, complex responsive processes suggest that change will naturally emerge in and around the organization as a result of daily micro interaction. As ideas and knowledge diffuse throughout the organization, its members will become increasingly capable of self-organizing in times of crisis, perhaps to the point at which the original CMT is rarely required to intervene. However, a management team that develops the habit of active engagement and enactment as a group, as well as with others and the environment, is most able to begin micro interactions within the organization that can bring about real transformation.

Schwenk (1995) described this process in terms of organizational learning, arguing that "when environmental change invalidates existing assumptions, organizational members articulate and advocate elements of the new knowledge structure. These are then combined through the activities of key decision makers...into a new knowledge structure which is communicated to the other members of the organization" (p. 478). Thus management does not become a separate, elitist part of the planning process but performs a dual function, as both liaison responding to the concerns of subordinates and diffusion agent communicating the new assumptions through the organizational network of relationships.

In chapter 5, we argued that knowledge management is a social process, not a set of procedures to generate and organize data. The outcome of knowledge management is the ability to reflect on the implications of knowledge and thus to use knowledge heuristically in order to identify and highlight the organization's guiding assumptions. These guiding assumptions give a reasonable amount of stability; put in complexity terminology, they provide an "attractor," a set of parameters that guide organizational behavior and decisions about actions to follow. At the same time, the attractor does not inhibit decision making in the manner of the negative feedback practiced by traditional management. Although it constrains wandering outside its parameters, an attractor has unlimited internal possibilities, and it therefore allows requisite variety that preserves the range of possible responses by which crisis managers can respond to changing exigencies. In this way, Johnson & Johnson responded to the Tylenol poisonings by bringing together its crisis team to decide first whether they were going to follow the company's mission statement that put customers before profits. Having affirmed this "attractor," the CMT—operating without any written crisis plan—was free to make a broad range of decisions as long as they did not stray beyond the guiding principles of the mission statement (Murphy, 1996).

The J&J case supports the argument that an explicit crisis plan is less important than coordinating a sense of what an organization stands for— that is, making explicit an attractor that guides how the organization will navigate the uncertainties and rapidly changing circumstances of a crisis. This sense accrues through team learning and dialogue. Earlier, in chapter 5, we pointed out that dialogue is an important component of team learning, helping to construct that shared sense of an organization. However, that shared sense does not imply consensus; rather, it indicates awareness among team members of multiple, sometimes irreconcilable, points of view. This view of dialogue was described in terms of a need for "joint action," or coordination of activity that can produce, and tolerate, "unintended and unpredictable outcomes," along with anticipated results (Heath et al., 2006, p. 344).

As has often proved to be the case, mainstream management and adaptive approaches differ about both procedures for and outcomes of dialogue. Communication theorists distinguish between a focus on content in dialogue and a focus on process. A content focus views the purpose of dialogue as achieving a result, generally consensus; it is goal oriented, and the dialogue facilitator tries to foster active listening and participative decision making. In contrast, the process view of dialogue is nondirective; it involves unpredictable routes toward insight into one's own beliefs and those of other group members. Hammond and Sanders (2002) termed this content-process dualism "the convergent-emergent tension," reflecting whether a dialogue is "converging on a problem or series of problems, or whether it is open, waiting for a mutual direction to emerge" (pp. 19–20).

Looking at dialogue in terms of crisis management, mainstream approaches favor goal orientation and consensus reflected in a unitary crisis plan. Complexity-based approaches favor open-ended discussions whose primary purpose is less to achieve policy or factual resolution than to achieve *"relational resolution* that develops from understanding each other's emotions, values, interests, and positions" (Heath et al., 2006, pp. 367–68; italics in original). Despite this greater open-endedness, the process-based approach often results in highly pragmatic outcomes: Mutual understanding helps to create a "workable level of uncertainty," as well as "allow[ing] the social system to converge on collective rather than random actions" (Hammond & Sanders, 2002, pp. 17, 19). This style of emergent dialogue assists expert learning, as team members recognize patterns of values and behaviors in their organization and arrive at general assumptions that guide responses to crisis.

In addition, because crises are typified by lack of information, we argued in chapter 5 that CMTs need to develop expertise, or intuition, which we defined as the ability to sense complete patterns where information is incomplete or uncertain. Based on this intuition, crisis managers can employ "bricolage," a type of improvisation that bases decisions on the knowledge at hand rather than waiting for more data. Johnson & Johnson's senior managers employed bricolage and improvisation to respond quickly to a bewildering situation rather than waiting until the poisoner was discovered (he or she was never found). This expertise, we argued, is affiliated with enactment, whereby organizations respond to crises through self-conscious actions, relying not on crisis plans or data so much as on an overall shared sense of guiding principles. This overall sense is developed during a "reflective process of planning" that precedes a crisis, regardless of specific "lists of do's and don't's or lessons learned" in a crisis plan itself (Weick, 1995, p. 52).

Of course, improvisation in itself is not enough to ensure a good outcome. For example, the handling of the Catholic Church sex abuse scandal proceeded via bricolage—by putting together whatever actions would keep the scandal quiet, such as relocating abusive priests. Similarly, NASA engineers employed their own style of improvisation to fix up unpredictable technology before space shuttle launches. To be productive, improvisation should grow out of team decision making (TDM) processes that foster "shared intuition" (Eisenhardt, 1989, 1999) or "team mind" (Klein, 1998). The aim is to create a setting favorable to collective learning. McKinney et al. (2005) described the coordinated cognitions and behavior of "swift action teams" such as airline cockpit crews: teams of relative strangers whose communication "can improve the shared mental model of a situation....These shared mental models are very helpful when information is ambiguous or must be acquired and shared in a timely manner" (pp. 206–7). Like the "heedful interrelating" of sense-making, the shared mental models of TDM are developed through frequent and regular collaborative interaction among group members. More than any other aspects, the abilities to have a successful dialogue and to improvise are essential to TDM and learning processes.

Culture and Leadership

In talking about organizational patterns, values, and general assumptions, we are essentially talking about organizational culture: "a set of shared philosophies, ideologies, values, beliefs, expectations, attitudes, assumptions, and norms" (Marra, 1998, p. 465). Organizational culture itself is emergent, developing through daily local interaction among people within the organization. Organizational actions thereby are embedded in their context, "all being value-laden and meaningful only in terms of their relation to other symbols" (Linstead & Grafton-Small, 1992, p. 334). Sometimes the cultural context creates a single, shorthand meaning that everyone in the group understands. Snowden (2002) gave an example of "a coded reference to past experience. 'You're doing a Margi' may be praise or blame—without context the phrase is meaningless" (p. 105). Culture thus functions to create rapid common understanding without the need to codify expertise laboriously.

At its best, culture incorporates multiple voices in the organization without demanding consensus. The reason is that "any event, organizational or otherwise, is capable of different interpretations by different interests, and hence an event 'contains' several meanings simultaneously" (Linstead & Grafton-Small, 1992, p. 336). Through dialogue, employees work out organizational culture as an emergent Burkean "wrangle in the marketplace" of ideas involving a "differential process of meaning construction, as different aims are pursued, different persuasive strategies employed to mobilize support or resistance and groups attempt to define or re-define their boundaries and membership" (Linstead & Grafton-Small, 1992, p. 336).

The relationship between communication, culture, and crises is one key to crisis response. For example, Marra (1998) ascribed the failure or success of crisis plans to the degree of communicative culture present within an organization: open or closed, hierarchical or flat, revealing or secretive. Similarly, Smallman and Weir (1999) focused on cultural factors as aggravating elements that blind organizations to an imminent crisis or keep them from handling it swiftly. The culture itself may create blind spots, or "information rejection, that is, information is systematically filtered out...according to the rules and structure of the organizational culture in which the communication process is set" (Smallman & Weir, 1999, p. 38). We have already seen the impact of culture on obliviousness to impending crises in Enron, NASA, and the Catholic Church. As Kersten (2005, p. 545) commented, "More often than not, it is the organization's standard operating practices, its paradigmatic or cultural outlook on life, its use and distribution of information, and its implicit or explicit expectations of its employees that shaped the key perceptions and decision-making events causing the crisis."

Compounding these blind spots, the potential distortion of organizational routines that occurs in a crisis situation may affect the ability of information to flow smoothly through networks inside and outside of an organization. Information flow will be least fluid in organizations with a strict hierarchical culture, in which communication is highly formalized. As a result, losses or interruptions that crises cause in formal channels will have a stronger impact on such rigid organizations than on more informal, loosely coupled structures in which information is exchanged through a flexible range of means, a dynamic "achieved process" that must be "worked at and continually reviewed" (Smallman & Weir, 1999, p. 35). Marra (2004) described the practical impact of these two approaches. He contrasted a hierarchical, authoritarian, planned approach to decision making in a crisis involving a student athlete with the approach favored by AT&T, in which employees were free to make decisions quickly without first obtaining permission from the top. He found that the AT&T approach was far more effective in mitigating the crisis, and he credited that success to "the ability of 'cogs' to make 'big wheel' decisions":

> Most organizations consist of people in separate categories: big wheels, cogs, and specialists....But when tension is running high, all work together as specialists among specialists on an equal footing....Then cogs can become big wheels. Whatever their status in the formal hierarchy, they are trained intensively every day so that—based on their experience—they can take complete command. (Pfeiffer, 1989, as cited in Marra, 2004, p. 320)

The type of diffused decision-making authority that Marra described appears to undercut traditional centralized authority, a focused leadership that mainstream experts consider necessary to coordinate crisis response. However, management theorists are quick to point out that complexity-based leadership does not mean abdicating the leadership function; rather, it means redefining what the leader does. In organizations that operate as complex adaptive systems, leaders are "not invested in establishing themselves as the ultimate authority"; instead of directing people, they "cultivate conditions where people could self-organise and restructure around the existing issues" (Lewin & Regine, 2003, p. 173). Opt (2008) stated the problem somewhat differently, explaining that "human beings *intervene* into, rather than *control*, the symbolic constitution of needs, relationship, and worldview. Human beings *affect*, but not control, the development of the communicatively constituted human social system. They *interact* with, rather than act on, others" (p. 234; italics in original). Thus influence rather than control is the chief characteristic of leadership in a complexity-based organization.

In contrast to the intervention perspective, traditional management thinking gives central place to the command-and-control elements of leadership: defining the mission and steering the organization toward clearly defined goals that realize that mission. Clearly, complexity-based leadership discourages these notions of control. According to Ashmos et al. (2000, p. 591), all organizations share similar problems of disorder, conflict, and ambiguity, but managers who adopt complexity thinking "will work with these problems rather than impose a simplified order on them." In these organizations, conflict and disarray are seen as inescapable and even desirable elements of the sensemaking process.

In practical terms, managers can create what we described in chapter 5 as the learning environment and learning space. These are not necessarily physical spaces—although managers who engage in complexity-based thinking may also create literal spaces (Lewin & Regine, 2003). Rather, learning environments and learning spaces refer to an organizational climate that facilitates team learning, without mandating the precise conditions or the outcome of learning. Creating these conditions requires managers to unlearn control-oriented practices and instead encourage learning by providing the environment—physical or cultural— in which it can take place. That environment might simply be an organizational climate in which employees feel free to talk about organizational practices, policies, and power structures or to engage in nonproductive activity (Rifkin & Fulop, 1997). These dialogues often have unintended outcomes that transform the parties involved in ways they could not have anticipated. However, dialogues generally do not effect change unless "someone of sufficient power in the institution/organization involved...could shelter the process and see to it that its results were implemented" (Heath et al., 2006, p. 350). Thus it is up to the manager both to create occasions for reflection and dialogue and then translate the resulting insights into actions.

As these characteristics imply, the knowledge/awareness aspect of crisis management is particularly used during precrisis environmental scanning, in which a CMT needs to appraise a situation, find patterns, identify areas of ignorance, and imagine a wide variety of potential responses. Knowledge/awareness underlies the second dimension of an expert organization: adaptability, or the capacity to respond, reappraise, and revise quickly.

Adaptability

One way to build on expert learning is to combine reflection with decision making, turning awareness into action. A particularly popular technique is scenario planning, best undertaken after organizations have identified patterns that suggest a potential crisis and are looking for ways to respond. Mainstream crisis management authors commonly urge that managers, to maintain expertise, perform simulations to test the crisis plan and keep it current (Caponigro, 2000; Coombs, 2007; Dyer, 1995; Fearn-Banks, 2007). The rationale is that simulations can expose facets of a crisis situation that managers have previously failed to consider.

In themselves, simulations do not provide adequate crisis training. For example, Klein (1998) observed a number of organizational CMTs as they carried out their simulations and called them "the worst ones we have observed" (p. 238). The particular teams that earned this soubriquet were led by the CEO; the other team members were lower level managers such as the director of security. The companies held training exercises and crisis management seminars a few times a year. Despite this training—which reflects at least the basic level recommended by the mainstream literature—the crisis teams suffered from problems ranging from communication troubles to a tendency to focus on minor details and lose sight of the larger situation. Team members hesitated to make decisions as they tried to gather all possible information before committing to a course of action. They failed to recognize cues and opportunities. There were power struggles within the team itself, as certain members attempted to take control and micromanage the work of others. Team members gave orders to subordinates but lacked awareness of how long it would take to execute those orders, throwing off the pace of the entire exercise. In the end, Klein pronounced himself "surprised by their incompetence" (1998, p. 238).

What may have undermined these simulation failures was action without reflection. We previously noted that mere improvisation to dodge a crisis seldom works. Likewise, simulations offer the chance for enactment, but simulations alone are not sufficient for a team to develop group intuition, a shared sense of identity, and the ability to act without complete information. Given the resources required for simulations, such a full-scale effort cannot be made very often. When they do occur, their value can be improved if, between simulations, the team practices its skills through training.

Addressing this problem, Gavetti and Levinthal (2000) proposed combining "offline" cognitive methods that do not require direct experience of a situation, such as scenario development and planning exercises, with the "online" results of direct experience—as well as "grey area" practices such as simulations. They found that experience contributed most to enhanced performance. However, adding offline processes shortened the learning cycle, reduced risk, and provided a broader array of options. Scenario planning, in particular, encourages managers to "think different" and imagine a situation in great detail, turning it into a sort of future narrative (Brown & Starkey, 2000; De Geus, 1999; Schwartz, 1998; Smallman & Weir, 1999). Scenario planning therefore provides an intense, ongoing discussion forum without the drawbacks of infrequent immersion in simulated crises.

The exercise of planning also allows teams to practice their reasoning processes without producing, as the final output, a set of procedures to which the organization is expected to adhere. Scenario planning is essentially a way of encouraging executives to leave behind assumptions that normally go unquestioned as a means of learning through mental exploration. It assumes that "our present ways of knowing, and what we already know, form an inadequate basis for learning about an uncertain future" (Brown & Starkey, 2000, p. 112). Despite the flexibility and open-endedness that these expert learning exercises encourage, they are carefully structured—it is just that the "goal" of flexibility and teamwork is quite different from the certainty aspired to in traditional crisis exercises.

It is important to keep in mind that openness to an uncertain future does not mean abandoning the past. As chapter 3 showed, complexity theory gives primacy to the history of a system, noting that patterns are continually reiterated, as they evolve by means of small changes that eventually accrete into overall configurations. By the same token, crisis planning teams should not unquestioningly adopt best practices from other organizations or from their own past experiences; because of the small changes that accrete through positive feedback, the same crisis never happens twice. Instead, "past practices...could be used as a means for increasing alertness and for creating a mental map to facilitate the discovery of innovative responses" (Thiétart & Forgues, 1997, p. 137). Past experiences can also serve as "sources of inspiration for new responses to an, as yet, unknown future" and thereby help to create the "repertoire of responses" needed to prepare for a highly contingent future (p. 137).

One of the most effective ways to put all of these skills to work is through improvised teamwork. An analogy with another type of team endeavor—a soccer game—provides some idea of how improvisation prepares organizations to cope with an uncertain environment. A soccer coach does not attempt to plan out every step of a match beforehand using analytical methods and to make sure team members are familiar with and have access to the plan. He or she knows that there is no way to predict exactly what will take place during the course of the game and that it is futile to try to control circumstances. Numerous factors can affect the play, from the weather to the conditioning of the players, their expectations, and those of any fans who may come to watch. (Have they been having a winning or a losing season? Is the other team one of the best, one of the worst, or in the middle of the league? Is either team in the running for a cup?) An unfamiliar field, a hostile crowd, poor morale, or overconfidence can all mean trouble. The coach also knows that sometimes a team plays well but loses the match regardless of performance.

Despite all these uncertainties, the skilled coach does not sit back and send the players out to face the other team unprepared. Instead, he or she trains them regularly, both individually and together. He or she has them practice teamwork over and over, until these moves nearly become second nature. During practice sessions, the coach tries to recreate as many different circumstances as possible, so that team members grow used to dealing with a wide variety of situations; they know how to appraise circumstances and spot openings. The coach also makes sure that each player is familiar with the unique skills of teammates and their individual weaknesses, so that everyone knows on whom to count for whatever the situation demands. In short, the coach does whatever he or she can to turn the players into an expert team: individuals aware of their mutual interdependencies, conscious of each others' strengths and weaknesses, and with the ability to rapidly draw distinctions and intuit patterns.

The complexity of organizational crises is even greater than the soccer match analogy suggests. Whereas sports events have clear goals, the goals in a crisis situation are not always clear and may even change over time. The rules are not known equally to everyone playing and may also be subject to change. Players might not even realize that there is a game in progress until it has already started. Sometimes there is no hard-and-fast rule about what it means to win or lose or how to tell when the game is over. In addition, during organizational exigencies, the players cannot always be certain which team they belong to—and, in fact, many players probably belong to several teams: employee, member of the community, customer. Players from different teams may be on the same side or may form alliances and even new teams. Groups of players may decide to form new teams. Individual players or teams may be dismissed at any time if others decide they should no longer be allowed to play. The field itself changes in shape and texture according to the actions of the different players. Over time—sometimes gradually, sometimes suddenly—a whole new game begins.

Given these shifting circumstances, no attempts to predict or plan can prepare players completely. Instead, the focus needs to be on making sure the players—the members of the organization and particularly its leadership and crisis team—are capable of understanding and acting on circumstances as they arise: that they can improvise. In fact, one of the best means of ensuring preparedness is through mindful improvisation—what the soccer team metaphor exemplifies. One reason that people balk at the thought of improvisation as strategy is that they mistake it for unskilled decision making, the type of unconsidered, escalating reaction that entangled Enron. Instead, successful improvisation requires a synthesis of skills and abilities honed to the point at which the individual or group can call on them as needed, in what Weick (2001) referred to as just-in-time strategy. Like many of the other practical approaches recommended in this chapter, improvisation is more suited to a complex, changing environment than to traditional planning methodologies. As Weick (2001, p. 151) observed: "When it is assumed that survival depends on variation, then a strategic plan becomes a threat because it restricts experimentation and the chance to learn that old assumptions no longer work." Effective improvisation closely resembles what Eisenhardt and Martin (2000) called dynamic capabilities. In relatively stable conditions, they resemble codified routines. However, in more turbulent settings, "they are simple, experiential, unstable processes that rely on quickly created new knowledge and iterative execution to produce adaptive, but unpredictable outcomes" (Eisenhardt & Martin, 2000, p. 1106). This type of response requires both advanced learning capabilities and extensive prior knowledge of the organization, its multiple embedded networks, and the context in which it operates.

Improvisation deals with the unforeseen; it works without a prior stipulation; and it works with the unexpected. Just as important, improvisation works as enactment, combining action with reflection; and it works with the same pattern-recognition skills that we earlier associated with expertise. For example, Klein (1998) described expert rock climbers' process of learning to identify leverage points during their climb. These points have no single common characteristic; they may be crevices or protrusions in the rock, something to be grasped by a hand, a notch just large enough to insert the toes, or a ledge too narrow to stand on but wide enough to take some of the weight off the upper body or to serve as a launching pad to jump to a larger shelf. What is more, there are no "absolute" leverage points: The environment (visibility, wet or dry, hot or cold) and condition of the climber (fresh or tired, relative strength, size, and weight) all play a part in determining what may be used. The leverage points cannot be identified in a photograph. The same holds will not work for everyone, even on the same climb. Rock climbers must learn to make rapid and effective real-life decisions; they must learn to improvise and to exercise adaptability.

Another way to conceptualize adaptability is in terms of "fitness landscapes," a concept from Kauffman's (1995, 2000) studies of evolution within complex biological systems. To model evolutionary processes, Kauffman envisioned species as located in a "landscape," or environment, populated by other species. Each species' needs impinge on the others' survival. Each species simultaneously attempts to maximize its fitness— its survivability—and the activities each species launches to improve its own position shift the fitness landscape shared by others, who like-wise respond, creating an ongoing series of interactions and adaptations interspersed with temporary periods of stability. Using network theory, Kauffman created various types of fitness landscapes that model organizations' success within their own environments. Organizational theorists have described this shifting world of fitness landscapes as "a discernible set of alternative possibilities that can be responded to but which require a repertoire of flexible responses. Contingencies can be managed but rarely optimally" (Boisot & Child, 1999, p. 244). In chapter 3 we discussed Ashby's (1954) law of requisite variety, which theorists have used to argue that organizations, like natural life forms, evolve most successfully when they "enhance their capacity to match the variety of the environments they encounter"; as their requisite variety improves, "so do their survival chances and reproductive fitness improve" (Boisot & Child, 1999, p. 238). The more turbulent and varied the environment, the greater the need to match environmental demands by keeping in play a range of possible responses. From this standpoint, the ability to improvise is one of the most important skills that crisis teams can cultivate.

This kind of improvisational fluency is one of many ways in which organizations can cultivate their adaptiveness, keeping in play a range of strategies that might dovetail with various aspects of a changeable environment. This adaptiveness complements other approaches that we have already discussed. First, it supports the redefinition of the leader as someone who guides rather than controls. Second, adaptiveness encourages the cultivation of close relationships among top management in a crisis team, requiring each to maintain a network of relationships with rank-and-file employees that provides input to the crisis team, as well as a web of adjacent micro interactions through which change can diffuse throughout the system. Knowledge/awareness and adaptation allow an organization to seize opportunities in a complex environment rather than resist change. In the next section, we argue that these qualities allow an organization to absorb complexity rather than attempt to reduce it.

Complexity Absorption

It is the effort to achieve certainty, stability, and control that fundamentally distinguishes mainstream crisis management from complexity-based thinking. For both managers and publics, one of the worst challenges in a crisis is the sense of being out of control, of not knowing what will happen next. Therefore, as Heath and Millar (2004, p. 9) pointed out, "A crisis can be viewed as a struggle for control. Persons who are affected by a crisis look to responsible parties to control their actions or to create actions that reduce the harm of the crisis." Yet crises are all about uncertainty and lack of control, a factor that can create a number of negative repercussions. Tyler (2005) argued that "it seems impractical if not unethical to keep insisting that managers must regain control.... [That] may only exacerbate what is already a highly stressful and difficult situation for most organizational employees" (p. 569). The strain of seeking to restore a perceived status quo or demonstrate control over ultimately uncontrollable circumstances can mean that these goals overshadow more productive ways of handling the situation at hand.

In contrast, complexity-based thinking affirms lack of control rather than avoiding it. A complexity mind-set urges managers to tolerate uncertainty, ambiguity, and change; to put less emphasis on managerial prediction-and-control responsibilities and more on a leader's ability to guide and influence an organization in a positive direction. Although renouncing the status quo leads to short-term managerial discomfort, in the longer term organizations that tolerate a variety of potential responses to crisis and pursue a range of possible outcomes often adapt more successfully to turbulent times than those that hold on to stability.

The two parallel approaches to crisis—complexity-based cultivation of requisite variety and a traditional goal orientation to restore the status quo—express themselves in a set of behaviors relating to complexity reduction or complexity absorption. On the one hand, traditional organizations often react to a turbulent, complex environment by choosing behavioral strategies aimed at complexity reduction, which attempt to increase control and predictability in a struggle to contain the perceived complexity. Most crisis management experts recommend this complexity reduction approach in order to reduce confusion and get the crisis off the table at the earliest possible moment.

In crisis management, therefore, a high valuation on stability and certainty reflects complexity reduction. Organizations that pursue a strategy of complexity reduction attempt to impose order on apparent anarchy by simplifying their internal structure, sharpening their goals, formalizing and centralizing decision-making processes, and seeking to achieve a state of predictable, stable equilibrium. Complexity reduction is the traditional approach taken by managers and often advocated by management books and MBA programs that define good managers as "those who achieve stability and balance in a system, and are able to minimize sudden and unpredictable change" (Ashmos et al., 2000, p. 580). Those who fail to do so are less favored in a modernist regime that values order and predictability (Holtzhausen, 2000).

On the other hand, organizations may instead attempt to adapt to turbulent times through complexity absorption. This type of approach aims to preserve "behavioural plasticity"; it involves "the creation of options and risk-hedging strategies" and tolerance for "multiple and sometimes conflicting representations of environmental variety" (Boisot & Child, 1999, p. 238). Complexity absorption therefore involves acceptance of rapid change and the ability to accommodate multiple possible responses.

In its preference for multiplicity and aversion to specialization, complexity absorption often runs counter to traditional approaches to crisis management—for example, advice that organizations develop one detailed crisis plan to meet each of six categories in a crisis typology (Pauchant & Mitroff, 1992). In contrast, complexity absorption means that each of the various options and representations may fit the problem situation less exactly than the goal-directed, data-driven plans often espoused by most crisis experts. However, the advantage of giving up exactitude and certainty lies in increased flexibility and adaptiveness, so that "the range of environmental contingencies that an organism can deal with in this way is greater than in a regime of specialization" (Boisot & Child, 1999, p. 238). Given the unpredictability of crises, it is more important to preserve options than to commit resources to relatively narrow possibilities.

In fact, this flexible approach is advocated by disaster experts. For example, after Hurricane Katrina hit New Orleans in 2005, Kathleen Tierney, director of the Natural Hazards Center, commented, "You don't plan for an individual event. You set up a framework where you are able, first of all, to analyze your vulnerabilities and then plan to address those vulnerabilities....It is not a principle...that one plans for a single disaster or type of disaster" (Flatow, September 16, 2005). This kind of framework leaves a margin of strategic ambiguity that, if the crisis management team has appropriate skills and expertise, provides a rough guide without the cognitive or procedural limitations of a more traditional plan.

Organizations that absorb complexity do more than simply preserve multiple options. They also use three other adaptive types of strategies (Ashmos et al., 2000; Gilpin & Murphy, 2005). First, they gather ongoing information about their own business and culture, their stakeholders, and evolving conditions in their business and social environment. Second, they give priority to relationships, both internal and external; these networks both generate fresh knowledge and aid sensemaking by creating an arena for multiple voices. Third, organizations that absorb complexity are willing to be flexible and to self-organize as they generate new information, then fresh knowledge, then revised goals. Each of these additional strategies flows from a fundamental principle of complexity-based crisis management: the preservation of a requisite variety of viewpoints and possible actions in response to a turbulent environment.

Of course, not all organizations need to absorb complexity. The need depends on the context: As long as events transpire in a historically predictable fashion, complexity-reduction techniques can be effective. In a predictable and stable environment, in which change happens slowly and crises are rare, organizations can afford to adopt a strategy of complexity reduction based on codified information, routines, and standards. That is the most efficient management approach, and one that characterizes the dominant crisis management paradigm. For example, public utilities follow this type of complexity reduction strategy with respect to weather exigencies, preplacing public service announcements with radio stations and producing prewritten news releases about repair schedules. These measures work well when the future is predictable; it is really only a question of when severe weather will occur, not whether it will. However, this form of complexity reduction does not work when the need goes beyond information dissemination, when public opinion becomes volatile and focuses on societal values and contingencies, as transpired in the case of Hurricane Katrina. In those cases, crisis managers need to absorb complexity by developing a range of possible responses that coevolve with changing events.

This kind of crisis-prone and turbulent environment undermines the predictability, stability, and control that the dominant paradigm requires. Instead, by giving up a measure of control and efficiency, organizations faced with crises gain critical adaptiveness that enhances their control over events in the long run.

In fact, despite the indirectness of using influence rather than control, organizations that practice complexity-based management can shape their own futures, at least to some extent. Complexity theory above all studies the emergence of order from unstable conditions. That order comes out of local interactions among individual agents, most of which are reasoned and not random. The eventual state of a complex system may be uncontrollable and unpredictable. However, even though the precise outcome cannot be foreseen, "the range of broad possibilities is, to some extent, determined by the simple rules, or the connections which were applied to generate the new order" (MacLean & MacIntosh, 2003, p. 150). From this standpoint, the character of the relationships that compose the organization operates as a type of parameter determining the character of the evolving organization, much as an initial algorithm shapes fractal patterns that emerge over a phase space. That is the reason that repeated crises strongly suggest a faulty organizational culture rather than bad luck or environmental pressures; the organizational culture sets the behavioral patterns that emerge over time. Organizational scholars who use complexity theory therefore view crisis as "a non-desirable situation which might in fact be created and perpetuated by the same organizational actors who try to solve it," so the crisis is "the consequence of deterministic rules which originate from the actions of the organizational actors themselves" (Thiétart & Forgues, 1997, p. 120).

If actors create a crisis, then they have the power to shape its course. Thus it is inaccurate to assume, as some do, that lack of a crisis-planning document, linear goals, or a command-and-control structure means that organizations can do nothing to prepare themselves for crises but passively react to circumstances. The types of expertise and enactment inherent in complexity absorption specifically regard active engagement as a key to simultaneously learning about and shaping events. That is the reason that complexity-absorbing organizations look very much like enacting organizations as described by Daft and Weick (2001). Enacting organizations assume the world to be indeterminate, yet they actively engage with it rather than passively reacting to occurrences. In comparison with complexity-reducing organizations, they are less likely to rely on hard data or analytical decision models and are more involved in testing actions, experimenting with new processes and programs, and attempting to shape the environment through their behavior. Enacting organizations are heavily invested in learning by doing. Like the effective decision makers in Dörner's (1996) simulations, managers in these organizations play an active part in the entire interpretation cycle, from awareness to sensemaking to learning.

In addition, there are clear similarities between enacting organizations—or ones that behave in a complexity-absorbing manner—and the model of the expert organization described in chapter 7. This expert model relies on relationships and interactions in an effort to influence the environment by applying the skills of sensemaking: acting on information and noting how those actions influence both the environment and the organization itself. These approaches focus on developing skills and knowledge, along with effective information sharing and learning processes, as a means of handling rapid, unforeseen change. These processes are flexible rather than rigid, situated rather than sweeping, suggestive rather than prescriptive. Through interaction among individuals and groups, both within and outside perceived boundaries, the expert organization engages in continuous learning while simultaneously enacting its knowledge. This approach creates the dynamic, emergent character of organizations that operate as complex systems and that therefore constantly self-organize and evolve.

Different organizations will have different ways of encouraging complexity absorption, some more successfully than others. Regardless of individual variations, however, all organizations can structure their change processes; all can influence the character of the change they want to implement. One way to do so is by understanding the "deep rules" that influence the organization's response to its environment (MacLean & MacIntosh, 2003) and then attempting to reform dysfunctional aspects of that response. By so defining their identity, organizations essentially supply their own attractors, and they can thereby shape the characters of their own futures, even though they cannot control or predict their details.

Conclusion

As should be evident by now, a complexity-based approach to crisis management poses a challenge to researchers and practitioners accustomed to thinking along positivist and rationalist lines. Organizational science is solidly entrenched in these modes of thinking, and changes may be hard-won. Managers and other experts who are heavily invested in the context of traditional crisis management may find some of the ideas advanced in this book unsettling. In particular, the ideas of relinquishing close planning and of depending on improvisation appear to work against precepts long valued in the management community.

In the end, however, what we are recommending is not a radical break but a further step in the evolution of a field. During the past few years, events have repeatedly shown that classic, goal-oriented, closely planned crisis management is not optimal in most exigencies. What we have done is to supply a new model—that of complex adaptive processes—that provides a full explanation of where and why traditional crisis management falls short, as well as a theoretical basis for the shortfall. In addition, we have suggested a comprehensive theory that guides such approaches, emphasizing the confluence of complexity theory, expert knowledge, and enacting organizations. This book itself is embedded in a growing context of scholarship that argues against a tightly managed approach and for participation by multiple voices in crisis preparations by generating identity/attractors, devising solutions to existing problems, and helping with repair efforts if a crisis strikes.

Broadly, we urge a paradigm shift for crisis management in which uncertainty, adaptiveness, and improvisation replace certainty, goal orientation, and control. We do not argue that complexity thinking should completely replace traditional management approaches in all cases, but we do recommend matching the tools to the job at hand. For example, there will be instances "where we have statistical confidence that interactions between variables are highly stable over time," such as association between educational level and salary (Elliott & Kiel, 1997, p. 71). In these cases, a classic control-and-prediction model works well. This is the realm of known limits—"the only legitimate domain of best practice" (Snowden, 2002, p. 106)—in which organizations can appropriately impose order and create predictable environments so they can conduct their customary business. However, by definition crises do not occupy this known space; complexity-based crisis planning works best in a realm of uncertainty, lack of control, and emotion. As McKie (2001) pointed out, reductive management beliefs should not disproportionately influence the "people-centered and unpredictable" (p. 80) world of communication and organizations.

At the risk of oversimplifying, we have drawn stark contrasts between complexity-based thinking and traditional crisis management in order to make our points more clearly. However, the two approaches are not always diametrically opposed. Indeed, many of our recommendations, such as a leader who facilitates change and a participative management, fit comfortably within traditional management thinking. These commonalities can make it easier for managers to evolve from current rationalist crisis planning approaches to an adaptive, complexity-based approach.

In this book we have made a start. However, the passage from theory to practice is essential if organizations are to meet the demands of an increasingly tightly coupled world. That will happen only if decision makers are persuaded that complexity theory has pragmatic value in an organizational context. Historically speaking, science does not become accepted as part of the mainstream unless those in a position of power are prepared to mobilize resources to support its legitimacy. In making that switch, managers can contribute to the emergence of a new type of crisis management that genuinely addresses the complexity of our turbulent world.

REFERENCES

Abel, T. (1998). Complex adaptive systems, evolutionism, and ecology within anthropology: Interdisciplinary research for understanding cultural and ecological dynamics. *Georgia Journal of Ecological Anthropology, 2*, 6–29.

Alexander, D. (2000). Scenario methodology for teaching principles of emergency management. *Disaster Prevention and Management, 9*(2), 89–97.

Alvesson, M., & Deetz, S. (2000). *Doing critical management research.* London: Sage.

Americans doubt safety of nation's food supply in wake of pet food contamination. (2007, April 3). *PR Newswire.* Retrieved June 15, 2007, from SmartBrief database.

Americans doubtful of food supply's safety: Survey. (2007, April 4). *Progressive Grocer.* Retrieved June 15, 2007, from LexisNexis Academic database.

Appelbaum, S. H., & Goransson, L. (1997). Transformational and adaptive learning within the learning organization: A framework for research and application. *Learning Organization, 4*(3), 115–28.

Argyris, C. (1977, September–October). Double loop learning in organizations. *Harvard Business Review,* 115–24.

Argyris, C. (1994, July–August). Good communication that blocks learning. *Harvard Business Review,* 77–85.

Ashby, R. W. (1954). *An introduction to cybernetics.* London: Methuen.

Ashmos, D. P., Duchon, D., & McDaniel, R. R., Jr. (2000). Organizational responses to complexity: The effect on organizational performance. *Journal of Organizational Change Management, 13*(6), 577–94.

Baca, M. E. (2007, May 1). Looking to baby your pet? *Minneapolis Star-Tribune,* p. 1E. Retrieved June 6, 2007, from LexisNexis Academic database.

Barley, S. R., & Tolbert, P. S. (1997). Institutionalization and structuration: Studying the links between action and institution. *Organization Studies, 18*(1), 93–117.

Barnett, C., & Pratt, M. G. (2000). From threat-rigidity to flexibility: Toward a learning model of autogenic crisis in organizations. *Journal of Organizational Change Management, 13*(1), 74–88.

Barton, L. (1993). *Crisis in organizations: Managing and communicating in the heat of chaos.* Cincinnati, OH: South-Western.

Barton, L. (2001). *Crisis in organizations: II.* Cincinnati, OH: South-Western.

Bazerman, M. H., & Watkins, M. D. (2004). *Predictable surprises: The disasters you should have seen coming and how to prevent them.* Boston: Harvard Business School Press.

Bechler, C. (2004). Reframing the organizational exigency: Taking a new approach in crisis research. In D. P. Millar & R. L. Heath (Eds.), *Responding to crisis: A rhetorical approach to crisis communication* (pp. 63–74). Mahwah, NJ: Erlbaum.

Becker, M. C. (2001). Managing dispersed knowledge: Organizational problems, managerial strategies, and their effectiveness. *Journal of Management Studies, 38*(7), 1037–51.

Behr, P., & Barbaro, M. (2003, August 29). No time to stop blackout, report finds; power surges were too sudden for human response, grid operator PJM says. *Washington Post.* Retrieved November 13, 2005 from http://shelob.ocis.temple.edu:2062/universe/document?_m=ca20b165-deed036c5c0cc77558fe0a44&_docnum=4&wchp=dGLbVlz-zSkVb&_m-d5=bd6b48e3bdc1f37a10b446e7b9c5b7a3.

Bell, K. (2007, March 23). Pet food manufacturer says it has no idea why animals have died. *Buffalo News,* p. A6.

Benoit, W. L. (1997). Image repair discourse and crisis communication. *Public Relations Review, 23*(2), 177–86.

Berger, C. R. (1997). Message production under uncertainty. In G. Philipsen & T. L. Albrecht (Eds.), *Developing communication theories* (pp. 29–55). Albany: State University of New York Press.

Birch, J. (1994). New factors in crisis planning and response. *Public Relations Quarterly, 39*(1), 31.

Blackler, F., & McDonald, S. (2000). Power, mastery and organizational learning. *Journal of Management Studies, 37*(6), 833–51.

Blankets with DDT spur outcry. (1992, December 16). *The Dallas Morning News,* p. A27.

Bodeen, C. (2007, April 12). *Pet food crisis shows China's food safety woes are an international concern.* Retrieved June 6, 2007, from LexisNexis Academic database.

Boisot, M. (2003). Is there a complexity beyond the reach of strategy? In E. Mitleton-Kelly (Ed.), *Complex systems and evolutionary perspectives on organisations: The application of complexity theory to organisations* (pp. 185–202). New York: Pergamon Press.

Boisot, M., & Child, J. (1999). Organizations as adaptive systems in complex environments: The case of China. *Organization Science, 10*(3), 237–52.

Boje, D. M. (2000). Phenomenal complexity theory and change at Disney: Response to Letiche. *Journal of Organizational Change Management, 13*(6), 558–66.

Boland, R. J., Jr., Tenkasi, R. V., & Te'eni, D. (1994). Designing information technology to support distributed cognition. *Organization Science, 5*(3), 456–75.

Botan, C. H. (1997). Ethics in strategic communication campaigns: The case for a new approach to public relations. *Journal of Business Communication, 34*(2), 188.

Boyd, J. (2000). Actional legitimation: No crisis necessary. *Journal of Public Relations Research, 12*(4), 341–53.

Brewton, C. (1987). Managing a crisis: A model for the lodging industry. *Cornell Hotel and Restaurant Administration Quarterly, 28*(3), 10–15.

Bridges, A. (2007, April 18). *Second tainted pet food ingredient found.* Retrieved June 1, 2007, from LexisNexis Academic database.

Briggs, J., & Peat, F. D. (1989). *Turbulent mirror: An illustrated guide to chaos theory and the science of wholeness.* New York: Harper & Row.

Bronn, P. S., & Olson, E. L. (1999). Mapping the strategic thinking of public relations managers in a crisis situation: An illustrative example using conjoint analysis. *Public Relations Review, 25*(3), 351–68.

Brown, A. D., & Starkey, K. (2000). Organizational identity and learning: A psychodynamic perspective. *Academy of Management Review, 25*(1), 102–20.

Brown, J. S., & Duguid, P. (2000). *The social life of information.* Boston, MA: Harvard Business School Press.

Brown, L. (2003). *Columbia Accident Investigation Board releases final report.* Retrieved June 21, 2007, from http://caib.nasa.gov/news/press_releases/pr030826.html.

Burke, P. (2000). *A social history of knowledge: From Gutenberg to Diderot.* Cambridge, UK: Polity Press.

Burnett, J. J. (1998). A strategic approach to managing crises. *Public Relations Review, 24*(4), 475–88.

Burros, M. (2006a, September 27). Tainted spinach brings demand for new rules. *The New York Times,* pp. F2, F5.

Burros, M. (2006b, December 7). Growing peril on path from field to plate. *The New York Times,* p. 8.

Burros, M. (2007, March 13). Government offers guidelines to fresh-food industry. *The New York Times,* pp. A1, A17.

Busby, J. S. (1999). The effectiveness of collective retrospection as a mechanism of organizational learning. *Journal of Applied Behavioral Science, 35*(1), 109–29.

Byrne, D. S. (1998). *Complexity theory and the social sciences: An introduction.* London: Routledge.

Cancel, A. E., Cameron, G. T., Sallot, L. M., & Mitrook, M. A. (1997). It depends: A contingency theory of accommodation in public relations. *Journal of Public Relations Research, 9*(1), 31–63.

Cancel, A. E., Mitrook, M. A., & Cameron, G. T. (1999). Testing the contingency theory of accommodation in public relations. *Public Relations Review, 25*(2), 171–97.

Canizares, A. (1999, December 14). Goldin stands by "faster, better, cheaper" credo. Retrieved June 21, 2007 from http://www.space.com/news/goldin_nasa_991214.html.

Cannon, D. R. (1999). Cause or control? The temporal dimension in failure sensemaking. *Journal of Applied Behavioral Science, 35*(4), 416–38.

Canon-Bowers, J. A., & Bell, H. H. (1997). Training decision makers for complex environments: Implications of the naturalistic decision making perspectives. In C. E. Zsambok & G. Klein (Eds.), *Naturalistic decision making* (pp. 89–110). Mahwah, NJ: Erlbaum.

Canon-Bowers, J. A., Salas, E., & Pruitt, J. S. (1996). Establishing the boundaries of a paradigm for decision-making research. *Human Factors, 38*(2), 193–205.

Caponigro, J. R. (2000). *The crisis counselor: A step-by-step guide to managing a business crisis.* Lincolnwood, IL: Contemporary Books.

Carneiro, A. (2000). How does knowledge management influence innovation and competitiveness? *Journal of Knowledge Management, 4*(2), 87.

Cheney, G., & Christensen, L. T. (2001). Organizational identity: Linkages between internal and external. In F. M. Jablin & L. L. Putnam (Eds.), *The new handbook of organizational communication: Advances in theory, research, and methods* (pp. 231–69). Thousand Oaks, CA: Sage.

China executes food safety chief for bribery. (2007, July 10). *Daily Mail.* Retrieved July 11, 2007 from http://www.dailymail.co.uk/pages/live/articles/news/worldnews.html?in_article_id=467427&in_page_id=1811.

Choo, C. W. (2001). The knowing organization as learning organization. *Education + Training, 43*(4/5), 197–205.

Christensen, L. T. (2007, May). License to critique: Corporate communication as polyphony. Paper presented at the annual meeting of the International Communication Association, San Francisco, CA.

Churchman, C. W. (1967). Wicked problems. *Management Science, 14*(4), B141–B142.

Cilliers, P. (1998). *Complexity and postmodernism.* London: Routledge.

Columbia Accident Investigation Board. (2003, August). *Report: Vol 1.* Retrieved June 21, 2007, from http://caib.nasa.gov/news/report/pdf/vol1/chapters/introduction.pdf.

Conan Doyle, A. (1894/1960). Silver Blaze. *The complete Sherlock Holmes.* New York: Doubleday.

Conrad, C. (2003). Setting the stage: Introduction to the special issue on "corporate meltdown." *Management Communication Quarterly, 17*(1), 5–19.

Cook, S. D. N., & Brown, J. S. (1999). Bridging epistemologies: The generative dance between organizational knowledge and organizational knowing. *Organization Science, 10*(4), 381–400.

Cooksey, R. W. (2001). What is complexity science? A contextually grounded tapestry of systemic dynamism, paradigm diversity, theoretical eclecticism. *Emergence, 3*(1), 77–103.

Coombs, W. T. (1999). *Ongoing crisis communication: Planning, managing and responding.* Thousand Oaks, CA: Sage.

Coombs, W. T. (2000). Crisis management: Advantages of a relational perspective. In J. A. Ledingham & S. D. Bruning (Eds.), *Public relations as relationship management: A relational approach to the study and practice of public relations* (pp. 73–93). Mahwah, NJ: Erlbaum.

Coombs, W. T. (2007). *Ongoing crisis communication: Planning, managing and responding* (2nd ed.). Thousand Oaks, CA: Sage.

Coombs, W. T., & Holladay, S. J. (2001). An extended examination of the crisis situations: A fusion of the relational management and symbolic approaches. *Journal of Public Relations Research, 13*(4), 321–40.

Cope, J., & Watts, G. (2000). Learning by doing: An exploration of experience, critical incidents and reflection in entrepreneurial learning. *Journal of Knowledge Management, 6*(3), 104–24.

Daft, R. L., & Weick, K. E. (1984). Toward a model of organizations as interpretive systems. *Academy of Management Review, 9*(2), 284–95.

Daft, R. L., & Weick, K. E. (2001). Toward a model of organizations as interpretation systems. In K. E. Weick (Ed.), *Making sense of the organization* (pp. 241–57). Oxford, UK: Blackwell.

Daneke, G. A. (1997). From metaphor to method: Nonlinear science and practical management. *International Journal of Organizational Analysis, 5*(3), 249–66.

D'Aveni, R. A., & Macmillan, I. C. (1990). Crisis and the content of managerial communications: A study of the focus of attention of top managers in surviving and failing firms. *Administrative Science Quarterly, 35,* 634–57.

Davenport, T. H., & Prusak, L. (1998). *Working knowledge: How organizations manage what they know.* Boston, MA: Harvard Business School Press.

Dawson, R. (2000). Knowledge capabilities as the focus of organizational development and strategy. *Journal of Knowledge Management, 4*(4), 320–27.

De Geus, A. (1997). *The living company.* London: Brealey.

Deetz, S. (1995). *Transforming communication, transforming business: Building responsive and responsible workplaces.* Cresskill, NJ: Hampton Press.

Dent, E. B. (1999). Complexity science: A worldview shift. *Emergence, 1*(4), 5–19.

Discard tainted blankets, groups told. (1992, December 13). *The Dallas Morning News,* p. 6A.

Dixon, M. A. (2004). Silencing the lambs: The Catholic Church's response to the 2002 sexual abuse scandal. *Journal of Communication and Religion, 27,* 63–86.

Dixon, N. M. (2000). *Common knowledge: How companies thrive by sharing what they know.* Boston, MA: Harvard Business School Press.

Dörner, D. (1996). *The logic of failure: Recognizing and avoiding error in complex situations.* Reading, MA: Perseus.

Dozier, D. M., Grunig, L. A., & Grunig, J. E. (1995). *Manager's guide to excellence in public relations and communication management.* Mahwah, NJ: Erlbaum.

Dyer, S. C. (1995). Getting people into the crisis communication plan. *Public Relations Quarterly, 40*(3), 38–40.

Easterby-Smith, M. (1997). Disciplines of organizational learning: Contributions and critiques. *Human Relations, 50*(9), 1085–1113.

Edwards, J. C. (2001). Self-fulfilling prophecy and escalating commitment. *Journal of Applied Behavioral Science, 37*(3), 343–60.

Eisenhardt, K. M. (1989). Making fast strategic decisions in high-velocity environments. *Academy of Management Journal, 32*(3), 543–76.

Eisenhardt, K. M. (1999). Strategy as strategic decision making. *Sloan Management Review, 40*(3), 65–72.

Eisenhardt, K., & Martin, J. (2000). Dynamic capabilities: What are they? *Strategic Management Journal, 21,* 1105–21.

Elliott, D., Smith, D., & McGuinness, M. (2000). Exploring the failure to learn: Crises and the barriers to learning. *Review of Business, 21*(3/4), 17–24.

Elliott, E., & Kiel, L. D. (1997). Nonlinear dynamics, complexity, and public policy: Use, misuse, and applicability. In R. A. Eve, S. Horsfall, & M. E. Lee (Eds.), *Chaos, complexity, and sociology: Myths, models, and theories* (pp. 64–78). Thousand Oaks, CA: Sage.

Enron named most innovative for sixth year. (2001, February 6). Retrieved July 7, 2007, from http://www.enron.com/corp/pressroom/releases/2001/ene/docs/15-MostInnovative-02-06-01-LTR.pdf.

Farr, K. (2000). Organizational learning and knowledge managers. *Work Study, 49*(1), 14–18.

Fearn-Banks, K. (2007). *Crisis communications: A casebook approach* (3rd ed.). Mahwah, NJ: Erlbaum.

Feds: Don't eat your spinach. (2006, September 15). *Grand Rapids Press,* p. A1.

Ferdig, M. A. (2000, April). Complexity theories: Perspectives for the social construction of organizational transformation. Paper presented at the meeting of the Midwest Academy of Management Annual Conference, Chicago.

Ferguson, S. D. (1994). *Mastering the public opinion challenge.* Burr Ridge, IL: Irwin.

Festinger, L. (1957). *A theory of cognitive dissonance.* Stanford, CA: Stanford University Press.

Finch, M. R., & Welker, L. S. (2004). Informed organizational improvisation: A metaphor and method for understanding, anticipating, and performatively constructing the organization's precrisis environment. In D. P. Millar & R. L. Heath (Eds.), *Responding to crisis: A rhetorical approach to crisis communication* (pp. 189–200). Mahwah, NJ: Erlbaum.

Fink, S. (1986). *Crisis management: Planning for the inevitable.* New York: AMACOM.

Fiol, C. M., & Lyles, M. A. (1985). Organizational learning. *Academy of Management Review, 10*(4), 803–13.

Fishman, D. A. (1999). ValuJet Flight 592: Crisis communication theory blended and extended. *Communication Quarterly, 47*(4), 345–75.

Flatow, I. (Host). (2005, September 16). Preparing for future disasters. *Talk of the Nation: Science Friday* [Radio broadcast]. Washington, DC: National Public Radio. Retrieved July 15, 2007 from http://www.npr.org/templates/story/story.php?storyId=4851388.

Franklin, B. (1743). *Poor Richard's almanac.* New York: Peter Pauper.

Frederick, W. C. (1998). Creatures, corporations, communities, chaos, complexity. *Business and Society, 37*(4), 358–89.

Fugel, J. A. (1996). Planning is critical to effective crisis communications. *Rural Telecommunications, 15*(3), 62–65.

Gavetti, G., & Levinthal, D. (2000, March). Looking forward and looking backward: Cognitive and experiential search. *Administrative Science Quarterly, 45*, 113–37.

Gerlach, L. P. (1987). Protest movements and the construction of risk. In B. B. Johnson & V. T. Covello (Eds.), *The social and cultural construction of risk* (pp. 103–45). Dordrecht, Netherlands: Reidel.

Gherardi, S. (1999). Learning as problem-driven or learning in the face of mystery? *Organization Studies, 20*(1), 101–24.

Giddens, A. (1984). *The constitution of society: Outline of a theory of structuration.* Cambridge, UK: Polity Press.

Gilpin, D. R. (2005). A complexity-based scrutiny of learning from organizational crises. In K. A. Richardson (Ed.), *Managing organizational complexity: Philosophy, theory, application* (pp. 374–88). Greenwich, CT: Information Age.

Gilpin, D. R. (in press). Narrating the organizational identity: Reframing the role of the news release. *Public Relations Review.*

Gilpin, D. R. & Murphy, P. (2005). Reframing crisis management through complexity. In C. H. Botan & V. Hazleton (Eds.), *Public Relations Theory II.* (pp. 375–92). Mahwah, NJ: Erlbaum.

Gladwell, M. (1996, January 22). Blowup. *The New Yorker, 71*, 32–36.

Goldberg, J., & Markóczy, L. (2000). Complex rhetoric and simple games. *Emergence, 2*(1), 72–100.

Goldman, A., & Lee, D. (2007, May 4). Reported pet deaths at 8500, FDA says. *Los Angeles Times*, p. C3. Retrieved June 6, 2007, from LexisNexis Academic database.

Gonzalez-Herrero, A., & Pratt, C. B. (1995). How to manage a crisis before—or whenever—it hits. *Public Relations Quarterly, 40*(1), 25–29.

Gotsi, M., & Wilson, A. M. (2001). Corporate reputation: Seeking a definition. *Corporate Communications: An International Journal, 6*(1), 24–30.

Gottschalk, J. A. (Ed.). (1993). *Crisis response: Inside stories on managing image under siege.* Washington, DC: Visible Ink Press.

Grunig, J. E. (2001). Two-way symmetrical public relations: Past, present, and future. In R. L. Heath (Ed.), *Handbook of public relations* (pp. 11–30). Thousand Oaks, CA: Sage.

Haeckel, S. H. (1999). *Adaptive enterprise: Creating and leading sense-and-respond organizations.* Boston: Harvard Business School Press.

Hammond, S. C., & Sanders, M. L. (2002). Dialogue as social self-organization: An introduction. *Emergence, 4*(4), 7–24.

Harvey, M. G., Novicevic, M. M., Buckley, M. R., & Ferris, G. R. (2001). A historic perspective on organizational ignorance. *Journal of Management Psychology, 16*(6), 449–68.

Hayek, F. A. (1945). The use of knowledge in society. *American Economic Review, 35*(4), 519–30.

Hearit, K. M. (1994). Apologies and public relations crises at Chrysler, Toshiba and Volvo. *Public Relations Review, 20*(2), 113–25.

Hearit, K. M., & Courtright, J. L. (2004). A symbolic approach to crisis management: Sears' defense of its auto repair policies. In D. P. Millar & R. L. Heath (Eds.), *Responding to crisis: A rhetorical approach to crisis communication* (pp. 201–12). Mahwah, NJ: Erlbaum.

Heath, R. L. (1997). *Strategic issues management: Organizations and public policy challenges.* Thousand Oaks, CA: Sage.

Heath, R. L. (2004). Telling a story: A narrative approach to communication during crisis. In D. P. Millar & R. L. Heath (Eds.), *Responding to crisis: A rhetorical approach to crisis communication* (pp. 167–88). Mahwah, NJ: Erlbaum.

Heath, R. L., & Millar, D. P. (2004). A rhetorical approach to crisis communication: Management, communication processes, and strategic responses. In D. P. Millar & R. L. Heath (Eds.), *Responding to crisis: A rhetorical approach to crisis communication* (1–17). Mahwah, NJ: Erlbaum.

Heath, R. L., Pearce, W. B., Shotter, J., Taylor, J. R., Kerstein, A., Zorn, T., et al. (2006). The processes of dialogue: Participation and legitimation. *Management Communication Quarterly, 19*(3), 341–75.

Heiss, B. M. (2006, June). Experts, actions, and concepts in transactive memory networks: Preserving the dynamic properties of complex organizational knowledge. Paper presented at the annual meeting of the International Communication Association, Dresden, Germany.

Henderson, D. (2007, April 21). Tainted pet food reaches human fare. *The Boston Globe.* Retrieved May 30, 2007, from http://www.boston.com/business/globe/articles/2007/04/21/tainted_pet_food_reaches_human_fare?mode=PF.

Holder, T. L. (2004). Constructing response during uncertainty: Organizing for crisis. In D. P. Millar & R. L. Heath (Eds.), *Responding to crisis: A rhetorical approach to crisis communication* (pp. 51–62). Mahwah, NJ: Erlbaum.

Holtzhausen, D. R. (2000). Postmodern valves in public relations. *Journal of Public Relations Research, 12*(1), 93–114.

Hosansky, D. (2002). Food safety. *CQ Researcher, 12*(38), 897-920.

Ice, R. (1991). Corporate publics and rhetorical strategies: The case of Union Carbide's Bhopal crisis. *Management Communication Quarterly, 4*(3), 341–62.

Introna, L. D. (2003). Complexity theory and organizational intervention? Dealing with (in)commensurability. In E. Mitleton-Kelly (Ed.), *Complex systems and evolutionary perspectives on organisations: The application of complexity theory to organisations* (pp. 205–19). New York: Pergamon Press.

Irvine, R. B., & Millar, D. P. (1996). Debunking the stereotypes of crisis management: The nature of business crises in the 1990s. In L. Barton (Ed.), *New avenues in risk and crisis management* (Vol. 5, pp. 51–63). Las Vegas: University of Nevada Las Vegas Small Business Development Center.

Janis, I. L. (1972). *Victims of groupthink: A psychological study of foreign-policy decisions and fiascoes.* Boston, MA: Houghton Mifflin.

Kahneman, D., & Tversky, A. (1979). Prospect theory: An analysis of decision under risk. *Econometrica, 47*(2), 263–92.

Karniol, R., & Ross, M. (1996). The motivational impact of temporal focus: Thinking about the future and the past. *Annual Review of Psychology, 47,* 593.

Kash, T. J., & Darling, J. R. (1998). Crisis management: Prevention, diagnosis and intervention. *Leadership and Organization Development Journal, 19*(4), 179–86.

Kauffman, J. A. (2005). Lost in space: A critique of NASA's crisis communications in the Columbia disaster. *Public Relations Review, 31,* 263–75.

Kauffman, S. (1995). *At home in the universe.* London: Penguin Books.

Kauffman, S. (2000). *Investigations.* New York: Oxford University Press.

Kent, M. L., & Taylor, M. (2002). Toward a dialogic theory of public relations. *Public Relations Review, 28*(1), 21–37.

Kersten, A. (2005). Crisis as usual: Organizational dysfunction and public relations. *Public Relations Review, 31*(4), 544–49.

Kersten, A., & Sidky, M. (2005). Re-aligning rationality: Crisis management and prisoner abuses in Iraq. *Public Relations Review, 31*(4), 471–78.

Kets de Vries, M. F. R., & Miller, D. (1984). *The neurotic organization.* San Francisco: Jossey-Bass.

Khatri, N., & Ng, H. A. (2000). The role of intuition in strategic decision making. *Human Relations, 53*(1), 57–86.

King, A. W., & Ranft, A. L. (2001). Capturing knowledge and knowing through improvisation. *Journal of Management, 27*(3), 255.

Klein, G. (1998). *Sources of power: How people make decisions.* Cambridge, MA: MIT Press.

Knights, D., Noble, F., Vurdubakis, T., & Willmott, H. (2001). Chasing shadows: Control, virtuality, and the production of trust. *Organization Studies, 22*(2), 311.

Koschmann, T. (1999). Toward a dialogic theory of learning: Bakhtin's contribution to understanding learning in settings of collaboration. In C. Hoadley (Ed.), *Computer support for collaborative learning* (pp. 308–13). Mahwah, NJ: Erlbaum.

Kuhn, T., & Ashcraft, K. L. (2003). Corporate scandal and the theory of the firm: Formulating the contributions of organizational communication studies. *Management Communication Quarterly, 17*(1), 20-57.

Lagadec, P. (1993). *Preventing chaos in a crisis: Strategies for prevention, control, and damage limitation* (J. M. Phelps, Trans.). New York: McGraw-Hill.

Laudon, K., & Starbuck, W. H. (1996). Organizational information and knowledge. In M. Warner (Ed.), *International encyclopedia of business and management* (pp. 3923–33). London: Routledge/Thompson Business Press.

Lerbinger, O. (1997). *The crisis manager: Facing risk and responsibility.* Mahwah, NJ: Erlbaum.

Letiche, H. (2000). Phenomenal complexity theory as informed by Bergson. *Journal of Organizational Change Management, 13*(6), 545–57.

Levett, G. P., & Guenov, M. D. (2000). A methodology for knowledge management implementation. *Journal of Knowledge Management, 4*(3), 258-70.

Levinthal, D. A., & Warglien, M. (1999). Landscape design: Designing for local action in complex worlds. *Organization Science, 10*(3), 342–57.

Lewin, R., & Regine, B. (2003). The core of adaptive organizations. In E. Mitleton-Kelly (Ed.), *Complex systems and evolutionary perspectives on organisations: The application of complexity theory to organisations* (pp. 167–83). New York: Pergamon Press.

Lin, R.-G. (2006, September 11). E. Coli spurs review of lettuce farms. *The Los Angeles Times,* p. B1.

Lindenmann, W. K. (1998). Measuring relationships is key to successful public relations. *Public Relations Quarterly, 43*(4), 18–27.

Linke, C. G. (1989). Crisis: Dealing with the unexpected. In B. Cantor & C. Burger (Eds.), *Experts in action: Inside public relations* (pp. 166–78). New York: Longman.

Linstead, S., & Grafton-Small, R. (1992). On reading organizational culture. *Organization Studies, 13*(3), 331–55.

Lippmann, W. (1922). *Public opinion.* New York: Free Press Paperbacks.

Lissack, M. R. (1997). Of chaos and complexity: Managerial insights from a new science. *Management Decision, 35*(3–4), 205–19.

Lissack, M. R. & Roos, J. (1999). *The next common sense: The e-manager's guide to mastering complexity.* London: Nicholas Brealey Publishing.

Lopes, G. (2007, May 2). FDA appoints Acheson food-safety czar; contamination spurs new post. *The Washington Times,* p. C08. Retrieved May 30, 2007, from LexisNexis Academic database.

Lorin, J. F. (2007, February 4). Consumers still worried about spinach after *E. coli* contamination. Retrieved June 1, 2007, from LexisNexis Academic database.

Lukaszewski, J. E. (1993). The Exxon Valdez paradox. In J. A. Gottschalk (Ed.), *Crisis: Inside stories on managing image under siege* (pp. 185–213). Detroit, MI: Visible Ink Press.

MacLean, D., & MacIntosh, R. (2003). Complex adaptive social systems: Towards a theory for practice. In E. Mitleton-Kelly (Ed.), *Complex systems and evolutionary perspectives on organisations: The application of complexity theory to organisations* (pp. 149–65). New York: Pergamon Press.

Magnier, M. (2007, May 30). The world: China sends message on food, drug scandals; a death sentence for an ex-official reflects the pressure on Beijing. *The Los Angeles Times,* p. A1.

Maier, C. T. (2005). Weathering the storm: Hauser's vernacular voices, public relations and the Roman Catholic Church's sexual abuse scandal. *Public Relations Review, 31*(2), 219–27.

Malagutti, V. (2004). *Buconero SpA: Dentro il crac Parmalat.* Rome: Laterza.

Malpas, J., & Wickham, G. (1995). Governance and failure: On the limits of sociology. *Australian and New Zealand Journal of Sociology, 31,* 37–50.

Marion, R. (1999). *The edge of organization: Chaos and complexity theories of formal social systems.* Thousand Oaks, CA: Sage.

Marquardt, M. J. (1996). *Building the learning organization.* New York: McGraw-Hill.

Marra, F. J. (1998). Crisis communication plans: Poor predictors of excellent crisis public relations. *Public Relations Review, 24*(4), 461–74.

Marra, F. J. (2004). Excellent crisis communication: Beyond crisis plans. In D. P. Millar & R. L. Heath (Eds.), *Responding to crisis: A rhetorical approach to crisis communication* (pp. 311–25). Mahwah, NJ: Erlbaum.

Mårtensson, M. (2000). A critical review of knowledge management as a management tool. *Journal of Knowledge Management, 4*(3), 204–16.

Martin, R. M., & Boynton, L. A. (2005). From liftoff to landing: NASA's crisis communications and resulting media coverage following the Challenger and Columbia tragedies. *Public Relations Review, 31,* 253–61.

Massey, J. E. (2001). Managing organizational legitimacy: Communication strategies for organizations in crisis. *Journal of Business Communication, 38*(2), 153–82.

Mathews, K. M., White, M. C., & Long, R. G. (1999). The problem of prediction and control in theoretical diversity and the promise of the complexity sciences. *Journal of Management Inquiry, 8*(1), 17–31.

McCampbell, S., Clare, L. M., & Gitters, S. H. (1999). Knowledge management: The new challenge for the 21st century. *Journal of Knowledge Management, 3*(3), 172–79.

McElroy, M. W. (2000). Integrating complexity theory, knowledge management and organizational learning. *Journal of Knowledge Management, 4*(3), 195–203.

McKelvey, B. (1999). Complexity theory in organization science: Seizing the promise or becoming a fad? *Emergence, 1*(1), 5–32.

McKelvey, B. (2003). Emergent order in firms: Complexity science vs. the entanglement trap. In E. Mitleton-Kelly (Ed.), *Complex systems and evolutionary perspectives on organisations: The application of complexity theory to organisations* (pp. 99–125). New York: Pergamon Press.

McKie, D. (2001). Updating public relations: "New science," research paradigms, and uneven developments. In R. L. Heath & G. Vasquez (Eds.), *Handbook of public relations* (pp. 75–91). Thousand Oaks, CA: Sage.

McKinney, E. H., Jr., Barker, J. R., Davis, K. J., & Smith, D. (2005). How swift starting action teams get off the ground: What United Flight 232 and airline flight crews can tell us about team communication. *Management Communication Quarterly, 19*(2), 198–237.

Megginson, D. (1996). Planned and emergent learning: A framework and a method. *Management Learning, 27*(4), 411–28.

Meyers, G. C., & Holusha, J. (1986). *When it hits the fan: Managing the nine crises of business.* Boston: Houghton Mifflin.

Millar, D. P., & Heath, R. L. (Eds.). (2004). *Responding to crisis: A rhetorical approach to crisis communication.* Mahwah, NJ: Erlbaum.

Millar, F. E., & Beck, D. B. (2004). Metaphors of crisis. In D. P. Millar & R. L. Heath (Eds.), *Responding to crisis: A rhetorical approach to crisis communication* (pp. 153–66). Mahwah, NJ: Erlbaum.

Miller, K. (2001). Quantitative research methods. In F. M. Jablin & L. L. Putnam (Eds.), *The new handbook of organizational communication: Advances in theory, research, and methods* (pp. 137–60). Thousand Oaks, CA: Sage.

Mirvis, P. H. (1996). Historical foundations of organizational learning. *Journal of Organizational Change Management, 9*(1), 13–31.

Mitleton-Kelly, E. (2003). Ten principles of complexity and enabling infrastructures. In E. Mitleton-Kelly (Ed.), *Complex systems and evolutionary perspectives on organisations: The application of complexity theory to organisations* (pp. 23–50). New York: Pergamon Press.

Mitroff, I. I. (2004). *Crisis leadership: Planning for the unthinkable.* Hoboken, NJ: Wiley.

Mitroff, I. I., & Anagnos, G. (2001). *Managing crises before they happen.* New York: AMACOM.

Mitroff, I. I., Harrington, L. K., & Gai, E. (1996). Thinking about the unthinkable. *Across the Board, 33*(8), 44–48.

Mitroff, I. I., & Pearson, C. M. (1993). *Crisis management: Diagnostic guide for improving your organization's crisis-preparedness.* San Francisco: Jossey-Bass.

Morin, E. (1992). For a crisiology. *Industrial and Environmental Crisis Quarterly, 7*(1), 5–21.

Murphy, A. G. (2001). The flight attendant dilemma: An analysis of communication and sensemaking during in-flight emergencies. *Journal of Applied Communication Research, 29*(1), 30–53.

Murphy, P. (1991). How "bad" PR decisions get made: A roster of faulty judgment heuristics. *Public Relations Review, 17*(2), 117–29.

Murphy, P. (1996). Chaos theory as a model for managing issues and crises. *Public Relations Review, 22*(2), 95–113.

Murphy, P. (2000). Symmetry, contingency, complexity: Accommodating uncertainty in public relations theory. *Public Relations Review, 26*(4), 447–62.

Murray, E., & Shohen, S. (1992). Lessons from the Tylenol tragedy on surviving a corporate crisis. *Medical Marketing and Media, 27*(2), 14–19.

National Commission on Terrorist Attacks upon the United States. (2004). Foresight—and hindsight. *The 9-11 Commission Report* (pp. 339–60). Retrieved July 14, 2007, from http://www.9-11commission.gov/report/911Report_Ch11.pdf.

Nidumolu, S. R., Subramani, M., & Aldrich, A. (2001). Situated learning and the situated knowledge web: Exploring the ground beneath knowledge management. *Journal of Management Information Systems, 18*(1), 115–50.

Nonaka, I., & Konno, N. (1998). The concept of "ba": Building a foundation for knowledge creation. *California Management Review, 40*(3), 40–54.

Opt, S. K. (2008). Public relations and the rhetoric of social intervention. In T. L. Hansen-Horn & B. Dostal Neff (Eds.), *Public relations: From theory to practice* (pp. 227–41). Boston: Pearson Education.

O'Rourke, R. J. (1996). Learning from crisis: When the dust settles. *Public Relations Strategist, 2*(2), 35–38.

Oswick, C., Anthony, P., Keenoy, T., & Mangham, I. L. (2000). A dialogic analysis of organizational learning. *Journal of Management Studies, 37*(6), 887–901.

O'Toole, L. (1999, August 6). *Mars society fights NASA budget cuts.* Retrieved June 21, 2007, from http://www.space.com/news/mars_cuts_806.html.

Palenchar, M. J. (2001). Media coverage of risk events: A framing comparison of two fatal manufacturing accidents. Paper presented at the Academy of Education in Journalism and Mass Communication (AEJMC) Conference, Washington, DC.

Paraskevas, A. (2006). Crisis management or crisis response system? A complexity science approach. *Management Decision, 44*(7), 892–907.

Pauchant, T. C., & Mitroff, I. A. (1992). *Transforming the crisis-prone organization: Preventing individual, organizational, and environmental tragedies.* San Francisco: Jossey-Bass.

Pearson, C. M., & Clair, J. A. (1998). Reframing crisis management. *Academy of Management Review, 23*(1), 59–76.

Penrose, J. M. (2000). The role of perception in crisis planning. *Public Relations Review, 26*(2), 155–71.

Pérez-Bustamante, G. (1999). Knowledge management in innovative organisations. *Journal of Knowledge Management, 3*(1), 6–17.

Perkel, C. (2007, March 17). GTA maker of pet foods issues recall; supplies house brands for major retailers. *The Toronto Star,* p. D18.

Perrow, C. (1984). *Normal accidents: Living with high risk technologies.* New York: Basic Books.

Petrick, J. A., Scherer, R. F., Brodzinski, J. D., Quinn, J. F., & Ainina, M. F. (1999). Global leadership skills and reputational capital: Intangible resources for sustainable competitive advantage. *Academy of Management Executive, 13*(1), 58–69.

Pfeffer, J., & Sutton, R. (1999). *The knowing–doing gap.* Boston: Harvard Business School Press.

Phuong, C. L. (2007, April 13). From the fields of China to the ports of Seattle pet food made headlines, but food for humans is tainted too, and very little gets inspected; with surging imports come safety concerns. *The Seattle Post-Intelligencer,* p. A1. Retrieved June 6, 2007, from LexisNexis Academic database.

Piaget, J. (1950). *Psychology of intelligence.* London: Routledge.

Polanyi, M. (1961). Knowing and being. *Mind, 70*(280), 458–70.

Pollan, M. (2006). *The omnivore's dilemma: A natural history of four meals.* New York: Penguin.

Poole, M. S., & Van de Ven, A. H. (1989). Using paradox to build management and organization theories. *Academy of Management Review, 14*(4), 562–78.

Poole, M. S., Van de Ven, A. H., Dooley, K., & Holmes, M. E. (2000). *Organizational change and innovation processes: Theory and methods for research.* New York: Oxford University Press.

Poulsen, J. (1996). When journalism loses its senses: On mad cow disease and ritual sacrifice. *Nordicom Review, 17,* 3–9.

Price, B. (1997). The myth of postmodern science. In R. A. Eve, S. Horsfall, & M. E. Lee (Eds.), *Chaos, complexity, and sociology: Myths, models, and theories* (pp. 3–13). Thousand Oaks, CA: Sage.

Ramée, J. (1987). Corporate crisis: The aftermath. *Management Solutions, 32*(2) 18–22.

Reeves, C. (2002). An orthodox heresy: Rhetoric and the science of prions. *Science Communication, 24*(1), 98–122.

Regester, M., & Larkin, J. (2005). *Risk issues and crisis management: A casebook of best practice* (3rd ed.). London: Kogan Page.

Ren, C. H. (2000). Understanding and managing the dynamics of linked crisis events. *Disaster Prevention and Management, 9*(1), 12–17.

Report of the Presidential Commission on the Space Shuttle Challenger Accident. (1986, February 3). *The contributing cause of the accident* (Chapter 5). Retrieved June 21, 2007, from http://science.ksc.nasa.gov/shuttle/missions/51-l/docs/rogers-commission/Chapter-5.txt.

Richardson, K. A., & Cilliers, P. (2001). What is complexity science? A view from different directions. *Emergence, 3*(1), 5–22.

Richardson, K. A., Cilliers, P., & Lissack, M. (2000, November). Complexity science: A "grey" science for the "stuff in between." Paper presented at the International Conference on Systems Thinking in Management, Geelong, Australia.

Richardson, K. A., Mathieson, G., & Cilliers, P. (2000). The theory and practice of complexity science: Epistemological considerations for military operational analysis. *SysteMexico, 1*(2), 25–66.

Rifkin, W., & Fulop, L. (1997). A review and case study of learning organizations. *The Learning Organization, 4*(4), 135–48.

Romanelli, E. (1999). Blind (but not unconditioned) variation: Problems of copying in sociocultural evolution. In J. A. C. Baum & B. McKelvey (Eds.), *Variations in organization science: In honor of Donald T. Campbell* (pp. 79–91). Thousand Oaks, CA: Sage.

Romme, A. G. L., & van Witteloostuijn, A. (1999). Circular organizing and triple loop learning. *Journal of Organizational Change Management, 12*(5), 439–53.

Rosenthal, C. (2007, June 3). Advice: Consider these books for pet recipes. *San Antonio Express-News,* p. 13J.

Ross, J., & Staw, B. M. (1993). Organizational escalation and exit: Lessons from the Shoreham nuclear power plant. *Academy of Management Journal, 36*(4), 701.

Roux-Dufort, C. (2000). Why organizations don't learn from crises: The perverse power of normalization. *Review of Business, 21*(3/4), 25–30.

Rudski, J. M., Lischner, M. I., & Albert, L. M. (1999). Superstitious rule generation is affected by probability and type of outcome. *Psychological Record, 49*(2), 245–60.

Rulke, D. L., & Rau, D. (2000). Investigating the encoding process of transactive memory development in group training. *Group and Organization Management, 25*(4), 373–96.

Scanlon, L., Tuukka, J. R., & Morton, G. (1978). Media coverage of a crisis: Better than reported, worse than necessary. *Journalism Quarterly, 55*, 66–72.

Schmit, J. (2007, January 29). E. coli's long gone, but spinach sales are still hurting. *USA Today,* p. 1B.

Schmitt, N. (1997). Naturalistic decision making in business and industrial organizations. In C. E. Zsambok & G. Klein (Eds.), *Naturalistic decision making* (pp. 91–98). Mahwah, NJ: Erlbaum.

Schwartz, H. S. (1987). On the psychodynamics of organizational disaster: The case of the space shuttle Challenger. *Columbia Journal of World Business, 22*(1), 59–67.

Schwartz, P. (1998). The art of the long view. West Sussex: John Wiley & Sons.

Schwenk, C. R. (1995). Strategic decision making. *Journal of Management, 21*(3), 471–93.

Seeger, M. W., & Ulmer, R. R. (2003). Explaining Enron: Communication and responsible leadership. *Management Communication Quarterly, 17*(1), 58–84.

Seligman, A. B. (1998). Trust and sociability: On the limits of confidence and role expectations. *American Journal of Economics and Sociology, 57*(4), 391–404.

Sellnow, T. L., & Seeger, M. (2001). Exploring the boundaries of crisis communication: The case of the 1997 Red River Valley flood. *Communication Studies, 52*(2), 153–67.

Sellnow, T. L., & Ulmer, R. R. (1995). Ambiguous argument as advocacy in organizational crisis communication. *Argumentation and Advocacy, 31*(3), 138–50.

Senge, P. (1990). *The fifth discipline: The art and practice of the learning organization.* New York: Doubleday Currency.

Senge, P., Kleiner, A., Roberts, C., Ross, R., Roth, G., & Smith, B. (1999). *The dance of change: The challenges of sustaining momentum in learning organizations.* London: Brealey.

Shell, A. (1993). In a crisis, what you say isn't always what the public hears. *Public Relations Journal, 49*(9), 10–11.

Simon, H. (1976). *Administrative behavior* (3rd ed.). New York: Free Press.

Sitkin, S. B., & Weingart, L. R. (1995). Determinants of risky decision-making behavior: A test of the mediating role of risk perceptions and propensity. *Academy of Management Journal, 38*(6), 1573–92.

Small, W. J. (1991). Exxon Valdez: How to spend billions and still get a black eye. *Public Relations Review, 17*(1), 9–25.

Smallman, C., & Weir, D. (1999). Communication and cultural distortion during crises. *Disaster Prevention and Management, 8*(1), 33–41.

Smith, D. (2000). On a wing and a prayer? Exploring the human components of technological failure. *Systems Research and Behavioral Science, 17*(6), 543–59.

Smith, G. E. (1997). Managerial problem solving: A problem-centered approach. In C. E. Zsambok & G. Klein (Eds.), *Naturalistic decision making* (pp. 371–80). Mahwah, NJ: Erlbaum.

Smith, R. S. (1979). How to plan for crisis communications. *Public Relations Journal, 35*(3), 17–18.

Snowden, D. (2002). Complex acts of knowing: Paradox and descriptive self-awareness. *Journal of Knowledge Management, 6*(2), 100–11.

Snowden, D. J. (2000). New wine in old wineskins: From organic to complex knowledge management through the use of story. *Emergence, 2*(4), 50–64.

Spencer, J. (1989). How to manage a crisis by planning ahead. *Canadian Manager, 14*(1), 12–13.

Stacey, R. D. (2001). *Complex responsive processes in organizations: Learning and knowledge creation.* London: Routledge.

Stacey, R. D., Griffin, D., & Shaw, P. (2000). *Complexity and management.* London: Routledge.

Starbuck, W. H. (1992). Strategizing in the real world. *International Journal of Technology Management, 8*(1/2), 77–85.

Stauber, J., & Rampton, S. (1995). *Toxic sludge is good for you: Lies, damn lies, and the public relations industry.* Monroe, ME: Common Courage.

Stenmark, D. (2001, August). The relationship between information and knowledge. Paper presented at the meeting of the IRIS 24 (Information Systems Research Seminar in Scandinavia), Bergen, Norway.

Stephens, D. (2007, June 4). [Letters to the editor]. *Pensacola News Journal.* Retrieved from http://www.pensacolanewsjournal.com/apps/pbcs.dll/article?AID=/20070604/OPINION/706040303/1020.

Stevens, B. (1999). Persuasion, probity, and paltering: The Prudential crisis. *Journal of Business Communication, 36*(4), 319–334.

Stocking, S. H. (1998). On drawing attention to ignorance. *Science Communication, 20*(1), 165–78.

Street, M. D., Robertson, C., & Geiger, S. W. (1997). Ethical decision making: The effects of escalating commitment. *Journal of Business Ethics, 16,* 1153–61.

Suchman, M. C. (1995). Managing legitimacy: Strategic and institutional approaches. *Academy of Management Review, 20*(3), 571–610.

Sullivan, P. (2007, April 6). Pet food recall expands as senator announces hearings on FDA investigation. *The Washington Post.* Retrieved June 15, 2007, from LexisNexis Academic database.

Sutcliffe, K. M. (2001). Organizational environments and organizational information processing. In F. M. Jablin & L. L. Putnam (Eds.), *The new handbook of organizational communication: Advances in theory, research, and methods* (pp. 197–230). Thousand Oaks, CA: Sage.

Taback, H. (1991). Preventing a crisis from getting out of hand. *Risk Management, 38*(10), 64–69.

Taylor, B. C., & Trujillo, N. (2001). Qualitative research methods. In F. M. Jablin & L. L. Putnam (Eds.), *The new handbook of organizational communication: Advances in theory, research, and methods* (pp. 161–94). Thousand Oaks, CA: Sage.

Taylor, M. (2000). Cultural variance as a challenge to global public relations: A case study of the Coca-Cola scare in Europe. *Public Relations Review, 26*(3), 277–93.

Thayer, W. (1998, April). An inside look at the scary world of food safety scares. *Frozen Food Age, 46,* 1, 12, 38.

Thiétart, R.-A., & Forgues, B. (1997). Action, structure and chaos. *Organization Studies, 18*(1), 119–43.

Thomas, J. B., Clark, S. M., & Gioia, D. A. (1993). Strategic sensemaking and organizational performance: Linkages among scanning, interpretation, action, and outcomes. *Academy of Management Journal, 36*(2), 239–70.

Thomas, J. B., Shankster, L. J., & Mathieu, J. E. (1994). Antecedents to organizational issue interpretation: The roles of single-level, cross-level and content clues. *Academy of Management Journal, 37*(5), 1252–84.

Thomsen, S. R. (1995). Using online databases in corporate issues management. *Public Relations Review, 21*(2), 103–22.

Tompkins, P. K. (2005). *Apollo, Challenger, Columbia: The decline of the space program: A study in organizational communication.* Los Angeles: Roxbury.

Tsoukas, H. (2000). Knowledge as action, organization as theory: Reflections on organizational knowledge. *Emergence, 2*(4), 104–12.

Tsoukas, H. (2005). *Complex knowledge.* London: Oxford University Press.

Tsoukas, H., & Vladimirou, E. (2001). What is organizational knowledge? *Journal of Management Studies, 38*(7), 973–93.

Tyler, L. (2005). Towards a postmodern understanding of crisis communication. *Public Relations Review, 31*(4), 566–71.

Tyre, M. J., & von Hippel, E. (1997). The situated nature of adaptive learning in organizations. *Organization Science, 8*(1), 71–83.

Ulmer, R. R., Sellnow, T. L., & Seeger, M. W. (2007). *Effective crisis communication: Moving from crisis to opportunity.* Thousand Oaks, CA: Sage.

Urry, J. (2003). *Global complexity.* Cambridge, UK: Polity.

van Ginneken, J. (2003). *Collective behavior and public opinion.* Mahwah, NJ: Erlbaum.

van Uden, J., Richardson, K. A., & Cilliers, P. (2001). Postmodernism revisited? Complexity science and the study of organisations. *Tamara: Journal of Critical Postmodern Organization Science, 1*(3), 53–67.

Varela, F. J. (1995). The re-enchantment of the concrete. In L. Steels & R. Brooks (Eds.), *The artificial life route to artificial intelligence: Building embodied, situated agents* (pp. 11–20). Mahwah, NJ: Erlbaum.

Vaughan, D. (1996). *The Challenger launch decision: Risky technology, culture, and deviance at NASA.* Chicago: University of Chicago Press.

Veysey, S. (2000). Reputation risk needs managing. *Business Insurance, 34*(25), 21–22.

Wallerstein, I. (1996). *Open the social sciences: Report of the Gulbenkian Commission on the Restructuring of the Social Sciences.* Stanford, CA: Stanford University Press.

Watzlawick, P. (1976). *How real is real?* New York: Random House.

Weick, K. E. (1988). Enacted sensemaking in crisis situations. *Journal of Management Studies, 25*(4), 305–17.

Weick, K. E. (1993). The collapse of sensemaking in organizations: The Mann Gulch disaster. *Administrative Science Quarterly, 38*(4), 628–52.

Weick, K. E. (1995). *Sensemaking in organizations.* Thousand Oaks, CA: Sage.

Weick, K. E. (2001). *Making sense of the organization.* Oxford, UK: Blackwell.

Weick, K. E., & Roberts, K. H. (1993). Collective mind in organizations: Heedful interrelating on flight decks. *Administrative Science Quarterly, 38*(3), 357–81.

Weise, E. (2007, June 5). Pet-owning bloggers mobilize on food front; reporters call for background information. *USA Today,* p. 3B. Retrieved June 6, 2007, from LexisNexis Academic database.

Weise, E. & Schmit, J. (2007). Melamine in pet food may not be accidental. *USA Today,* Money.

Weiss, R., & Trejos, N. (2007, May 2). Crisis over pet food extracting healthy cost. *The Washington Post,* p. D01.

Wicks, D. (2001). Institutionalized mindsets of invulnerability: Differentiated institutional fields and the antecedents of organizational crisis. *Organization Studies, 22*(4), 659–92.

Williams, D. E., & Olaniran, B. A. (1994). Exxon's decision-making flaws: The hypervigilant response to the Valdez grounding. *Public Relations Review, 20,* 5–18.

Williams, D. E., & Olaniran, B. A. (1998). Expanding the crisis planning function: Introducing elements of risk communication to crisis communication practice. *Public Relations Review, 24*(3), 387–400.

Williams, S. L., & Moffitt, M. A. (1997). Corporate image as an impression formation process: Prioritizing personal, organizational, and environmental audience factors. *Journal of Public Relations Research, 9*(4), 237–58.

Wolfe, T. (1979). *The right stuff.* New York: Farrar, Straus, & Giroux.

Yarbrough, C. R., Cameron, G. T., Sallot, L. M., & McWilliams, A. (1998). Tough calls to make: Contingency theory and the Centennial Olympic Games. *Journal of Communication Management, 3*(1), 39–56.

Zezima, K. (2007, March 23). Rat poison found in tainted pet food. *The New York Times.* Retrieved June 13, 2007, from http://www.nytimes.com/2007/03/23/us/23cnd-petfood.html?ei=5088&en=76b4f6cecb2542 9f&ex=1332302400&partner=rssnyt&emc=rss&pagewanted#.

Zsambok, C. E. (1997). Naturalistic decision making research and improving team decision making. In C. E. Zsambok & G. Klein (Eds.), *Naturalistic decision making* (pp. 111–20). Mahwah, NJ: Erlbaum.

INDEX

Clair, J. A., 15, 16, 17, 18, 115, 134,
 139, 150–51
Clare, L. M., 53
Clark, S. M., 21, 162
CMP. *See* crisis management plan
CMT. *See* crisis management team
Coca-Cola scare in Europe, 3, 38
coevolution, 28
cognitive dissonance theory, 86
cognitive normalization, 154
cognitive skills, 98
collaborative dialogue, 70
collective accomplishment, 100
collective knowledge, 57–59
collective learning, 69
Columbia shuttle disaster, 47–49, 51,
 56, 78
commodity view, of
 knowledge, 56–57
community view, of
 knowledge, 56–57
competencies, 98
complexity, 24. *See also* complexity-
 based thinking
 approach to postcrisis
 evaluation, 148–51
 of assimilation, 50–68
 dominant paradigm reframed
 for, 107–11, 108*t*–109*t*
 of information, 50–68
 learning and, 110–11
 reduction of, 173–74
 relationships and, 114–21, 146–47
 specialization resulting from
 increase in, 89
 trust viewed by, 118
 of understanding, 69–84
complexity absorption
 context influencing, 174–75
 relationships and, 175
 shifting paradigms of, 159*t*, 172–76
 strategies in, 174
complexity-based thinking, 33–34
 challenges of, 176
 mainstream thinking *vs.,* 157–77
 methodological corollaries of, 34
complexity theory, 6, 23–34. *See also*
 complex system(s)
 approaches to, 32–34
 chaos theory *vs.,* 38–39
 definition of, 24
 and organizational crises, 7
 systems thinking *vs.,* 40

complex organizational systems. *See*
 complex system(s)
complex recovery, 146–56
complex system(s), 12
 adaptability in, 25–27
 vs. complicated systems, 25
 control in, 35–43
 definition of, 6, 24
 distinguishing features of, 25*t*
 environment integral to, 31
 fractals and, 28–29, 29*f*
 group as incompressible, 58
 history in, 30, 35–36, 169
 individual life as, 87
 instability in, 30
 interacting agents 119, in, 24–25
 interaction among components
 of, 35–37
 irreducibility of, 31–32, 36
 predictability in, 35–43
 principles of, 24–32
 self-organization in, 28–29
 traditional statistical methods
 challenged by, 36
complicated systems, *vs.* complex
 systems, 25
Conan-Doyle, A., 127
Conrad, C., 4
context-sensitive decision making, 51
contextual determinants, of
 escalation, 142
contextual path dependency, 37
control, in complex systems, 35–43
Cook, S. D. N., 55, 56, 58, 62, 63, 64
Cooksey, R. W., 34
Coombs, W. T., 5, 14, 16, 19, 20, 21,
 51, 59, 83, 115, 116, 118, 120, 121,
 122, 124,127, 135, 136, 147, 148,
 151, 168
Cope, J., 69, 75, 76
cosmology episode, 15, 50, 76
Courtright, J. L., 5, 56
credibility
 pet food contamination
 and, 116–17
 relationships influenced by, 116–17
 terminal, 116
crises
 assumptions challenged
 after, 146–56
 assumptions challenged
 during, 134–45
 cause defining, 15